Published in 2011 by Stewart, Tabori & Chang
An imprint of ABRAMS

Library of Congress Cataloging-in-Publication Data:

Stoller, Debbie.
Bust DIY guide to life / by Debbie Stoller and
Laurie Henzel.
     p. cm.
"STC Craft/A Melanie Falick book."
ISBN 978-1-58479-896-5 (alk. paper)
1. Home economics. I. Henzel, Laurie. II. Bust
(New York, N.Y.) III. Title.
TX145.S863 2011
640—dc22
     2010052494

Editor: Liana Allday
Designer: Anna Christian
Production Manager: Tina Cameron

The text of this book was composed in Avenir.

Printed and bound in the United States.
10 9 8 7 6 5 4 3 2 1

Stewart, Tabori & Chang books are available at special discounts when
purchased in quantity for premiums and promotions as well as fundraising
or educational use. Special editions can also be created to specification.
For details, contact specialsales@abramsbooks.com or the address below.

THE ART OF BOOKS SINCE 1949
115 West 18th Street
New York, NY 10011
www.abramsbooks.com

THE BUST DIY GUIDE TO LIFE

Contents

the BUST DIY Guide to Life

MAKING *your* WAY *through* EVERY DAY

Laurie Henzel & Debbie Stoller

STC Craft | A Melanie Falick Book

STEWART, TABORI & CHANG   NEW YORK

Part Three

HEALTH & BEAUTY

Part Four

EAT, DRINK & BE MERRY

Part Five

MOVING & SHAKING

Introduction

When we first started *BUST* magazine back in 1993, we never would have predicted that some day we'd be putting together a book about DIY. In fact, crafting wasn't on our minds at all back then. In those days, our main goal was to create a magazine that would be different than any other women's magazine on the newsstand. Instead of making our readers feel inadequate, we would celebrate them—and ourselves—just as we are. We would print the stories no other magazine would dare: about our confusion and at times ambivalence about relationships, careers, motherhood, and what our lives—we, the first generation of women to be raised on feminism—would or should be like. While other women's magazines ran stories about how to please your man, we'd encourage our readers to learn how to please themselves; instead of schooling women on how to climb the corporate ladder, we'd advise on how to fulfill oneself creatively; where other magazines told women how to lose weight, we'd emphasize that all sizes are beautiful.

But maybe the fact that we've become so involved with DIY shouldn't come as such a surprise. After all, *BUST* itself was an entirely DIY endeavor. When we came up with the idea for the magazine, we were three girls—myself, Laurie Henzel, and Marcelle Karp—working at low-level jobs at a children's TV network. We didn't know anything about business plans, investors, profit margins, or other things that most entrepreneurs would consider when starting a new business venture. That's because we considered *BUST* to be more of a *cause* than a commodity. This was long before blogs, so our only option for getting our voice out there was to create a printed magazine, and we set out in search of a way to get that first issue made without any money at all. We began by asking our writerly friends and colleagues if they had stories about their lives that they felt weren't being told by the mainstream media, and if so, if they would like to contribute. Most of the people we approached were so excited about finally getting a forum where their voices could be heard that they were more than happy to oblige. Then we asked our graphic designer colleagues at the TV network if they'd be willing to help lay out the magazine during their off-hours. They too, were excited about the project, and got right to work, cutting and pasting the designs for each story by hand.

Within a few months we had our first issue, printed out on regular old copier paper, filled with first-person stories, artwork, fiction, and more. We stayed late at the office to surreptitiously make copies and got sore wrists from stapling them all together. But finally, there they were: 500 copies of our little "magazine," or 'zine, as this kind of homemade publication is called. Back in the early '90s, thanks to the newly accessible desktop publishing tools, there were so many of these 'zines that there were entire stores devoted to them, and independent bookstores and record stores usually had a few shelves reserved for their display. We sent *BUST* out to all these places, asking them to sell the mag for us, and it quickly sold out. We had to create another 500 copies—once again, late at night at our day-job office—to meet the demand. Soon we even began to receive fan mail—letters from folks who told us how much they enjoyed the magazine, how much it meant to them, how it made them feel so much less alone.

That bit of encouragement was all we needed to keep going. We started working on a second issue, and pooled our money together to get it printed. And then a third issue. And with each new issue, we improved the magazine just a little bit. We went from photocopies to newsprint, and then eventually from newsprint to glossy paper. We didn't give up our day jobs, but *BUST* kept us excited and fulfilled as we grew our circulation bit by bit. In 2000, we partnered with a dot-com company that gave us a budget and some office space, and allowed us to finally quit our day jobs and work on *BUST* full-time. But when the dot-com bubble burst one short year later, so did our partnership. It was tough to lose our backing, but we pulled ourselves up by our bra straps. At this point there were just two of us running the mag—myself on the editorial side of things and Laurie heading up design. We set up shop at Laurie's house and started the magazine again, and that's how we've carried on for the past ten years (although we now have an actual office and a full-fledged staff). Today, *BUST* continues to be a completely woman-owned, woman-run independent operation, with no owners or investors to tell us what we can and can't publish. And how did we get here? Yup; we did it ourselves.

In the early years of the magazine our stories were mostly first-person narratives (our contributors were so anxious to get these untold women's stories out there), but as we grew, and our audience grew, we began publishing more reported stories, more interviews with women we admired (Björk, Tina Fey, Amy Sedaris, Amy Poehler, Yoko Ono, Gloria Steinem, Missy Elliott, Kathleen Hanna, Kim Gordon, Chloë Sevigny, Miranda July, Rosario Dawson—to name but a few), and more "service"-type pieces—advice columns and so on. Then, in 1997, we introduced a new crafting column, She's Crafty, in which we planned to start publishing all kinds of DIY ideas. At that time, no one could imagine a magazine aimed at young women that would encourage such old-fashioned activities as soap-making, knitting your own clothes, or learning to make dinner from scratch. And in particular, what would a magazine that considered itself feminist be doing publishing such things? Cooking? Crocheting? These were exactly the types of things our feminist mothers had tried so hard to free us from; why would we voluntarily decide to go back?

But for us, there were plenty of reasons to promote DIY in our magazine, and the first and foremost of these was directly tied to our feminist roots. After all, for centuries, women had been entrusted with creating everything they needed to keep a family clothed, cleaned, and fed. They had to know how to make soap; they had to be able to weave fabric and sew or knit clothing for their family; they had to be able to create nutritious meals and preserve a harvest so that the family wouldn't go hungry in the middle of winter. These skills were necessary for survival, and women must have taken just as much pride in their ability to carry them out as men did in their ability to build a home or hunt a wild boar. But eventually, as soap, clothing, and even fully prepared frozen meals became available for purchase, knowing how to create these things became less and less important. To the women's movement of the '60s and '70s, achieving freedom from these tedious chores was the path to salvation. Up until then, women had been given the short end of the broomstick, they argued, stuck at home with the cleaning, cooking, and sewing, while the real action—and only chance at financial independence—was outside, in the work world, an arena that men had tried so hard to keep women out of for so long. Convinced that women had so much more to contribute to the world than kids and casseroles, feminists fought their way out of their homes and slammed the door behind them, hoping that they, and their daughters, would never find themselves trapped there again.

But by the time their daughters grew up, in the '80s and '90s, a new strategy was taking hold. Rather than rejecting all those things that our feminist foremothers had considered oppressive, we chose to re-examine them, and sometimes reclaim them, making them our own. Was sewing really such a suffocating and unsatisfying task, or did it just seem oppressive because women had been limited to performing this task and held back from performing others? And was this sense of oppression multiplied by the fact that the tasks themselves weren't given much value? After all, the women who performed this work were never really given credit for their skill and experience. We found ourselves thinking, as feminists, that instead of shutting the door on these skills, perhaps we should be celebrating them. Couldn't there be both pleasure and pride in creating something with our own hands or cooking a nice meal from scratch? Our moms didn't need to worry—of course we were all going after careers as well. We just didn't necessarily want to eat take out for the rest of our lives.

That's what we were thinking when we published our first She's Crafty column. In her intro to the column, author Erika Bardot tried to calm down any readers who might object to seeing this sort of thing in *BUST*: "Doing housey-crafty things is fun and relaxing, either solo or with your gaggle." She went on to explain how to make homemade herbal bath teas to treat various ailments. The story ran, and we didn't get any hate mail. We had let the crafting cat out of the bag, and by 2000 we had added Chef Rossi's recipes to the mix. Rossi was a particularly good choice for the mag as her approach was ballsy in tone and casual in method (instead of directing precise measurements, Rossi advised using "coffee-cupfuls" and "dollops" of ingredients). She kept things light and fun, and was the perfect person to introduce the joy of cooking to our readers.

Bringing back these "housey-girly" things just felt so good, so right. In fact, we were so excited about our new approach to these previously disdained and discarded skills that in the spring of 2001 we devoted an entire issue to the topic. Our "Homegirls" issue—one of my personal favorites of all time—celebrated the "womanly arts" without apology, including a story on women who made their living by crafting, a thoughtful essay on why the time was ripe for young feminists to reclaim the domestic skills our foremothers had rejected, and an interview with Amy Sedaris in which she revealed her love of baking and cooking and shared her recipe for cheese balls, among other articles. At the back of the issue we had a section called "The Bad Girl's Guide to Good Housekeeping," and there we compiled favorite recipes, useful housecleaning and laundry tips, simple cures to make at home, instructions on how to craft a box for your sex toys, and lots more, all collected from reader submissions. To me, it was truly a breakthrough issue, in which we made a strong case for seeing women's work from a new angle, and making peace with it; embracing it not only because knowing these things could improve the quality of our lives, but also because engaging in many of them was just plain fun. Our readers rejoiced, many letting us know how grateful they were to see proof that feminism and the home front need not be at odds with each other. "I like to cook and sew, but that doesn't mean that I'm spitting on the ERA," one reader wrote. "It's time for the world to understand that,"

Eventually, our interest in DIY grew so much that it required its own section in the magazine. Before we knew it, the do-it-yourself ethos infiltrated other areas of *BUST* as well, including our beauty and fashion coverage. While our style sensibility had always strayed away from mainstream fashion trends and instead leaned toward vintage looks and independent designers, soon we were including stories on how to dye your own hair and sew your own skirt; how to recycle your baggy jeans into cute, fitted shorts and convert your moth-eaten sweaters into a nice scarf; how to craft your own ring and string your own necklace. When an ambitious intern revealed that she was obsessed with learning how to create various historic and ethnic hairstyles and proposed writing a column on this topic, we were happy to accept. And after we wrote about a woman who had started a business re-creating vintage makeup products, we asked her to write a column for us so that our readers could learn how to create a wide range of looks for themselves.

But DIY is not just about making things—it's also about making a life. Aside from learning how to knit a scarf, we wanted our readers to learn how to create a life on their own terms: to find work that is satisfying; to be brave enough to travel the world on their own; to manage their own finances; and especially, to make sure that certain traditions and milestones in their lives—such as getting married or giving birth—were as personal and individualized as they deserved to be. And so, over the years, we have run stories on how to buy a house, how to go into business for yourself, how to make basic home repairs, how to have an indie wedding, how to give birth naturally, and many, many more.

In the 15 years since we introduced that very first DIY column, things have changed a lot. The days when crafting was looked down on are long gone. Today there's a growing DIY movement and even a DIY culture. Hundreds of thousands of young women and men have gone into business for themselves, handcrafting everything from jewelry to jumpers and selling them on the Internet or in specialty shops. Here at BUST, we even started our own craft fair in New York City back in 2006 to help support these clever ladies and gents—the BUST Magazine Craftacular—and since then it has expanded to five events a year in New York City, Los Angeles, and London. Not coincidentally, shortly after we published our first crafting column, I got into knitting big-time, wrote about it in BUST, and started a small group at a NYC café to teach knitting to anyone who was interested. From that tiny Stitch 'n Bitch group grew both a bestselling book series and a community, with over 1,000 groups worldwide today. The need to create and to learn how to be self-sufficient has also been taken up as a cause. Many people are looking for ways to opt out of a global corporate culture that encourages them to buy, buy, buy, with little regard for a product's impact on the environment or on the people who work in factories and modern-day sweatshops to make it. For these people, DIY is both the answer and the antidote.

As early promoters and staunch supporters of the DIY movement, we thought it was high time we collected the best of our do-it-yourself knowledge into a single fat volume. Looking at them all together, we feel these articles do a good job honoring the skills and traditions that women have developed and devoted themselves to for centuries, and updating them for an entirely new generation of women (and men). Here, then, are DIY ideas for everything from how to style your home to how to style your hair; from how to grow your own food to how to prepare it; how to support your immune system naturally to how to support yourself financially. We hope these stories will encourage you to be truly independent; that they will empower you to be genuinely self-sufficient; and that they will inspire you to be limitlessly creative. But don't just take our word for it—get on out there and do it yourself.

Debbie Stoller

PART ONE

BUST-IER HOMES & GARDENS

best week ever

DIY TEA TOWELS TAKE IT DAY BY DAY // Debbie Stoller

Vintage "days of the week" dish towels are typically embroidered with a kitten doing the laundry on Monday or a Dutch girl sewing on Wednesday, but now you can make them in a design more suited to your life. Monday is TV, Tuesday is takeout, Wednesday is your Stitch 'n Bitch, Thursday is yoga night, Friday is party night, Saturday is date night, and Sunday is potluck night. And since you might not have the time to stitch seven towels, these are done with fabric paint.

materials

Tracing paper or vellum

Iron-on transfer pencil or pen

7 flour-sack towels

Straight pins

Iron and ironing board

10" metal paint hoop with blotter (the Aunt Martha's brand is great) or a 10" embroidery hoop and paper towels

Fine-tip paintbrush

Fabric paint in purple, rose, teal, cherry, chartreuse, dark yellow, pine, and rust

1 Photocopy the seven designs on page 16, enlarging each one by 150 percent.

2 Lay one design underneath a sheet of tracing paper or vellum, and lightly trace over all the lines with your iron-on transfer pencil or pen (you want to make the lines as fine as possible). Place the transfer with your pencil lines facing down on top of the towel where you'd like the design to go and pin it in place.

3 Heat your iron on the cotton setting, then press it down on the transfer, shifting your iron back and forth. Refer to the instructions for your transfer pen or pencil for how long to keep ironing.

4 If you've got a paint hoop with blotter, place the blotter over the metal base hoop first, lay the towel on top, and fix the towel in place, taut, with the hoop. If you have a standard embroidery hoop, you'll be using it in exactly the opposite way from what you're used to. Place the tea towel facedown over the smaller hoop, cover it with a layer or two of paper towels, and press on the larger hoop to hold both pieces taut. Flip the whole thing over and place it on a sturdy work surface.

5 After practicing on scrap fabric, carefully paint over each line of the transferred design, using whatever color you prefer. Allow the paint to dry according to the instructions. Heat set with the iron, if needed.

6 Repeat with each of the towels and designs to make the full set.

Monday

Tuesday

Wednesday

Thursday

Friday

Saturday

Enlarge each
template by
150 percent.

Sunday

easy-peasy pot holder

SEW A HOT PAD // Derek Fagerstrom and Lauren Smith

materials

Two 8" squares of heavyweight fabric, such as canvas or bark cloth (no flammable synthetics!)

One or two 8" squares of cotton batting

Iron and ironing board

Straight pins

36" extra-wide, double-fold seam binding

Sewing machine and matching thread

Scissors

Bring a little kitsch to your kitchen by sewing up a super-simple pot holder. They're so easy to make, you can whip one up for your best friend's next birthday and make a few to keep around your house while you're at it.

1 Sandwich your fabric and batting squares together. Put the batting in the middle, with each fabric piece facing right side out.

2 Heat the iron. Starting at a corner, pin the seam binding around your squares to encase the raw edges of the fabric, easing the corners into shape with the iron (this takes a little patience, but the corners will eventually lie flat when pressed). The tail end of the seam binding will be 4" longer than the perimeter of the pot holder. Leave this tail attached.

3 Using the sewing machine, stitch around the pot holder close to the inside of the seam binding, making sure to catch the bottom layer of the binding. Stitch along the tail of the binding.

4 Fold the raw edge of the seam-binding tail ½" to the wrong side and press. Fold the tail down again to create a 1½" loop. Pin and stitch the loop into place, then trim any loose threads.

- -

One layer of batting should do the trick, but for extra thickness, use two layers of batting.

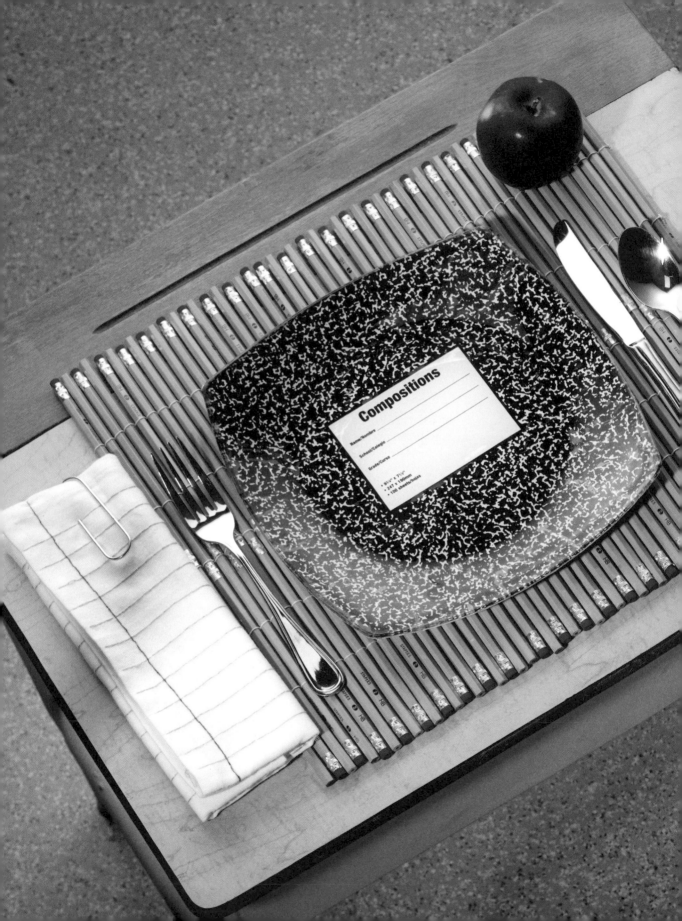

you got served

MAKE A TRENDSETTING PLACE SETTING // Tracie Egan Morrissey and Callie Watts

Ah, the smell of fresh, new pencils, wide-ruled notebooks, and bubble gum under desks. These cool homemade place settings will take you back to your school days, but you can easily make them with the motif of your choice—chopsticks and origami paper, perhaps? Use your imagination and soon you'll be serving it up.

pencil place mat

materials

98 unsharpened No. 2 pencils

Super Glue

Hammer (if needed)

Five 54" lengths thin nylon cord

1 To make this sharp-lookin' place mat, pull the erasers out of 49 of the pencils. Drop some Super Glue in the metal part (where the eraser was) and wedge the unsharpened end of a pencil that still has its eraser into the hole. You may want to tap it with a hammer to get it in all the way—just make sure it's in straight. Repeat until you have 49 doubled-up pencils, and let the glue dry.

2 To weave the pencils together, fold one of the nylon cords in half and slip a pencil into the loop. Cross the ends of the cord around the pencil. Place another pencil next to the first one and again cross the cord around it. (The cord end that crossed over the first pencil will go under this second one, while the cord that crossed under the first pencil will now cross over.)

3 Continue until all the pencils have been added, arranging them so that they alternate, eraser end to unsharpened end.

4 Weave in the remaining pieces of nylon, spacing the cords evenly. Tighten the cords so the pencils are as close together as possible. Tie and trim the ends.

composition book plate

materials

Clear glass plate

Scanned printout or photocopy of a marble composition book cover, sized to fit dimensions of plate

Mod Podge or other decoupage glue

Craft brush

Plastic spoon

X-ACTO knife

Matte acrylic sealer

1 To create this classy plate, clean the plate, then coat the back of it with decoupage glue. Also coat the front of the marble image, then position the right side of the image onto the back of the plate. Gently press away any wrinkles with a plastic spoon. Lightly coat the back of the image with the decoupage glue and let dry.

2 Trim the overhanging paper edges with an X-ACTO knife and scrape off any thick goo spots. Spray the back of the plate with a few light coats of sealer. Let dry and clean. Note that these plates are hand-wash only—don't go putting them in the dishwasher!

wide-ruled loose-leaf napkin

materials

Iron and ironing board

White linen napkin

Straightedge

Pencil

Embroidery hoop (or sewing machine)

Light blue and dark pink embroidery floss (or regular thread in the same colors)

Giant paper clip

1 To make the school-ruled napkin, iron the napkin and lay it flat on a clean surface. Using a straight edge and a pencil, draw horizontal lines across the entire napkin, ¾" apart. Draw a vertical line 1" from the left and right edges.

2 Place the napkin in the embroidery hoop or in your sewing machine. Separate two strands from the light blue embroidery floss (or use light blue thread in the machine), and follow along the horizontal lines. If hand-stitching, use a backstitch to embroider ⅛"-long stitches.

3 Embroider or sew the same way along the vertical lines, using dark pink embroidery floss or thread. The back of the napkin will most likely look sloppy after stitching, so if you want, you can fold the napkin lengthwise, ugly side in, and sew the sides together.

4 To complete the effect, use a giant paper clip as a napkin holder.

rolling-in-dough duvet

STENCIL & STITCH SOME SWEET DREAMS // Callie Watts and Lori Forty Weaver

materials

Masking tape

10 sheets 8 ½"-by-11" lightweight card stock

Spray mount

Five 8 ½"-by-11" copies of the diamond graphic

X-ACTO knife

2 full-sized flat sheets (or the size that matches your duvet)

Blue and gold fabric paint

Foam brush

One 8 ½"-by-11" photocopy of the dollar sign graphic

Large piece of scrap cloth (for covering sheet while ironing it)

Iron and ironing board

Straight pins

Sewing machine and matching thread

5 blinged-out buttons

Buttonhole foot

Seam ripper

The same ol', same ol' mass-produced crap can make your place seem weary and worn. Instead of picking up covers identical to the ones your bff found at the big-box shop, take "making your bed" to the next level with this blinged-out DIY duvet cover. With just an afternoon and some inexpensive supplies, you'll be hittin' the hay your way.

1 Tape together nine pieces of card stock, cutting one of the pieces to make a stencil that's 70" long by 11" wide. Lightly spray the back of the diamond printouts with spray mount and stick them to the card stock, spaced so the widest points are 7¾" apart. With an X-ACTO knife, cut out the solid-colored parts of the images.

2 Lay one of the sheets on the floor, right side up. Spray the back of the long stencil with spray mount, and place it on the sheet so the tops of the diamonds are 4" below the decorative hem at the top and the center diamond is exactly in the center of the sheet. Using blue fabric paint and a foam brush, stipple the paint over the stencil, dabbing the brush on the fabric like you're sponge painting. Don't use too much paint at once, and make sure the stencil is pressed firmly in place. Let it dry.

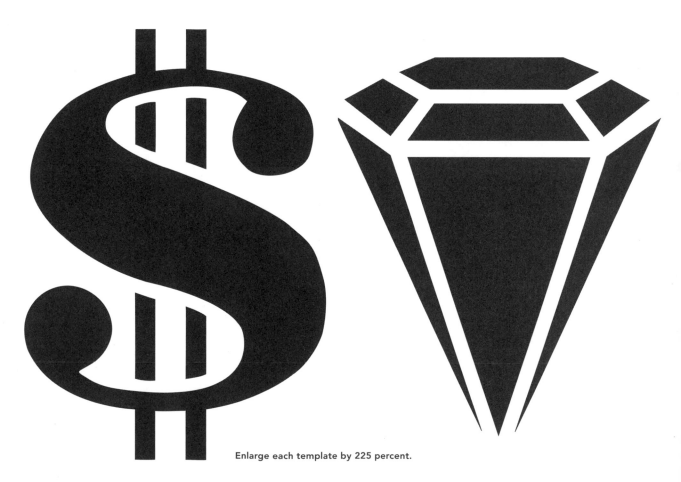

Enlarge each template by 225 percent.

3 Peel the stencil off the sheet. Wipe any paint off the back of the stencil and make sure the surface is still sticky (if not, apply spray mount again). Move the stencil to the left and down so the tops of the diamonds are 9" from the bottoms of the ones in the existing row and staggered between them. Beginning with the first diamond on the left, paint every other diamond. Make a third row of diamonds, centered like the first row; paint every diamond on this row. For the fourth row of diamonds, shift the stencil to the right of the first row so the diamonds are again staggered; beginning with the first diamond on the right, paint every other one. Finish with a fifth row of diamonds, just like the first row.

4 Make a stencil with the dollar sign using the remaining piece of card stock. Use gold fabric paint to fill in the spaces you skipped in rows two and four, centering the stencil between the diamonds. Leave the sheet to dry, then, with a cloth covering it, iron the sheet to set the paint.

5 To sew together the duvet cover, put one sheet on top of the other with the right sides facing each other. Pin along the edges of the sheet, leaving the bottom edge open. Sew a ½" hem along the sides and top of the sheets. Turn the cover right side out. Fold the bottom edge of the top sheet under 1½", pin it, and sew it down. Pin the lower edge of the bottom sheet the same way and sew it down. Pin the bottom edge of the two sheets together and sew 26" in from each side, leaving a 35" opening in the middle. Sew the buttons, evenly spaced, along the bottom inside hem. Sew corresponding buttonholes in the top sheet and use the seam ripper to cut the buttonhole openings. Now you're ready to stuff your diamond-studded duvet cover! Sleep tight.

spice it up

RACK UP YOUR SPICES IN AN OLD SUITCASE // Lori Forty Weaver

materials

Old hard-sided suitcase with flat sides (check your local thrift or vintage store)

Enough cute fabric to cover the interior (if needed)

Pencil (optional)

Scissors

Magna-Tac 809 or other fabric glue

Tape measure

2 pieces 1"-thick wood

Table saw or handsaw

Paint or wood stain

Paintbrush

Drill with ⅛" countersink and screwdriver bit

Eight 1⅝" flat top wood screws

Ribbon

Frame mounting kit, complete with 2 picture frame hooks and screws

Wire

Add some vintage flair to your digs by making a super spice rack from an upcycled suitcase. You'll need one made of hard material with flat sides, so it will hang flush against your wall. The bottom of the suitcase (the part that holds the bulk of your clothes) should be deeper than the top.

1 If the inside of your suitcase isn't too shabby, feel free to keep the original lining. If the interior is looking beat up, cover it with the fabric. Here's how: lay a piece of the fabric on a surface, then lay the closed suitcase on the fabric and trace around it. Flip the suitcase over and trace again on another section of fabric. Cut out the pieces, then spread a thin layer of fabric glue on the inside of your suitcase and secure the fabric in place with the right side facing out. With the suitcase open, measure the height and circumference of the inner walls on the bottom half. Cut a strip of fabric ¼" taller and ½" longer than your measurements. Use fabric glue to attach the strip, right side out, to the wall of the suitcase. Tuck in ¼" at the top and ends of the strip so the raw edges are hidden. Let dry.

2 To make the shelves, measure the width (from the handle side to the hinge side) and depth of the bottom of your suitcase. Cut two pieces of 1"-thick wood to these measurements. You can use a table saw or a handsaw (or find a hardware store that will cut the pieces for you). Paint or stain the shelves and let them dry.

3 To install the shelves, line them up just above and just below the suitcase handle. You may need to adjust the placement depending on the size, shape, or location of your suitcase's handle and closures. Making sure the first shelf is level, hold it in place, then use a drill and ⅛" countersink bit to drill two guide holes from the outside of the suitcase into each end of the wood. Repeat for the second shelf. Switch to a screwdriver bit and insert the screws through the guide holes and into the shelves.

4 To hold your spices in place, cut two pieces of ribbon 1" longer than your shelves. Secure a ribbon about 1" above each shelf by gluing ½" of each of the ribbon's ends to the interior sides of your suitcase. To hang your spice rack, use the drill to secure the picture frame hooks to the outside of your suitcase so the screws enter the back of your top shelf; use wire to hang. Fill with your fave flaves and get cookin'.

art of glass

MAKE GLASSWARE MORE FETCHING WITH DIY ETCHING // Caitlin Sasser

materials

Drinking glasses (must be made of, well, glass)

Masking tape

Fancy stickers (see tip)

Rubber gloves

Armour Etch or other glass etching cream

Plastic-coated paper plates

Bristle brush

figure 1

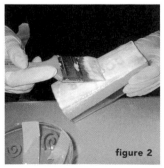

figure 2

Sure, you can spend months searching for a perfectly quirky set of glasses to complement your vintage Pyrex, or you can just make your own right now. Create a customized set with a few cheap glasses, some stickers, and a jar of etching cream. Then, the next time you throw a party, your guests will be sure not to mix up their drinks.

1 Wash and dry your glassware thoroughly to remove any manufacturing grime or grease.

2 Use the masking tape to tape off sections of glass you want to protect from the etching cream. Be sure the tape is pressed tightly to the glass to make a straight line. If it's buckled, the etching cream will seep under the seam.

3 Slap some stickers on there (see figure 1). Remember, anywhere there is a sticker, the glass will come out clear. Make sure you really rub the stickers on so that they make a good, tight seal with the glass to avoid seepage—wherever the etching cream touches the glass, the surface will be etched.

4 Before you use the etching cream, put on some rubber gloves. This step is important, because this etching cream is caustic. For real—it will burn you. Pour a little etching cream out onto the plastic-coated plate. (The cream will ooze through uncoated paper plates and make a gooey mess.) Use your brush to liberally apply the cream on the glass (see figure 2). Cover all surfaces very thoroughly, smearing cream over all the stickers and up to the taped edges, being sure to use lots of it. If you're stingy with it, you'll end up with streaks, which you won't be able to fix. Leave the cream on for 10 to 15 minutes.

5 Again wearing rubber gloves, and using plenty of warm water, rinse the glasses off in the sink. Wash the basin out thoroughly when you're done, too, so you don't accidentally etch your sink!

6 Peel off the stickers, wash the glasses with soap and water, dry them, and—voilà!—you have an awesomely cute set of etched glassware.

- -

We like using stickers made of vellum because they have defined edges and come off easily at the end of the project. Select stickers with good definition and great shapes. For lettering, choose stickers that have the centers of closed letters cut out.

tie one on

APRONS TO MAKE YOU LOOK BITCHIN' IN THE KITCHEN // Amy Karol

An apron is a playfully nostalgic, must-have kitchen accessory. Best of all, you can make your own, even if your sewing skills would make June Cleaver cringe.

the berry easy apron

materials

Men's long-sleeved dress shirt in large or extra large

Scissors

Freezer paper (found in most grocery stores near the waxed paper)

Pencil

X-ACTO knife

Iron and ironing board

Red and green fabric paint and foam paintbrush

1 Lay the shirt flat with the back facing up. On one side, cut from the hem to the armpit, just inside the side seam. Then cut from the underarm down to the cuff. Repeat on other side. Cut across about 2" above the back yoke and then down each arm through the cuffs, removing the back panel of the shirt (figure 1).

2 Photocopy the cherry design (figure 2) and trace it onto the dull side of the freezer paper. Cut it out with the knife to make your stencil (discard the center cut-out and use the cherry outline). Heat the iron and iron the stencil onto the shirt, with the shiny side of the paper facing the fabric. Now iron another piece of freezer paper onto the underside of the shirt, behind the stencil. This will prevent the paint from bleeding through.

3 Fill in the pattern in the stencil with fabric paint, and allow it to dry for at least 12 hours. Peel off the freezer paper from both sides and then heat-set, following the paint manufacturer's instructions.

4 Fold over the shirt's shoulders, so you have a straight line from the top of one arm to the other (figure 3). Then fold down the top another 2" to 4", adjusting the length to suit you. Iron flat. To wear this fine apron, just tie the arms around your waist.

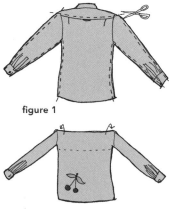

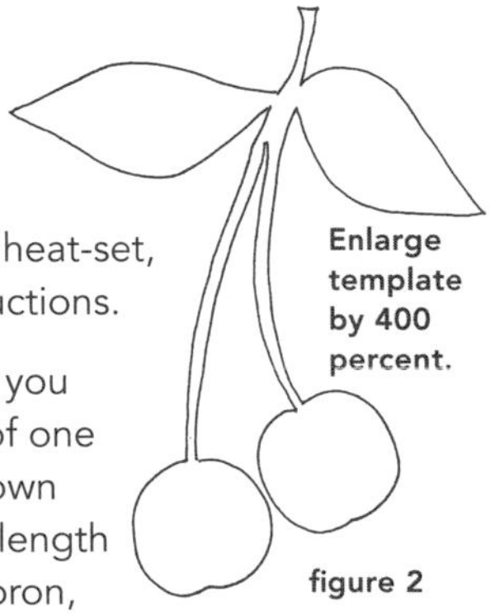

figure 1

figure 3

Enlarge template by 400 percent.

figure 2

the sassy circle

materials

38" square of prewashed cotton fabric (a vintage sheet works great)

Pencil

Scissors

9 yards ½"-wide double-fold bias tape

Sewing machine and matching thread

5 ½" square of contrasting fabric

Iron and ironing board

Straight pins

1 Fold the large fabric square in half with right sides together, and then in half again to make a square. Draw a large quarter circle along the outer open edge with a pencil and cut along the line. Then draw a small quarter circle 4" from the folded corner of the fabric and cut (figure 1).

2 Unfold your fabric. It should look like a doughnut approximately 38" in diameter with an 8" hole in the middle. Trim the doughnut if it's not perfect. On one side of the doughnut, cut a straight line from the outer edge to the hole (figure 2). Sew bias tape along the outer edge of the doughnut and the cut sides. Use a medium-wide zigzag stitch so you'll be sure to hit both edges of the tape.

3 Fold the contrasting fabric in half and round one unfolded corner on one side by cutting it. Unfold the fabric and apply bias tape to the U-shape you created (not the top) using zigzag stitch (figure 3). This will be your pocket. Fold the top down ½" and stitch across to hem it. Press and set the pocket aside.

4 Cut two 2-yard strips of bias tape. Unfold and iron them flat, then pin them, wrong sides together. Fold in the ends at an angle. Stitch the strips together along the outside edges, using a straight stitch, to make a waistband (figure 4).

5 Fold the waistband tape in half and center it over the top of the apron, enclosing the raw edge. Zigzag stitch it on through all layers (figure 5). The loose tape at either end will be your apron ties.

6 Try on your apron and pin the pocket where you think it looks good. Sew the pocket onto the apron with a straight stitch. Just don't sew across the top of the pocket.

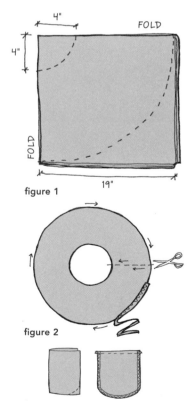

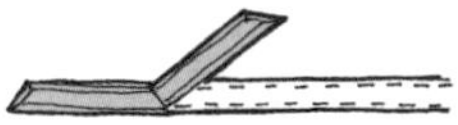

figure 1

figure 2

figure 3

figure 4

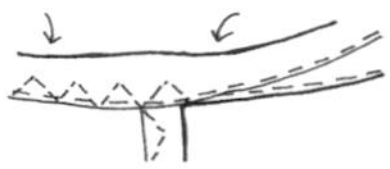

figure 5

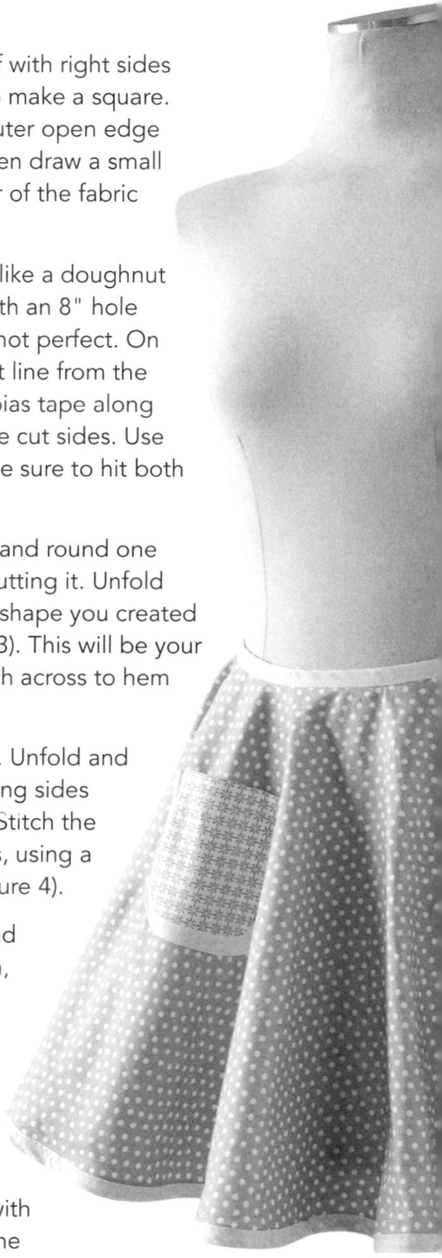

in the bag

MAKE A FAUX PLASTIC BAG AND MATCHING COIN PURSE // Jennifer Reichert

Plastic bags are lurking at the end of grocery lines everywhere, then tucked away under the kitchen sink. They can carry sweaty gym clothes, scoop up doggy poop, and line trash cans, but they can also float in the ocean, strangling animals that mistake them for food, and lie dormant in landfills, where they won't ever decompose. To decrease the number of bags you consume, why not make your own unique reusable tote? Whip up a coin purse made from a receipt and soon you'll be passing up plastic each time you shop.

materials

1 plastic grocery bag

¾ yard white, nonstretch medium-weight cotton fabric, such as twill or sateen

¾ yard lining fabric (we used red gingham)

Tailor's chalk or transfer pen

Straight pins

Scissors

Iron and ironing board

Sewing machine and matching thread

Photocopy of the "Thank You" template

Transfer paper

Stylus

Embroidery hoop or stabilizer

Embroidery needle

4 skeins red embroidery floss

1 To create your pattern, smooth out your plastic grocery bag, cut the bottom and the tops of the handles open, and pull out the sides so it lies completely flat. Iron your fabrics and fold them in half widthwise. Lay the plastic bag on top of the folded main fabric and, using chalk or a transfer pen, trace around the bottom and sides of the bag (adding ⅝" for seam allowance). Trace around the handles, continuing to add ⅝". To wear the bag over your shoulder, increase the length of the handles at the top by 3".

2 Lay your folded main fabric on top of the folded lining fabric. Pin the two together and cut along your traced line to make the four pieces of your bag: two lining pieces and two outer ones.

3 To make the inside pocket, measure the width of your bag and cut a rectangle of lining fabric 7" by the measured width. Fold the top edge over ¼" and then ¼" again. Iron flat. Sew a straight stitch to hem the edge. Lay the pocket upside-down on top of one lining piece with the right sides together and the hemmed pocket edge aligned 3" below the bottom of the bag. Pin the raw edge to the lining and sew across. Fold the pocket up and iron it flat. To create sections in your pocket, pin and sew seams from the bottom of the pocket to the top, backstitching at the beginning and end of your seams.

Enlarge template by 250 percent.

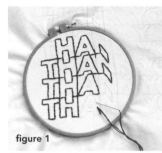

figure 1

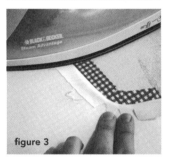

figure 2

figure 3

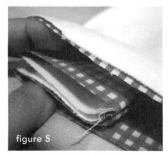

figure 4

figure 5

4 To embroider your design, take one outer bag piece and lay it flat. Center the "Thank You" graphic on the right side and pin the corners to the fabric. Slip a sheet of transfer paper underneath. Trace the design on your photocopy using a stylus. Check that the whole design has transferred to the fabric, then remove the papers.

5 Stabilize the fabric as you embroider by using the embroidery hoop. Use split stitch (see page 111) and six strands of floss to create the outlines (figure 1), then use satin stitch to fill in the letters.

6 Now it's time to sew your bag. Lay out the lining pieces with the right sides facing. Pin the tops of the handles and sew them together. Iron the seams flat. Repeat for the outer fabric pieces. Open up the outer bag piece and lining piece and lay both out flat, with right sides together. Pin around the inner edge of the handles, matching up seams, and sew (figure 2). Clip curves and trim any extra fabric from the seams.

7 Fold the outer edges of the top fabric's handles in ⅝" and iron the folds flat, clipping curves where necessary (figure 3). Turn the pieces over and repeat on the lining-fabric side.

8 Turn the bag right side out. Iron the inner handle seam. Match up the outer edges of the handles and topstitch them together, as close to the edge as possible. Turn the outer fabric so that the right sides are together, and pin them along the side seams. Match the linings' right sides together, and pin them along the side seams, making sure to catch the pocket sides between the lining pieces; sew. Trim any extra fabric and turn the bag right side out.

9 To finish the handles and create the side gussets, fold each handle in half lengthwise, with the lining on the inside of the fold (figure 4). Pin them in place. Sew along the top seam of the handle (it's called "stitching in the ditch") to secure the fold. Continue folding the sides of the bag in, creating a gusset. The side seam should be approximately 3" in from the fold, making a 6" gusset (figure 5). Pin to hold the fold in place. Sew a ¼" seam along the bottom of the bag, through all layers. Trim the seam allowance to ⅛". Turn the bag inside out, with the right sides facing. Sew a seam ⅜" from the folded edge, capturing the raw edge inside the new seam. Turn the bag right side out and press.

sales receipt coin purse

materials

Receipt

Printable T-shirt transfer paper

Inkjet printer

Piece of white fabric 5" wide and about 2" longer than your receipt

White zipper at least half as long as your receipt

Straight pins

Sewing machine with zipper foot and white thread

Iron and ironing board

1 Find a grocery store receipt twice as long as you want your change purse to be wide. Scan the receipt into an imaging program, then crop and straighten it. Reverse the image and print it onto the transfer paper.

2 Following the transfer instructions, transfer the receipt image onto the fabric.

3 Cut out the image, allowing for a ⅝" seam allowance on all sides.

4 Fold the fabric in half lengthwise, wrong sides together. Lay the closed zipper along one edge, face down. Pin one side of the zipper tape in place and sew it on, using a zipper foot. Sew across the zipper end and trim the zipper to size, if needed.

5 Unzip the zipper and pin the other side to the remaining top edge. Pin and sew it in place. Rezip.

6 Turn the pouch inside out and match up the side seams. Pin and sew the side seams.

7 Turn the pouch right side out. Sew ¼" from the bottom of the pouch, then trim the allowance to ⅛" and turn the pouch inside out. Sew ⅜" from the folded edge. Turn the pouch right side out and press.

this mug's for you

CUSTOMIZE YOUR DRINKWARE WITH DIY DECALS // Melinda Hikida

No matter the weather, it's probably safe to assume that at least one of your daily beverages makes its appearance in a mug. So why not make your drinkware your own by adding a customized design? Decorating mugs with water-slide decals is simple and inexpensive, and if you've got gift giving on the brain, the end result makes a great, personalized prezzie.

materials

Clear water-slide printer paper (get inkjet or laser paper depending on your printer type; available at www.carolcreations.biz)

Water-slide decal fixative (available at www.carolcreations.biz)

Soft sponge (your fixative should come with one)

Scissors

Shallow bowl

Plain mug

1 Start by finding an image you'd like to use as a decoration on your mug. Use any image you want as long as it fits on your mug and can be printed on paper; simple, two-toned images work best.

2 Print your image on a piece of water-slide paper and let the ink dry for 30 minutes.

3 Use your fixative to set the ink on the water-slide paper. The smell of the fixative is very strong, so make sure you do this in a well-ventilated area. Pour a puddle of fixative on the center of your image; you want a fairly thick coat (2–3 mm) so don't be shy. Then very, very gently use a soft sponge to spread the fixative around until the image is completely covered (try not to exert any pressure when doing this). To make sure the image is thoroughly covered, hold the paper up to a light so you can see where the fixative stops.

4 Once the image is covered, let it dry for 8 hours, then use sharp scissors to cut the image out close to the lines.

5 Fill a shallow bowl with warm water and completely submerge the decal. Let it sit in water until it starts to separate from the paper (about 1 minute). You can check its readiness by sliding the decal and paper between your fingers to see if it is moving away from the paper. But keep the image on the paper until you are ready to put it on your mug.

6 Decide where on your mug you want to place the image and wet the spot slightly with your fingers. (This enables you to move the image around once it's on the mug.) Hold one end of the decal and slowly pull the paper off, then place the decal on the mug. You can slide it around until it's exactly where you want it. Smooth out any air bubbles with your finger. Tip: Wait a few minutes (but no longer) until some of the water has evaporated, then smooth out any remaining air bubbles.

7 Let the decal dry for 24 hours, then christen your customized drinkware with a delicious mug of hot chocolate. Note: If you happen to have a dishwasher, don't put your water-slide-decaled mugs in it! Wash them by hand instead.

happy feet

SEW UP SOME SHOE STORAGE // Tara Marks

Too many shoes and not enough places to stash 'em? With fresh fabrics and a little sewing know-how, you can craft up an over-the-door organizer and store up to 16 pairs of your cute kicks in style.

materials

Scissors

1½ yards 60"-wide cotton fabric in a cool pattern for the background

Straight pins

Sewing machine and thread in the color of your choice

1 yard 60"-wide cotton fabric in a complementary solid for the shoe pouches

Measuring tape

Pencil

Bias tape or ribbon to match the pouch fabric (optional)

2 over-the-door hooks (available at any hardware store)

Buttonhole foot

Seam ripper

1 Cut a piece of your patterned fabric to 60" by 53". Fold it in half the long way, right sides together. Trim off the selvage so that your folded piece measures about 29" across. Pin and sew around the three open edges with your sewing machine, leaving an opening big enough to fit your fist through. Turn the fabric right side out, pulling it through the opening, then fold in the hem and sew the hole closed.

2 Next, take your yard of solid fabric, fold it in half lengthwise, and then fold it lengthwise again. Cut along the folds so you end up with four strips measuring 9" by 60" each. Pin and sew a hem along both long sides of each piece; this will become the top and bottom edge of each shoe pouch.

3 Create the rows of your shoe organizer by arranging the four strips evenly on top of your patterned fabric (right sides facing out) with the bottom strip flush with the bottom edge of the background. Leave 3" of background fabric visible between each row; there'll be about 5" visible at the top. Fold in and pin the side edges of each strip so the rows are secured to the background on both sides.

With all this extra storage to stash your shoes, you may need to buy more to fill it up!

4 To create the pouches, lay a measuring tape along the top of each row and, using a pencil, mark 7" intervals on the background fabric. Then mark 15" intervals along the top of each strip. Line up the 7" background marks with the 15" marks on each strip and pin them (thus creating the pockets). Sew a vertical line with your machine to secure the pocket sides. Now you have four rows, with four sections in each row. To close the pouches at the bottom, gather the loose fabric in each section by pulling it out, then flattening it so the extra falls toward the middle, making a sort of pleat; pin this in place. Sew along the bottom of each row.

5 If you want to hide the pleats, place bias tape or ribbon (matching your solid fabric) on top of the exposed edges along the bottom of each row, then pin and sew it in place. Snip any long thread you see hanging.

6 To finish, position the over-the-door hooks on the door where you want to hang your organizer. Replace the standard presser foot on your sewing machine with the buttonhole foot and sew two buttonholes in the top portion of the organizer—1" from the top and 3" from each side is a pretty safe bet for locations. Using a seam ripper, cut the buttonhole openings. Hang the organizer by sliding the buttonholes onto the hooks—and presto!

curtain call

STITCH YOUR OWN SHOWER CURTAIN // Djerba Goldfinger

Spending hours in the bathroom staring at an ugly beige shower curtain is downright criminal when you can create an alternative in an afternoon. This one can be sewn up with just about any kind of fabric—whatever you choose, it's better than that old moldy thing you have hanging now, isn't it?

materials

5 yards fabric of your choice, 45"–60" wide

Scissors

Sewing machine or needle and matching thread

Iron and ironing board

Straight pins

Grommet kit containing at least ten ⅜" grommets and the necessary setting tools (available at most fabric stores and some hardware stores)

Rubber mallet or hammer

Vinyl shower curtain liner

10 shower curtain hooks or rings

1 Cut the fabric in half horizontally so that you have two 2½-yard-long pieces.

2 Sew the two pieces, right sides together, using a ½" seam, to make a rectangle that is 90" to 120" across. Iron the seam flat after you've sewn it. You can be fancy and finish the edges of this seam if you want, but the liner is going to cover it in the end.

3 To finish the borders of the shower curtain, with the wrong side of the fabric facing up, fold ½" in on the left- and right-side edges, and press with an iron. Then turn the hem over again 1¼" and press. Pin it down and sew 1⅛" from the outside edge (or ⅛" from the hem's folded edge). Make a larger hem on the bottom the same way, folding in the usual ½" to start, then making the second fold 2¾" and stitching 2⅝" from the bottom edge. Make an even larger hem at the top by making the second fold 3¾" and stitching 3⅝" from the top edge.

4 On the top hem of the curtain, 1" from the top edge, use pins to mark where your grommets will go. Place your first and last grommets 2¼" in from the sides, then space the eight remaining grommets evenly between them.

5 Attach the grommets to the fabric, following the instructions that come with the kit. (Alternatively, if you have a sewing machine and know how to make buttonholes, you can make ten 1"-wide vertical buttonholes instead.)

6 Hang the curtain together with the vinyl liner using the shower curtain rings.

7 Take a shower, smelly.

office space

DIY DESK SET // Callie Watts

Deck out your desk with these DIY office supplies and you'll whistle while you work. Boring office supplies have nothing on homemade accordion files, magazine holders, binder clips, magnetic strips, and bulletin boards. With these odds and ends in hand, you won't mind the daily grind.

magazine holder

materials

Large map

Cheap cardboard magazine holder

Mod Podge or other decoupage glue

Gorilla Glue or other strong multipurpose glue

1 Lay the old map facedown on your work surface, then open the magazine holder so that it is flat and place it on the map. Trace the outline of the holder, adding 1" all around, and cut out the shape. Cut a second piece of map ⅛" smaller than the cardboard all around.

2 Using the same method as above, decoupage the larger piece of map to the outside of the holder and the smaller piece to the inside. Let dry and fold the holder back into shape, regluing it where necessary with Gorilla Glue.

If a map motif isn't your thing, switch it up by using decorative wrapping paper.

accordion file

materials

X-ACTO knife

Straightedge ruler

Nine 9½"-by-11½" envelopes in heavy stock, flaps sealed

Large map

2 pieces 11½"-by-12½" cardboard

Mod Podge or other decoupage glue

Glue brush

3 pieces 12" square card stock

Gorilla Glue or other strong multipurpose glue

Two 4½"-by-5½" horseshoe handles

4 nut-and-bolt pairs (the size needed to attach your handles—we used ⅝" bolts and #8-32 nuts)

Decorative toggle

Sticky notes and flags (optional)

1 Using the X-ACTO and a straight edge, trim off about ¹⁄₁₆" from the bottom of each envelope (the sealed flap end—made stronger by the sealed flaps—will serve as the bottom of each section of your accordion file).

2 To make the decorative file covers, cut two rectangles from the map that are 1" larger all around than the cardboard pieces. Cover one side of each cardboard piece by applying decoupage glue a little bit at a time; start at one corner of a map piece, pressing it onto the board and smoothing it out as you go. Fold the excess map over the edges and secure them with glue. Let the glue dry, then coat the entire front with decoupage glue. Brush the glue onto the folded-over edges and a little bit onto the board backs as well. Let dry. Cut two pieces of card stock slightly smaller than the cardboard, and glue each to an inside cover.

3 To make the piece that will connect your covers, cut the cardstock to 8"-by-11½", then mark every ½" along both short edges. Fold the card stock like a fan, accordion-style, making a crease at each mark. Apply Gorilla Glue to the right side of each fold's valley and attach the uncut side of an envelope to each crease, pressing the edge down firmly until dry.

4 Glue the outermost envelopes to the inside of the cardboard covers. Let dry.

5 Close your file and hold a horseshoe handle in position at each side of the top, making sure the handles are centered. Lightly mark the holes, then use the X-ACTO to punch through the cardboard. Attach each handle with two bolts and nuts. Center a decorative toggle at the top of the covers and attach it with Gorilla Glue. Finally, glue the sticky notes and flags to the inside cover.

To make a smaller accordion file, follow the instructions above using smaller envelopes for the pockets. When making the accordion piece, cut card stock to the same width as your envelopes but 1" shorter in length. Instead of adding a handle and toggle, keep it closed with a large rubber band.

magnetic clip strip

materials

Paper clips

Binder clips

Adhesive magnetic strip
(cut to desired length)

Newspaper

Spray paint in desired color

Clear topcoat spray

Gorilla Glue or other strong
multipurpose glue

Tiny ribbon

Scraps of map

Mod Podge or other
decoupage glue

Glue brush

To complete your desk set, gather paper clips, binder clips, and a magnetic strip. Spread them out on a newspaper-covered work surface; spray-paint them and seal with a clear topcoat spray. Glue pieces of tiny ribbon to the tops of the paper clips and let dry. Stick these to your magnetic strip for holding notes and photos. Decorate your binder clips by cutting pieces of an old map to the size of the clip, and attaching the pieces with decoupage glue.

magnetic bulletin board

If a magnetic strip isn't enough, whip up a magnetic bulletin board.

Just paint a piece of plywood with magnetic paint and let dry. Make sure you get the edges, too, if you don't want an unfinished look. It takes at least two coats of magnetic paint to get a strong bond (follow the instructions on the container); make sure it dries completely between coats. Attach eyelet screws to the back of the board and tie on picture framing wire for hanging. Mount the board using a picture hanging kit.

computer pajamas

LET YOUR SYSTEM SNOOZE IN STYLE // Lori Forty Weaver

Give back to your Mac or add some Windows dressing with this simple laptop cozy. In no time, your compy will be comfier and cozier in its jammies than you are sleeping in your favorite old T-shirt. And it'll keep the dust off, too.

materials

Tape measure

Scissors

Two fabrics of your choice (choose pieces large enough to fit around your laptop plus 6")

Sewing machine and matching thread

Batting or fiberfill

Iron and ironing board

2 pieces Velcro tape, about 1" each

1 Measure the entire circumference of your closed laptop, both widthwise and lengthwise. Divide the widthwise measurement in half and add 1". Add 5" to the length to allow for the flap.

2 Cut two pieces of fabric—one for the outside and one for the lining—to these measurements. Place them right sides together and sew along one short edge leaving a ½" seam allowance. Flip the fabric right side out and fold with wrong sides together. Sew side edges together, leaving a ½" seam allowance, beginning at the closed end and ending 4½" short of the other end. This open end will become the flap.

3 Fill with batting or fiberfill (enough to keep your computer protected) up to the open flap area. Fold the bottom of the case up to the lower edge of the flap and mark the center bottom. Unfold the case and stitch along this line to give the case some structure and keep the padding in place, and also stitch where the padding stops at the flap. Turn over so the right side of the inner fabric is facing you and fold the bottom up to meet the bottom of the flap; pin and stitch the sides, ending at the beginning of the flap and leaving a ½" seam allowance. Turn the case right side out and fold the raw edges along all three sides of the flap to the inside and iron down. Hand stitch around to close the edges of the flap.

4 Affix the Velcro pieces to the flap and front of the case to make a closure. Now you're ready to take your portable 'puter out into the wild!

take it or sleeve it

DECORATE WITH RECORDS // Erica Chandler, Tracie Egan Morrissey, and Callie Watts

materials

Heavy-duty single-hole punch

**9 record sleeves
(sans records)**

Fishing line

Do the mental-ward-white walls in your bachelorette pad leave you feeling less *That Girl!* and more *Girl, Interrupted*? Instead of lamenting what your walls lack, put your jams on your walls and your ass on the floor with this rockin' décor idea.

1 Punch holes in the corners of the record sleeves.

2 Using fishing line, tie the records together in three strips of three, leaving about 4 ½" between the records. Double knot the fishing line at the bottom corner of the first sleeve, run the line through the top hole of the next sleeve, then double it back up and secure it with another knot. (The knots slip out of fishing line easily, so make them really tight.) Once you have your record strip done, tie fishing line across the top two holes of the first record to hang it.

3 Hang the strips about 4 ½" apart on the wall.

cover up

STAMP OUT BIG SPENDING WITH DIY WALLPAPER // Taarna Grimsley and Callie Watts

materials

Black-and-white image
for stamp design
(photocopy or printout)

Rubber-stamp block

Colorless blender marker

X-ACTO knife or block-print
cutting tool

Stamp pad in desired color

Several sheets of card stock
about the size of your stamp

Rubber cement

½"-thick piece of wood
cut slightly larger than
your stamp

Roll of 90-pound drawing
paper

Matte-finish wall paint in
desired color, plus paint
roller and roller tray

Small paintbrush (for
touchups, if needed)

Glue pad

Fun Flock in a color that
matches stamping ink
(available at most stamp
stores)

Wallpaper paste and
glue brush, or stapler

Wallpaper is back in a big way, and it doesn't look like that peach-and-teal-flowered stuff your mom put in the bathroom in 1993. Nowadays, wallpaper is used sparingly and with finesse. Instead of covering a whole room in plaid, choose one or two walls to highlight. Still, all that paper gets expensive. So if you wanna wrap your walls in gorgeous paper without blowing your wad, use a stamp and some Fun Flock to make your own.

1 Place your image facedown on the rubber-stamp block. Hold the paper in place and run the transparent blender marker over the backside of your image to transfer it. Using the X-ACTO for simple designs or a block-print cutting tool for complicated ones, carefully cut out the parts of the image you want to be negative (the ink will print whatever you do not cut out). Once you are done cutting, test your stamp: blot it on a stamp pad, press it to a piece of card stock, pressing firmly and evenly, then remove. If the printed image doesn't look right, simply wash the ink off the block and deepen your cuts or make more of them. Repeat the test until you are satisfied. Use rubber cement to attach the stamp to the wood backing.

2 To figure out how many strips of wallpaper you'll need, divide the width of the wall by the width of your roll of paper. Using the X-ACTO knife, cut the necessary number of strips to the height of the wall. Paint the paper any color you want, using matte-finish paint, and let it dry.

3 Decide on a stamping pattern—you can keep the spacing consistent by measuring and marking the paper lightly with a pencil where you want the images to be. Cover your stamp with ink by blotting it on the stamp pad. Position the stamp, then apply heavy, even pressure. Keep your pattern consistent by lining up each strip as you go.

Don't worry too much about little smudges and stray marks; you can paint over them after you finish stamping if necessary.

4 Make your wallpaper look extra fancy by flocking the stamped image. To do this, wash the ink off your stamp. Blot it on a glue pad, then press it evenly onto the printed image. Using your fingers, dust the Fun Flock over the glue, then tap the excess off. Let the wallpaper dry completely.

5 To hang your wallpaper, apply paste to the back of the paper with a glue brush. For a less-permanent fix, you can staple the paper to your wall.

Try this recipe for nontoxic wallpaper paste from Care2.com: Combine 1 cup flour (wheat, corn, or rice) and 3 teaspoons alum in a double boiler. Add enough water to make it the consistency of heavy cream; stir until blended. Heat, stirring constantly, until the mixture has thickened to a gravy texture. Let cool. Stir in 10 drops clove oil.

dear diary

HOMEMADE JOURNALS TO WRITE HOME ABOUT // Samantha Hahn

materials

5"-by-4" piece of cardboard or heavy card stock

6"-by-5" piece of fabric

Hot glue gun and glue

Scissors

Short stack of paper, such as recycled printer paper, vellum, or watercolor paper

Pinking shears

Stapler

Origami paper or additional fabric (optional)

Make a mini-journal to fill with notes-to-self, doodles, or your deepest, darkest secrets. Its wee size makes it perfect for purses, so you can record your brilliant thoughts on the go.

1 Fold the 5"-by-4" piece of cardboard or card stock in half (like a card).

2 Affix your fabric to the outside of the cardboard by hot-gluing around the edges of the flattened cardboard and centering your piece of fabric on top. Then fold the cover to make sure you didn't adhere it too tightly.

3 Once dry, make diagonal cuts in the corners of the fabric that sticks out, so you can fold the excess fabric to the inside.

4 Hot-glue a thin line around the inside edges of the cardboard, then fold the fabric and affix to the inside cover. You may need additional glue where the fabric overlaps.

5 For your journal's pages, cut a short stack of paper about 4½" by 3½". Cut with pinking shears if you want your pages to have zigzag edges. Fold the stack in half (like a card) and staple twice in the crease to hold the pages together. Be sure not to use too much paper or the cover won't close.

6 Hot-glue a line down the inside center of the cardboard. Align the edge of your folded-paper pile with the crease; hold till dry. Further secure the pages by gluing the first and last to the cardboard.

7 Make the inside covers pretty by gluing origami paper or additional fabric over them.

glowing by the book

MAKE YOUR OWN LAMP // Lori Forty Weaver

materials

4 hardback books

Paintbrush

White craft glue

Heavy weight
(like a big dictionary)

Ruler or T square

Drill and ⅜" bit

Thin pen

Chopstick or thin dowel
(less than ⅜")

Extra-strong craft adhesive,
such as E-6000

2 or 3 C-clamps

Lamp kit (available from
any hardware store)

X-ACTO knife

Lampshade of your choice

Lightbulb

Think your concentration could use some illumination? If the lamps at the megamart don't brighten your day, follow the light and craft one yourself with a few used books. You don't need book-learnin' to get 'em stacked and turn it on. The work time is short, but drying time is long, so give yourself a couple days. Then, put on your reading glasses, get a big cup of tea, and read a book next to your book light. Crackling fireplace optional.

1 After you've raided your grandma's library (or the thrift store) for some books to create the base of your lamp, get started by holding a book closed but upright, with the spine on a table. Using a brush and the white glue, coat the edges of the book's pages with a thin layer; gravity is your friend, so be sure to let a little glue drip down between the pages to give you a nice solid seal. Repeat for all the books, then stack them and weight them with something heavy like more books. Let the books dry overnight, or for at least a few hours.

2 To create a path through your stack of books for the lamp wires to run through, select the book that you want at the top of your stack. With a ruler or T square, locate the center of the book's front cover, and drill straight through all the pages and the back cover. Decide how you want the base of your lamp to look—don't go for perfection, give the pile some character—and stack the books in order. Stick a thin pen through the hole you just made in the top book, and mark the second book's cover. Then drill straight through the second book at this mark. Repeat this mark-and-drill process for each book in your stack.

3 Push a chopstick through the holes to clear out any debris. Leave the chopstick in the bottom book as a guide for the stack—it will keep the books from moving and obscuring your hole as you assemble the base of your lamp.

Spread craft adhesive on the front cover, slide the next book onto the chopstick and into position. Repeat this step until you've stacked all the books. Once they've all been glued, check for gaps between the books or pages and brush on extra white glue if necessary. Use the C-clamps to hold the stack in place while it dries overnight. Leave the chopstick where it is, to prevent any glue from obstructing your hole. When the glue is dry, remove the chopstick.

4 Feed the wire from your lamp kit through the hole from the bottom up and add the fixture, following the instructions that come with the kit. You may want to use some craft adhesive to keep the fixture in place on the base. To allow the lamp to sit flat once you've wired it, create a groove for the cord by using the X-ACTO to cut a sliver between the hole in the bottom book cover to the back edge. Top off your lamp with a shade, screw in a bulb, and enjoy your snazzy new reading light!

picture yourself

MAKE IMAGE-TRANSFER PILLOWS // Kara Valle

materials

Newspapers

Black-and-white photocopies or laser printouts of image

Two square pieces of light-colored, woven cotton fabric, larger than image

Masking tape

Paintbrush

Paint solvent containing methylene chloride, such as Goof Off

Tool for burnishing (an old toothbrush works well)

Straight pins

Tailor's chalk or fabric marking pen

Sewing machine or needle and matching thread

Fiberfill

Is there something you wanna wake up snuggled next to every morning? Whether it's a cute pup or your celeb crush, just find an image and transfer it onto a pillow. Once you've got the knack for making solvent-image transfers, the possibilities are endless: Transfer a family photo for your mom on Mother's Day . . . or maybe some hardcore porn for your favorite pervy friend on her birthday.

1 Solvents are highly toxic, so choose a work surface in a well-ventilated area and line it with newspapers. Place the cotton fabric on the work surface, then position the image printout facedown on top of it. (Lightly tape the paper in place so it doesn't move around, but don't cover the image, or it won't transfer.)

2 Brush solvent onto the back of the image until you can see the picture through it; don't paint on too much or you might smudge it. The solvent evaporates really quickly, so work only in small sections.

3 Burnish (rub really hard) the back of the image to ensure a detailed transfer. You can check under a corner to see how your transfer is taking, but be careful not to move or shift the paper because it will be impossible to realign. If there are parts that haven't been transferred, continue applying the solvent and burnishing until you get the desired look and feel.

4 Allow the transfer to air-dry by a window or outside to clear any fumes.

5 To make the pillow: Pin the two pieces of fabric, right sides together. Using chalk or fabric marking pen, trace around the image shape, ¾" from image. Following the chalked line, sew a ¼" seam around the pillow, leaving a 3" opening at the bottom. Turn the fabric right side out, stuff with fiberfill, and whipstitch (see page 110) the opening closed.

push it real good

CRAFT A PUSH-LIGHT WALL FIXTURE // Alexandra Diaz, Tracie Egan Morrisey, and Callie Watts

materials

Hot glue gun and glue

18 heavy-duty magnets

9 push lights in the style of your choice, fitted with the required batteries

34" square metal sheet (not aluminum—it isn't magnetic)

4 nails

Convert your well-lit chat room into make-out central with this mood-setting, magnetic wall hanging/light fixture.

1 Using the glue gun, attach two heavy-duty magnets to the back of each push light.

2 Hang the metal sheet on your wall by hammering two nails beneath it at an angle, and two more at the top to secure it in place.

3 Place the lights on the metal sheet wherever you want.

ice, ice candle

COOL CANDLES MADE FROM SCRATCH // Maria Binns

If you're planning to spend the evening indoors, set the mood (and the table) with these chunky, cool-as-ice candles. You can buy new wax chunks for these—or recycle old white wax candles (just smash them inside a resealable freezer bag until you have meltable chunks). Wax, wax dye, and candlewicks are available at most craft-supply stores and candle-supply stores or online.

materials

Empty quart milk carton

Scissors

Candlewick

Ruler

Pencil

Fun-Tak or other reusable mounting putty

Wax

Double boiler or a metal bowl set in a larger saucepan (use old, cheap cookware from a thrift store)

Wax dye coloring chips

Ice

Resealable freezer bag

1 Wash and dry the inside of the milk carton. Cut the top off at the height you want your candle to be and cut a length of candlewick 2" taller than that. Fill the bottom of your double boiler with water and heat it to simmering on the stove.

2 Knot one end of the wick around a pencil, leaving a tail about 1½" long. Place a chunk of Fun-Tak onto the other end of the wick, and stick it to the inside center of the milk carton's bottom, with the pencil resting on top of the carton to keep it in place.

3 Fill the carton with wax chunks, then remove the wax chunks and transfer them to the top of the double boiler; melt slowly over low heat (figure 1).

4 When the wax is melted, add a dye color chip and stir until mixed. Repeat until you have the color you want.

figure 1   figure 2

5 Place several handfuls of ice in a sealed bag, and smash it to your desired size. Large chunks of ice will melt to leave big holes in your candle, while little pieces will create a pattern of smaller spaces in the wax. Fill the milk carton with ice up to 1" below the top, making sure that the wick remains in position.

6 Pour the melted wax into the carton, covering all the ice (figure 2). The wax will harden around the ice, which will then melt away.

7 Let the candle cool for about an hour, then pour out the water. Tear away the carton to reveal your candle, and prepare to light up.

For variety, experiment with different containers, such as drink cans or molds from candle-supply stores. Try using an assortment of ice-chunk sizes, or dye your wax with an assortment of colors.

you light up my life

DIY CANDLE LANTERNS // Maria Binns

Let your love light shine with a hand-crafted gypsy lantern. Make one to set the mood at dinner, or dozens to light up a backyard bash. Use a tea light for a softer glow or a votive candle for extra illumination.

materials

Tape measure

Glass jar

Scissors

8 ½"-by-11" sheet of paper

Pencil

Pinking shears

Thin, patterned cotton fabric

Interfacing (if needed)

Iron and ironing board (if needed)

Straight pins

Sewing machine or needle and matching thread

Hot glue gun and glue

Wire cutters

18-gauge copper or silver wire

Square pliers

Tea light or votive

1 Measure the circumference of the mouth of your jar. Divide this number by four and add 1". Cut a rectangular piece of paper to this width and to the height of the jar plus 3".

2 With a pencil, mark a point on one long edge of the strip of paper about 2" from the bottom. Fold the paper in half lengthwise and make an undulating cut from the mark you made to the center bottom of the strip, so that the piece, when unfolded, will resemble the shape shown in figure 1.

3 Use this pattern to cut out four pieces of fabric with pinking shears. If your cotton is particularly thin, you can iron on some interfacing to give it more structure.

4 Pin two pieces edge to edge with the wrong sides facing each other, and sew the edge, leaving a ½" seam allowance. Pin another piece on, again matching the edges with wrong sides facing; sew. Sew on the fourth piece and then stitch the final seam to make the pouch-shaped lantern cover. The seams will show on the outside of your lantern, so if you'd like a more finished look, hem the raw edges.

5 Slide the jar into the lantern cover. Using the hot glue gun, apply glue around the outer edge of the mouth of your jar. Press the top of the fabric onto the glue.

6 Cut 12" of wire for the lantern's handle. Twist a small loop in the center of the wire, then bend the sides into a crescent shape. With your pliers, bend each end of the wire upward into a little U shape.

7 Cut another 20" of wire. Hold the wire handle in position against the top of the jar, then wrap the second piece of wire around and around the mouth of the jar and into each U-shaped end to keep the handle in place. When you've wrapped the entire length of wire, twist the ends together to hold it.

8 Place a tea light or votive in the jar and hang.

figure 1

these little lights of mine

LIVING ROOM STRING LIGHTS // Heidi Andrea Rhodes

materials

4 cups water

Medium saucepan

Large bowl

Wooden spoon

½ cup flour

Strand of holiday lights

Water balloons or small balloons (one for every other bulb on your light strand)

Newspapers

Rubber gloves (optional)

Scissors

White string (you can buy a ball of it for a couple bucks at any craft-supply store)

Tweezers

Ever wished you could live under the night sky but suspected you should leave those glow-in-the-dark star stickers to your eleven-year-old niece? These clever lanterns, made with little more than string and holiday lights, create a celestial ambience without the middle-school mood. The best part is that they're super cheap to make, so you can save your money for a real trip to the city of romance.

1 Pour 2 cups of the water into the saucepan and place it over high heat. In the bowl, mix the flour with the remaining 2 cups water. When the water in the pan boils, add the flour mixture to it, stir, and bring to a boil again. Pour the mixture into the bowl. You just made paste!

2 Let the paste cool a bit so you don't burn your hands. Meanwhile, count every other bulb on your light strand and count out the same number of balloons. Blow up the balloons to the desired size (3½" to 4" in diameter) and tie them. Spread out some old newspapers to protect your work surface. Put on gloves if you want to.

3 Cut a long piece of string (start with about an arm's length; you can always add more) and dip it in the cooled paste. Run the string between your fingers to get rid of excess mix and then begin to wrap the string around a balloon. Do this until the balloon, minus its knot, is quite thickly covered in gooey string (figure 1)—cut and use another string if needed. Tie a separate dry string to the balloon knot and hang it where it won't be disturbed. The paste will drip, so lay some more newspaper underneath to catch it (figure 2). Repeat until you have finished all the balloons.

4 Let the lanterns hang until they are completely dry— this may take up to 48 hours. If you continue with moist spots remaining, you may encounter problems. Once the string is dry, pop the balloons and remove the balloon carcasses with a pair of tweezers (figure 3). Slip every other bulb into a string ball. Hang the light strand from a wall or ceiling and voilà! Pour your drink of choice and imagine that you are, indeed, dancing under the moon in Paris.

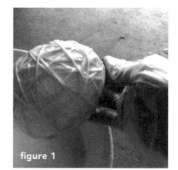
figure 1

figure 2

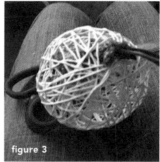
figure 3

These lanterns create an ethereal "could-be-dancing-under-the-moon-in-Paris" sort of feeling.

quilty pleasure

STITCH UP SOME HEADPHONES TO HANG IN YOUR HOME // Kim Thomas

materials

Quilting ruler

Rotary cutter

Cutting board

1½ yards black fabric

½ yard black patterned fabric

Sewing machine

Thread in black, silver, and a color that complements the silk brocade

Iron and ironing board

½ yard silk brocade

Scissors

Pattern (see page 63) printed onto 8½"-by-11" paper

¼ yard silver metallic fabric

Straight pins

Low-loft quilt batting

Safety pins

Double-fold bias quilt binding tape in a color that complements the silk brocade

22" length of wood dowel

Headphones sum up a lot of life experiences: the backseat of your parents' car during a cross-country trek, the school bus on that eighth-grade field trip, the daily haul from your nine-to-five. Celebrate your love of music by hanging pretty quilted headphones on your wall. Use these instructions to make a 20"-by-24" wall hanging to take quilting from olden ways to nowadays.

1 Using your ruler, rotary cutter, and cutting board, cut twelve 1½"-by-22" strips from the black fabric. Do the same with the black patterned fabric.

2 Note: Use a ¼" seam allowance throughout the pattern. Create strip pairs by sewing one solid black strip lengthwise to one black-pattern strip, right sides together, until you have 12 pairs. Sew all pairs together lengthwise, alternating black fabric and black-pattern fabric, until you have one piece.

3 Iron the piece flat on both sides. Use your rotary cutter to cut 1½" strips across the piece, giving you strips of squares. Sew these together lengthwise, rotating the strips to make a checkerboard pattern (turn half of them around so you are sewing a black square to a pattern square each time). The finished blocks will measure 1" on each side and the background piece will measure about 22" by 26". Iron the piece.

4 To make the border, cut two 2½"-by-22" pieces and two 2½"-by-30" pieces from the silk brocade fabric. First, sew the shorter pieces to the top and bottom of the background piece and, using a low or silk setting, iron them open so you have one flat piece. Next, sew the longer pieces to the sides, making sure to sew the edges of the border pieces together. Iron the whole piece flat.

5 To make the headphones, you'll first need to cut out the pattern pieces from the paper. Next, cut each piece of the headphones from its corresponding fabric as indicated on the pattern piece. Note that the dashed lines on the pattern are stitching lines, not cutting lines.

6 Lay the pieces out on your quilt to see how the finished headphones will look and pin them in place to the background.

7 Appliqué the pieces into place using a satin stitch technique: Place your sewing machine on the zigzag setting and the stitch width at as low a setting as you can manage. Remove the smaller pinned pieces so you can start by appliquéing the larger ones, and place the machine foot on the edge of the piece you are appliquéing. Stitch around the edge of this piece, as well as along the decorative stitch lines, making sure the stitch is going through both the base piece and the headphone piece. The smaller the stitch width, the harder it is to catch both pieces, so practice on scraps of fabric. Repeat the appliqué process with all the remaining pieces, using the silver thread when appliquéing the silver pieces, the black for the black portion of the headphones, and the complementary thread for the brocade.

8 Once you have affixed all pieces of the headphones, cut a piece of the solid black fabric to the size of your finished quilt plus 2" on each side—this will be the backing. Also cut the batting to this size.

9 Lay the backing fabric face down, then the batting, and then place the front of the quilt face up on top, smoothing it out to make the layers even. Safety-pin the layers together, starting in the middle and smoothing it out toward the edges.

10 Put all three layers under your sewing machine. Using black thread and a normal straight-stitch setting, quilt all three layers together by stitching in the ditch (meaning, sewing directly into all of the seams). Start with the blocks in the middle of the headphones, sewing the rows across and up and down. Then sew around the inside and outside of the headphones, tracing the headphones fabric with your stitch. Sew the rows on the outside of the headphones across and up and down until all the rows are completed. Trim the sides of the quilt using your rotary cutter and ruler so all edges are even.

11 Grab your double-fold binding tape and, leaving it folded, pin one folded edge along the back edge of the quilt. Stitch on the binding's pinned edge all the way around the quilt. Then fold the binding over the quilt edge and pin it in place on the front of the quilt. Sew the binding onto the front as close to its folded edge as you can.

12 To make your quilt hangable, cut two 2"-by-4" strips out of the black fabric. Sew the ends of each piece together to make a loop. Sew a loop into each end of the back of the quilt, just behind the seam where the background piece meets the silk border—that way you won't be able to see the sewing marks on the front. Put your wood dowel through the loops.

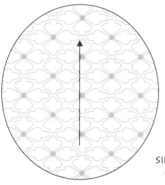

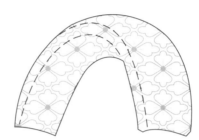

SILK BROCADE FABRIC

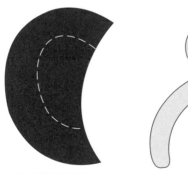

BLACK FABRIC

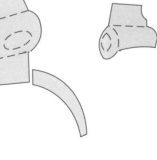

SILVER FABRIC

Enlarge pattern pieces by 400 percent.

let it snow

MAKE AN INDOOR WINTER WONDERLAND

That first snowy day of the year always makes the world feel magical . . . until it turns into brown slush and the salt ruins your favorite boots. If you really want to make it a snow day every day, you can easily whip up some wintry crafts. Turn a small jar into a snow globe using plastic toys and glitter; string some pom-poms and beads to deck your halls; and glue up some sparkly snowflakes to hang on the wall.

snow globe // Jennifer Knapp

materials

Baby-food jar, cleaned and label removed

Primer (DecoArt Primer-Sealer is a good one to try)

Acrylic craft paint in the color of your choice

Epoxy craft glue

Small plastic toys

Dish soap

1 tablespoon glitter or metallic confetti

1 Paint the outside of the jar cap with primer and let it dry.

2 Paint the cap with acrylic paint, allow it to dry, and using epoxy, attach plastic toys to the inside of the cap. Fill the jar almost to the top with water and add a small squirt of dish soap. Add the glitter.

3 Screw the cap on tightly. Turn the jar upside down and shake. It's snowing!

pom-pom garland // Alicia Paulson

materials

Sewing needle and
upholstery thread

Plastic beads in a variety of
shapes and colors (available
at most craft-supply stores)

Ready-made pom-poms
(available at most craft-
supply stores)

1 Cut a piece of upholstery thread to the length you want
your garland to be (ours was about 10').

2 Thread one end through a needle, then slip the needle
through your beads and the middle of your pom-poms,
creating a pattern by alternating colors and styles. Leave a
few uncovered inches of thread at each end.

3 Loop each end of the thread and secure with a knot for
hanging.

frosty flakes // Monica Ewing

materials

Craft sticks

Protractor

Hot glue gun and glue

White spray paint

Drop cloth or newspapers

Round 12 mm rhinestones, glitter, and fake snow (optional)

½"-wide ribbon and double-stick foam tape (for hanging on wall)

Scissors

1 To make the snowflake on the left: Start by gluing six craft sticks together at 60-degree angles into an asterisk shape. Use a protractor to make sure your angles are accurate. Glue two sticks to the end of each arm of the asterisk to triple the length of the arm and set aside. Glue six sticks in a hexagon shape. Center the hexagon on the extended asterisk so that each point of the hexagon rests on an arm of the asterisk. Secure with glue. Glue four sticks in a diamond shape to the end of each of the snowflake's six arms to complete. Skip to step 3.

2 To make the snowflake on the right: Start by gluing six craft sticks together at 60-degree angles into an asterisk shape. Use a protractor to make sure your angles are accurate. Create starlike points by gluing two more craft sticks to the end of each arm; lay them all out before gluing to make sure your points connect and aren't wonky. Glue two sticks to the end of each arm of the original asterisk to triple the length of the arm. To complete the snowflake, glue two more sticks to each arm where the second and third sticks of the extended arm meet, creating a V shape.

3 Once you've assembled your snowflakes, lay out a drop cloth or newspaper. Spray-paint each side of your snowflake with two coats of paint, making sure to cover the edges. Let dry overnight.

4 For added flare, glue rhinestones to the tips of the snowflake, or cover it with glitter or fake snow. Let dry.

5 To hang your snowflakes, cut a long piece of ribbon. Use double-stick foam tape to secure one end of the ribbon to the back of the snowflake's top and the other end to the very top of your wall.

a stitch in time

HAND-STITCH YOUR OWN CLOCK // Tracie Egan Morrissey

materials

Pencil

8 ½" embroidery hoop

Cardboard at least
8 ½" square

10" square of 18-count
evenweave cross-stitch
fabric

Short-shaft quartz
movement clock kit

X-ACTO knife

Clock face cross-stitch
pattern (page 70)

Red and black embroidery
floss

Embroidery needle

AA battery

Scissors

The right clock can really bring a room together. Not only can it tell you the time, it can also tell a story . . . especially when you've made your own by cross-stitching its face.

1 Trace the outline of the small inner piece of the embroidery hoop on the cardboard. Cut out the circle you traced and set it aside. Next, place the cross-stitch fabric in the hoop, making sure it is pulled taut. To create the hole for your clock mechanism, locate the center of the fabric and use the X-ACTO to remove a tiny patch of fabric that measures four squares on each side (the cross-stitch fabric is made up of these little squares).

2 To cross-stitch the pattern for the clock face, separate two strands of thread from your embroidery floss and thread your needle. Using the pattern as a guide, start at either the top or bottom, using white floss. First sew a half stitch: Bring your needle and thread up through the bottom left-hand corner of a square and make a diagonal stitch, pulling it back down through the upper right-hand corner of the square. Draw the thread down vertically and bring it up through the bottom right-hand corner of the square. Make another diagonal stitch in the upper right-hand corner of the next square to the right.

Who needs a new rug when you've got custom clockery to tie it all together?

Work the entire row this way in the color you're using (skip squares that are a different color on the pattern and go back to do those later). Then work backward in a similar fashion, so that your diagonal stitches angle the opposite direction and you form a line of X-shaped stitches. Make sure that these crossing stitches are all slanted in the same direction, or the finished project will look uneven.

3 Once you've finished filling in all of the stitches, reinforce the starburst outlines by making a backstitch in one strand of thread along the outside of the shapes. To backstitch, first secure your thread by making a few stitches at the back of your fabric. Then, bring the stitch up (through the back) one hole away from where you started. Stitch back one stitch toward where you started. Continue making stitches in this fashion to create the outline.

4 When you've completed your embroidery, rearrange your fabric, making sure that it is tight and centered in the embroidery hoop. Take the cardboard cutout and pop it into the back of the hoop. With a pencil, trace the hole for the movement's shaft onto the cardboard. Remove the cardboard from the hoop, and use your X-ACTO to cut out the hole you traced.

5 Pop the cardboard back into the hoop, insert the clock movement into the holes, and secure it with the supplied washer. Assemble the rest of the movement as directed by the kit instructions and insert the battery. Carefully trim off and discard any excess fabric around the edge of the hoop.

Cross-Stitch Pattern

nice rack

MAKE SHELVES FROM RECYCLED BOOKS // Callie Watts

Interesting wall shelves are hard to come by. It seems they're either cheap particleboard or overpriced particleboard. Either way: boring! If you have some vintage books lying around that are sweet to look at but no longer serve any purpose, you can quickly turn them into shelves. It takes just three easy steps to bang them out! All you need to do is glue, drill, and stack.

materials

Stack of books at least 4" tall

Liquid Nails or other crazy-strong glue

Two 4" corner braces

1 Choose the book you want at the bottom of your shelf, open it to the back cover, and glue a corner brace on at each end so that it'll be hidden inside the cover with the other side of the brace poking up perpendicularly. Close the book.

2 Glue the rest of the books together to form an attractive stack tall enough to cover the braces when they are placed on top of the base book. Set aside and let your glue dry for 24 hours.

3 Hang the braced-up book on the wall and then glue the stack onto the base book. Add more random loose books so your guests can't judge a book by its cover.

tool time

MAKING BASIC HOME REPAIRS // Erin Donnelly

For years we've been relying on boyfriends, landlords, and professionals to do work we should be able to do ourselves without being hit on, paying an arm and a leg, or being exposed to an unsightly derriere. Being self-reliant when it comes to minor repairs will not only prevent these unfortunate circumstances, but it is also a great way to assert your independence.

how to hang an object

materials

Nails

Picture hangers

Hammer

Power drill and
assorted drill bits

Anchors

Screws

Screwdriver

Stud finder

Level

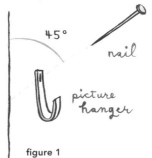

figure 1

BEFORE YOU BEGIN
You need to determine two things: (1) what type of walls you have and (2) the weight of the object you're hanging. If you live in a prewar walk-up, you probably have plaster-and-lath walls. If it's a house built later than that, you probably have drywall. If you don't know, ask your apartment manager or check your inspection report from when you bought your house.

TO HANG A LIGHT OBJECT ON DRYWALL
Place a nail through a picture hanger with the hook facing you. Hold it against the wall and hammer at a downward 45-degree angle (figure 1). (Watch those thumbs—and be careful when hammering into drywall—if you pound too hard, you'll end up with a gaping hole in your wall and a pissed-off landlord.) Once the nail is in deep enough to allow your artwork to lie flush to the wall, hang the picture by the wire across its back and center it.

TO HANG A HEAVIER OBJECT ON DRYWALL
Drill a hole into the wall using your power drill. *Warning: If you hit strong resistance when drilling into the wall, stop— you may have hit a pipe.* The drilled hole should be the exact size of the anchor you are using. (What is an anchor, you ask? It is a plastic casing that wraps around a screw, acting as a support system. Once drilled into the wall, the

casing spreads out, holding your screw tight against the wall and keeping the object you're hanging steady.) Once you've created the hole in your wall, tap your anchor into the hole, insert the screw, and tighten it. You're all set.

TO HANG A REALLY HEAVY OBJECT ON DRYWALL

figure 2

If you're hanging a large painting or flat-screen TV, you'll need to find the stud behind your wall before you hang it. Studs are beams of wood that hold up the infrastructure of your walls and are typically located about 16" apart—if you put a nail or an anchor into a wall willy-nilly, you will likely insert it into a hollow spot, giving the anchor nothing to hold on to, or worse, a pipe. To find a stud, you'll need a stud finder—an electronic device with a light that flashes when you wave it over a stud (though they don't work so well if you have textured walls). Once you've found your stud (figure 2), insert an anchor and screw as described above.

TO HANG SOMETHING ON A BRICK OR CONCRETE WALL

Drill a hole in the wall using a masonry bit, since a regular bit will break off. Then insert an anchor into the hole, followed by the screw, as described above.

TO HANG A SHELF

Depending on how long your shelf is, you'll need at least two wall brackets to support it. Use your stud finder to locate the center of the wall stud and place your first bracket over it, using a pencil to mark the placement of the mounting screws on the wall. Next, drill a hole, then screw the bracket in with screws that are long enough to go through the wall stud by 1" or more. Follow the same directions for your second bracket, making sure to find another wall stud (which will be about 16" from the first one). Use a level on the first bracket to ensure a straight line before drilling. Finally, place your shelf on top of the brackets and screw the shorter screws into the shelf to hold it in place. Be sure your screws are twisted tight, and don't put a super-heavy object on a lightweight shelf or you could get hit in the head.

how to regrout shower tiles and reseal your tub

materials

Tile cleaner
(bleach works well)

Grout saw

Sponge

Grout

Rubber float

Squeegee

Dry towel

Sealant (optional)

Rubber gloves

Cleaning agent
(Comet, Ajax, etc.)

Bathroom caulk in a color
that matches your grout

Putty knife

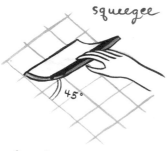

squeegee

45°

figure 1

REGROUT THE TILES

1 Start off by using a tile cleaner to remove any mildew or soap scum, then take a grout saw, use some elbow grease, and scrape off the old grout that's between the tiles. Run a sponge over the tile to remove any debris.

2 Mix your grout (read the instructions that accompany it) and apply it to the entire surface, using a rubber float or sponge to spread the grout over the entire tile surface— not just the edges where the individual tiles meet. Pull a damp squeegee across the tile's surface at a 45-degree angle to remove any excess (figure 1).

3 Wait until the grout is firm but no longer wet and use a damp sponge to remove additional excess grout. Then use a dry towel to wipe off any material that's still left. Give your shower a couple of days to dry fully before you go hopping in there with your loofah—yes, that means not bathing.

4 To go the extra mile, you can also spread a sealant over the tiles—once they've thoroughly dried—to waterproof them and reinforce all the hard work you just did.

RESEAL THE TUB

1 You'll have to treat the tiles that border your tub (i.e., where the tub meets the wall) a little differently than the walls. When this area is filled with too much dried grout or caulk, it may not be able to withstand the slight movements (yes, your tub moves) that are bound to happen. Start by scraping off the old grout from the tiles that meet your tub by using your trusty old grout saw. Next, put on your gloves and give your tub a good cleaning with water and bleach or whatever cleaning agent you like best. Let the tub and its surrounding tiles dry thoroughly.

2 Fill the tub with water, which will help keep it from shifting later on. Yes, you may get wet.

3 Now, holding your tube of caulk at a 45-degree angle, carefully fill in the joints (where the tiles meet and touch your tub), being sure to caulk all along the perimeter of your tub. Smooth out the caulk using a wet finger, or use your putty knife to remove excess caulk so it doesn't look quite so Frankenstein-ish.

4 Wait until the caulk has partially dried (roughly half a day, or at least a few hours) before you drain the tub. Once your tiles have had at least a full day to dry completely, the tub will be crack-free and safe to use again.

awl yeah! what to keep in your toolbox

These essential items will help you out of many domestic jams. If buying new is not in the budget, check out estate sales and secondhand shops.

adjustable wrench Used for tightening/ loosening screws and bolts, an adjustable wrench lets you fit the tool to a range of sizes.

awl This tool, which looks like an ice pick, is used to puncture holes in materials like wood or leather and is handy in many situations.

duct tape The quintessential multipurpose aid.

hammer Look for one with a fiberglass handle to help cushion your hand.

level The glass-encased bubbles in this rulerlike straightedge tool will tell you if your object is horizontal or vertical (i.e., straight) and is essential for hanging pictures and shelves.

nut driver A screwdriver for nuts and bolts, this has a rounded head. It's good to have these in a variety of sizes.

pliers Used for gripping, cutting, or bending. Slip-joint pliers have ridged jaws and can be adjusted. Needle-nose pliers look similar to a bird's beak and are used for more precise jobs.

power drill Consider it a screwdriver on steroids. Use it for drilling holes and driving in and/or removing screws. Look for cordless, lightweight models with reversible functions that will give you more control.

putty knife This scraper-type tool is used to remove grout and/or paint from flat surfaces.

screwdrivers You should have both a flat-head and a Phillips screwdriver. A flat head is just that— a screwdriver with a flat, almost knife-like tip that can be inserted into screws with simple slots; the Phillips head has an X at its tip and is used on screws that have the corresponding cross. Having each in a variety of sizes is recommended.

how to unclog a sink drain

materials

Plunger

Pipe wrench

Rubber gloves

Bucket

Drain auger (also known as a snake)

pipe wrench

figure 1

Sometimes it's easier— and safer—to bring in a professional, especially if the home improvement project involves a gas leak, electrical wiring, or anything that could result in your being blown to bits. There's no shame in getting help, and when the expert arrives, don't be afraid to ask questions.

PLUNGER METHOD

First try using a plunger to unclog the pipes. (And if you normally use your plunger in your toilet, please, for the love of God, wash it first!) Place the plunger over the drain and fill the sink with enough fresh water to cover the rubber. (This will help with suction.) You know the drill: pump the plunger up and down until the water drains. It can sometimes take at least a full minute of plunging before this happens—be patient.

CLEANING THE TRAP

Not getting any love from the plunger? Try clearing out the trap, the U-shaped pipe under the sink (figure 1). Make sure to put a stopper in the sink drain (or you'll have a sloppy, gross mess), then use a pipe wrench to loosen the two metal slip nuts on the trap. Gently unscrew the nuts by hand and remove the trap. Clear out any material you find there (might want to use some rubber gloves for this one). The bucket will come in handy here—use it to contain the nasty gunk that's been caught in your trap. When you're done, replace the trap, taking care not to screw the slip nuts too tightly.

SNAKE METHOD

Drain augers—also known as snakes—are essentially a spiral cable with a handle on one end. (You can rent a snake at hardware stores if you don't happen to have one lying around.) It's important to exercise caution when using one of these babies—they can damage the porcelain on your sink or toilet if you're not careful. Insert the end of the snake into the drain opening and turn the handle on the coiled end, cranking the snake down the drain until you feel resistance and it hits the clog. Try rotating the snake to break up the mess, or pull it out and see what the little guy has fished out. Rinse out the drain with water to further clear it. To avoid future clogs, you should rinse away food debris with cold water at full blast, occasionally toss some ice cubes down your garbage disposal (if you have one)—and, oh, yeah, stop using your sink as a trash can.

squish, squash

RID YOUR HOME OF COCKROACHES // Keph Senett

You finally found a sweet apartment to call home, only to discover several hundred tiny problems: Your roomies are roaches. You could follow your gut and grab the cat, toss a Molotov cocktail, and run—or follow these steps to keep the roaches from encroaching.

CLEAN SCENE
The little buggers live to eat, so give them an immaculate reception. Be fastidious, especially in the kitchen. Store food in sealed, airtight containers, take out the trash daily, and frequently wash surfaces with a bleach-and-water solution to kill the eggs they leave behind.

ROCK OUT WITH YOUR CAULK OUT
Once your place is spotless, seal it off. Run a line of caulking where wall meets floor. Secure the perimeter by repairing and sealing larger fissures. Put weather stripping along the bottom of your door to prevent unwanted visitors.

POWDERS AND ACIDS AND TRAPS—OH, MY!
Sprinkle boric acid (available at hardware stores) in problem areas, like under appliances. It sticks to the roaches that crawl through it and as they clean themselves and each other, they'll spread the poison through the colony. Boric acid is natural, but it may be toxic to your pets. For a harmless and affordable alternative, try baking soda and a bit of sugar. Diatomaceous earth, sold by the pound at hardware stores, is another green and pet-safe antipest powder.

Traps are inexpensive and—bonus—keep the bodies contained. You can fashion a natural one by combining borax, sugar, chopped onion, cornstarch, and water, then roll the mixture into pellets. Place these roach balls in an open Ziploc bag. But remember, traps work by attracting roaches, so use this method sparingly.

SPRAY IT FORWARD
Commercial sprays like Raid can zap bugs into submission, but you can kill only what you can see, and insecticides contain toxins that are bad for you and your four-legged friends. Keep the area well ventilated and don't spray near food or dishes. If you absolutely need an on-the-spot roach killer, vinegar is a non-toxic option.

WATER WARY
Roaches need water, so keep those dirty dishes from piling up in your sink and make a habit of plugging your drains. This will prevent them from sidling up for a drink and using your pipes to cruise to and from your pad.

in case of emergency

SAVE YOUR ASS IN A DISASTER // Jessica Leigh Lebos

Quick! A storm has knocked out power and cell towers for your city and electricity won't be restored for at least 72 hours. Faced with no phone, Internet, or open grocery stores, you (A) curl up in a ball with your dying iPod and wait for FEMA to come to the rescue; (B) light candle nubs, work your way through the contents of your refrigerator, and pray that the mayo doesn't get warm enough to spawn salmonella; or (C) break out your stash of protein bars, water, and extra flashlight batteries, then implement the action plan you decided on at the last neighborhood potluck.

If you answered C, you're way in the minority (and way ahead). For all the rest of you, heeding this advice will help you keep your head when you need it most because—contrary to what your grandma may have told you—getting caught wearing holey underpants is not the worst thing that can happen in an emergency.

ACT FAST
If you're fortunate enough to have advance notice of impending doom, don't be lazy: Heed evacuation updates from authorities via radio and television—you can even sign up with local media outlets for text updates. If you need to evacuate, first gather up birth certificates, Social Security cards, and other important personal papers as well as any meds; then go for photo albums and other sentimentals. Know alternative routes out of your city and make plans for accommodations. If you have pets, keep a list of animal-friendly hotels on hand so you can book a room for you and your pet quickly. The roads will be choked, so fill your tank before leaving town and grab a jug of antifreeze—cars easily overheat on slow highway crawls.

HAVE A MEETING PLAN
If disaster strikes without warning, deciding now where to meet up with friends, family members, roomies, or neighbors can minimize chaos. Check with your city government to find out which schools and public buildings are designated relief sites and choose one that's centrally located. Use the buddy system and pair elderly or disabled folks with someone who will make sure they're safe.

STOCK UP

Have a stash filled with items that will help you survive being stuck at home for three days without power and running water. It may seem like an intimidating undertaking, but we're not talking about stocking a bomb shelter for Armageddon. A basic emergency survival kit should contain provisions for each member of your household for three days. Ready-made kits are available online, or you can inexpensively compile a DIY version in a plastic container (see below).

diy disaster kit

These essential items will help you out of any emergency. Additionally, you should familiarize yourself with the possible freak weather and industrial risks in your area. Check out the "Disasters & Maps" tab on FEMA.gov before disaster hits (i.e., while the lights are still on). Where you live will impact specific items you might want to put in your kit.

nonperishable foods   (like nuts, dried fruit, protein bars, canned goods, and pet food)

water   (one gallon per person per day for three days)

can opener

pocketknife/multitool

first-aid kit

flashlight

batteries

waterproof matches and lighters

heavy gloves   (for handling debris)

solar- or crank-powered radio

thermal blankets

resealable freezer bags   (to keep things dry in case of a flood)

toilet paper

bucket   (useful for hauling—and can double as a toilet)

extra cell-phone battery

condoms or extra birth control
(just because there's danger outside doesn't mean you should take risks between the sheets)

three days' supply of prescription meds

tampons/pads

toothbrush and toothpaste

whistle   (to get the attention of emergency workers if needed)

pepper spray   (for defense, if things go really downhill)

get it together

ORGANIZE YOUR HOVEL WITH THESE TERRIFIC TIPS // Susan Beal

Having trouble finding your favorite black bra? Need room in your cupboard for more than just cans of soup? Organizing all the random stuff in your house can be a lot easier than you think. Just a few new ways of sorting and storing can help you find anything in a snap. And no, you don't need to drop beaucoup bucks at a container store. Here are some tips on how to get it together.

LIKE GOES WITH LIKE

This principle really makes it easier to remember where you put something and helps you figure out where to put new items. Apply the idea to everything you store—and use your own logic. For example, you might want to store all your baking supplies in the same area. And if there's something you don't use very often or only use seasonally— say, camping equipment—put it together in a bin and stash it in an accessible place away from the things you do use often.

DON'T OVERDO IT

Try reorganizing a room for 15 or 20 minutes at a time—set a timer and just go for it. You'll be amazed at what you get done in such a short amount of time! If you're going for a longer haul than 20 minutes, don't forget to take breaks. And always reward yourself when you're done. Anything you do decide to part with should be removed from the room as soon as possible before you start to

put it back. If you have a basement, hide it there until donation time. A storage unit will do, too.

IN THE KITCHEN

Lazy Susans (or as they should be called, efficient Susans) are perfect on shelves or in cabinets. For taller things like bottles of olive oil or sauces, a single one works well. Try using double-decker lazy Susans for cans of food or spice jars, so you can fit twice as many things in the same amount of space.

Try putting all the random stuff that just doesn't stack or sort well (like bulk rice or bags of pasta) in a big basket on an accessible shelf. Or you can store staples like rice, beans, and grains in big glass mason jars, which are pretty, functional, and cheap. You might even want to reuse pasta sauce jars and other containers you'd usually put in the recycle bin. That beloved Swedish behemoth, IKEA, has great kitchen containers—even magnetic strips for knives. Use these items, but don't go crazy. If it seems impractical for how you live, it probably is. Dogs don't care if their treats come in a fun-looking container.

Three-ring binders are great for clipped recipes, how-tos, or inspiring photos from magazines. Tuck papers of all sizes into the plastic sleeves to keep them neat and accessible. This has the added bonus of keeping gooey fingers from fudging up your instructions. Store the binders next to the cookbooks, and you'll always have great ideas at your fingertips.

IN THE LIVING ROOM

Set aside a specific place for current mail, a spot for magazines, and a place for stuff that needs to leave the house, such as library books or movie rentals. Once you get in the habit of stashing things in the right places, it makes it a lot easier to find the bills or the DVDs before it's too late. Vintage dinner platters make great spots for keys, change, and other little things that otherwise vanish into the bottoms of purses. Create a spot to stash your stuff in the same way every day and you'll never forget where you put your transit pass.

IN THE BEDROOM

To streamline a lingerie drawer, use a cardboard box as a divider, separating bras, underwear, and slips into their own little worlds so you don't have to pull every last thing out to find the only bra you can wear with that one dress.

Plastic drawers (like those you can get at Target) can be used to store clothes you don't wear often. Put a few on the closet floor and store purses and bags on top. Use the inside of the door for a shoe rack (learn how to sew one up on page 36).

LOOK UP

Don't forget about all the valuable storage and organization space available higher up. If your ceiling is high enough, install shelves above your windows to house plants or knickknacks you can't part with but don't want cluttering up tables and windowsills. Use these shelves for books, too, especially ones with pretty bindings.

STAY DISCIPLINED

Once you get organized, a great way to stay organized is to go through your stuff a couple of times a year. Or, even better, every time you bring something new in, take something you're no longer using to Goodwill. By following these few simple suggestions, you'll be on your way to finding the things you want when you want them instead of running around in a bra looking for your socks.

spring cleaning for dirty girls

MAKE YOUR HOME SHINE WITH NATURAL CLEANING TIPS // Jenny Rose Ryan

materials

Big pot

Assorted essential oils
(if you want), a small bottle
of tea tree oil, and some
lemon oil

Fans

Big bucket

Dr. Bronner's Lavender
Liquid Soap (or whichever
scent you like best)

Rags

Broom

Newspaper

Spray bottle

Big, cheap gallon bottle of
distilled white vinegar

Enormous box of
baking soda specifically
for cleaning (add a few
drops of essential oil for
a special hippie scent)

Average-sized box
of borax (look in the
detergent aisle)

Toilet brush

Scrub brush

Grandma was onto something when she used the most common household items to clean up after the riffraff (a.k.a., your uncles and mom). The following simple tips, tricks, and products will keep your home fresh, your chemical sensitivities at bay, and your pocketbook unscathed.

1 To get you in the cleaning mood, put a pot of water on the stove, add a few drops of tea tree oil, and set it a-boiling. Not only will this bubbling brew put you in the springtime spirit, the evaporating water will rehydrate the dry winter air.

2 Now, open all the windows, turn up the tunes, and blow out winter's dust and doom with a few strategically placed fans. To really clean out the cobwebs, fill a big bucket with hot water and a generous squirt of Dr. Bronner's soap. Dunk a clean rag in the bucket, wring it out, and drape it over the bristles of a broom. Skim the broom along the intersection where the ceiling and wall meet. When the rag is dingy and gross, rinse and repeat. After you've attacked the cobwebs, rinse out the bucket and refill it with more hot water and Dr. Bronner's. Grab a clean rag and wash the walls in the same top-to-bottom fashion. Spiffy!

3 To clean windows and mirrors, spray them with a bit of water (it's true—no other cleaner is necessary) and wipe them with newspaper until dry. Using newspaper keeps streaks at bay and also repurposes that crossword puzzle you tried to do last Sunday.

4 In the kitchen, dump some vinegar onto a clean rag and wash down countertops and tabletops, the fronts of drawers and cabinets, your stovetop, and both the inside and outside of your refrigerator. For stubborn gunk, baking soda can be used as a mild abrasive. It is especially good at brightening old ceramic sinks, but it also makes stainless-steel basins sparkle. If your sinks are extra dingy, sprinkle on some borax for its hot bleaching action, let it sit for a few minutes, then scrub. You might also want to make a gentle cleaner by putting a small squirt of Dr. Bronner's in a spray bottle and topping it off with water. You can use this concoction to wipe up surfaces between cleaning frenzies.

5 After the walls, appliances, and surfaces are clean, sweep the floors and use borax or baking soda to scrub up any dried-on crap. Make another bucket of hot water and Dr. Bronner's and mop the floor. Set the fans circulating throughout the room to dry the floor quickly. If it's hardwood, don't leave any puddles or you could damage the finish.

6 In the bathroom, grab your friend borax again and sprinkle a quarter cup or so in the toilet. Let it sit for a while, then scrub with a toilet brush and flush. Sprinkle a few tablespoons of borax in the tub and sink and rake it over with a brush to remove rings and mildew.

7 For wood, add a few drops of lemon oil to a half cup warm water, spray it on a slightly damp soft cotton cloth, and gently wipe down surfaces. For carpets, dump 1 cup borax powder or baking soda into a pint jar with a tight-fitting lid, and add 20 to 40 drops essential oil. Replace the lid and shake well. Sprinkle the powder on your carpet and leave it for a few hours or overnight, then vacuum it up.

If you use borax, keep pets away from the stuff until it's all cleaned up; it can cause respiratory and skin irritation.

it's laundromatic

BECOME A LAUNDRY QUEEN // Sarah Brown

Laundry commercials tout women's time-honored tradition of laundry doin'
like it's some sort of herstory to be celebrated. But, see, none of us likes the
chore. Plus it's become too complicated, what with aisles and aisles of cleaning
products and specific washing directions on everything from a lace camisole to
the most laid-back pair of jeans. To help take the mystery out of washing clothes,
here are nine tips that will turn you into a laundry queen. It's so much nicer
without the washboard, isn't it?

1 Separating clothes by color isn't absolutely necessary. How many of us have a complete load of whites anyway? If you wash everything on a cold temp, the color won't run, so save money and time by throwing it all into the same machine. That said, if it's your favorite piece of clothing in the whole wide world or if it's the first time you're washing a very colorful piece, you might feel better if you wash it separately.

2 Washing everything in cold water will not only keep colors from running, but it will also extend the lives of the clothes and save money on your utility bill.

3 Don't overload the machine with clothes and be sure to use the right type of soap for your machine. It's also important to use soap in the right quantity instead of just dumping a bunch in! Overusing soap leaves scum on your clothes, so read the box or bottle to find out how much you need and fill accordingly.

4 Bleach is usually used for that famed "white wash" as well as for disinfection, but it's not absolutely necessary. A hot-water wash will also kill germs. (Just be sure to separate your colors from your whites if you go the hot-water route.)

5 Almost everything can be thrown in the machine, even your daintiest little undergarments. Use the delicate cycle or the hand-wash setting if your machine has it (it's nice to think of little robot hands massaging your delicates, isn't it?). Use really mild soap for delicates and lay clothes flat to dry rather than putting them in the dryer.

6 Fabric softener or dryer sheets won't really soften your clothes any more than forty-five minutes in the dryer will. It just makes them smell nice. (Nothing wrong with that.)

7 A couple of tennis balls in the dryer will help fluff duvets, sleeping bags, down vests, and anything else you own that happens to be fluffy. Shoes will do the same thing, so if you have an old pair of kicks that need washing, throw them in with the towels and fluffy bedding.

8 Use a collapsible drying rack instead of the dryer whenever possible, especially for delicate or synthetic fabrics that don't fare well in intense heat. If a garment dries fast in the dryer, it will be dry in about a day on a rack (sooner, if you live in a dry area or if it's a hot day). If you have outdoor space, you can also set up a retractable clothesline and let the sunshine do the work for you.

9 Would you leave a hairdryer on when you leave the house? Then don't leave your clothes dryer on even if you're just stepping out for a moment. The things are huge fire hazards, especially at high heat. You'll also want to make sure the lint traps are clean. Vacuum them frequently, and check the exhaust leading outside, too.

get that spill out of that twill

GETTING RID OF STAINS // Lauren Smith

Into each life some stains must fall, and a busy girl's bound to wind up with some spillage. But stains don't have to mean the end of your favorite shirt. To treat these common culprits, all you need is some elbow grease and a few familiar household items—you'll be back in your white trousers in no time.

BEER
Rinse the stain in cold water. Prepare a mixture of 1 cup lukewarm water with 1 teaspoon mild dishwashing liquid. Pour this on the beer stain and blot with a clean cloth. Rinse with cold water and launder. If some stain remains, repeat the process.

BLOOD
Rinse the stain in cold saltwater as soon as possible. If the stain has dried, soak it for up to 30 minutes. Then soak the stain in a mixture of an enzyme detergent and cold saltwater, or blot the mixture on the stain. If the stain remains, make a solution of 1 part white vinegar and 1 part water and apply it to the stain with an eyedropper. Allow to sit a few minutes and wash.

COFFEE
To rinse out a stain from straight-up black coffee, make a solution of 1 part white vinegar and 1 part water. Apply it to the stain with an eyedropper, allow to sit a few minutes, then wash. If you took the coffee with two lumps, also rinse with cold water. For a milk stain, use an all-purpose commercial stain remover.

LIPSTICK
First, use an all-purpose commercial stain remover. If any lipstick color remains, make a solution of 1 part white vinegar and 1 part water and apply it to the stain with an eyedropper. Allow to sit a few minutes, then wash.

RED WINE
If possible, treat the stain immediately by rinsing the area with club soda, cold water, or even white wine. Sprinkle salt on the stain and let it stand for a minute, then rinse in cold water. If still necessary, dab the area with denatured alcohol. To remove any leftover stain, flush with a mild bleach (mix 1 part bleach with 10 parts water)—just make sure the item is color safe.

wash this way

USE YOUR HANDS TO GIVE DRY CLEANING THE FINGER // Emily Horton

Dry cleaning sucks; it costs a fortune and the process is chock-full of chemicals. Luckily, most of those "dry clean only" pieces—including wool, cashmere, linen, and fine cotton—are perfectly hand-washable with a little soap and water. (Unfortunately, silk and rayon are especially fussy, so those are still better off left to the professionals.) Hand-washing is far easier on fabric than dry cleaning, so those delicates will stay lovely longer, and your cashmeres will be softer than ever. As an extra bonus, you'll save cash and the planet.

materials

Deep basin (your kitchen sink is perfect)

1 to 2 tablespoons mild liquid soap (we recommend vegetable-oil-based castile soap)

Like-colored clothing to be washed

Dry towels

Drying rack (optional)

1 If your clothes have any stains, spot-treat them before you wash (see the facing page).

2 Fill the basin with lukewarm water and add the mild liquid soap—do not use detergents; they are too harsh.

3 Give the water a good swish, add a couple of pieces of clothing at a time, and swirl them for 3 to 5 minutes. Be gentle; agitation is what causes fibers like wool to shrink.

4 Empty your basin and refill it with cool water to swish away the suds.

5 After rinsing, fold each piece and gently squeeze out the water—wringing is a no-no. Lay the pieces flat on dry towels and roll them up, pressing out excess water.

6 Transfer your pieces to the drying rack, or, if you can keep your cat from nesting in them, simply lay them on a towel on the floor. Wool and fine knits need to dry flat—be sure to shape them while they are still wet so that they retain their prewash size.

the lazy environmentalist

EASY WAYS TO LIVE GREEN AND SAVE GREEN // Maggie Marton

Lots of environmentalists have great ideas for how we can save the planet, but these suggestions are often lofty and unrealistic. So, how can we make a difference without the big, scary cost and effort? Just target five simple areas for conservation: water, power, recyclables, errands, and self-care. The steps below are broken down by levels of effort required. Select one of the tips to implement today, or try them all. With time, maybe that fast-degrading toilet paper won't seem so bad after all.

SAVE IT, DON'T SPRAY IT

Some people put a bucket in the shower before the water warms, collect the cold water running down the drain, and use it to water plants. Good for them, but most of us do not want a skanky, water-filled bucket sitting in the bathroom. We can do far simpler things to conserve water.

Laziest

A great way to save water without lifting a finger is to use your dishwasher. Running a full dishwasher uses less water than hand-washing all your dirty dishes. Turn off the heated-dry feature of your dishwasher and let your dishes drip-dry to save even more energy—and money.

Pretty Lazy

Choose drought-tolerant native plants for your garden. Talk to a local garden center about good choices for your region. This way, a little rain can do the job of watering.

Easiest on Your Wallet

Reducing a few extra minutes of water flow each day makes a huge difference over time. Turn your faucet off while brushing your teeth and washing your face and hands. Try to cut a minute off your shower time and replace your showerhead with a low-flow model. You won't notice the difference, but your water bill will.

Challenging

Find ways to reuse water. If you have a fish tank, use the water you remove when cleaning the tank to water plants. When you soak a new water filter, you can use that carbonized water in houseplants, too. Install rain barrels under your downspouts and use this to water your garden.

Bonus

Buy a dual-flush toilet. It's a big purchase and potentially a big installation. But with two flush options, you can choose how much water you use per flush—less for a number one, more for a number two—which saves an enormous amount of water over time.

UNPLUG IT

When you unplug your cell from the power cord, the outlet stays active and continues to drain energy. Unplug the cord, save some energy, and save some money on your electric bill. Here are some other simple steps that would make Edison proud.

Laziest

Keep the freezer full. It will operate more efficiently and you'll have plenty of easy-to-prepare meals on hand.

Pretty Lazy

A fun way to save some energy is through the use of dimmer switches, which are inexpensive and simple to install. Soft lighting hides blemishes, creates a sexy atmosphere, and lowers the bottom line on your electric bill.

Easiest on Your Wallet

Focus on everyday power savings. Flip off any light not in use. Keep your computer on sleep mode. Better yet, turn it off when you're done. Turn off all unused peripherals (printer, scanner, fax, etc.). Also, appliances with an LED light, like most coffeemakers, are secret energy drainers. Unplug them when not in use to save even more money. An easy way to remember to take this extra step: plug all your computer or entertainment equipment into a power strip that you can switch off after you shut down.

Challenging

Swap your incandescent bulbs for compact fluorescent lightbulbs, or CFLs. Each bulb you switch saves money through the life of that bulb. The catch, though, is that CFLs are more efficient only for lights that are on for 15 minutes or more at a time.

Bonus

Say you're in the market for a new microwave or DVD player. Buy Energy Star–qualified appliances and electronics and you'll conserve energy and save some serious cash over the life of the product. Also, LCD televisions use less energy than traditional models. That's a great excuse to trade up your TV!

REUSE IT OR LOSE IT

Of course, recycling is crucial, but any chance to reuse can be fun, creative, and money saving.

Laziest

Dig up that old library card and check out or rent DVDs instead of buying. Get your flicks delivered right to your mailbox and you not only avoid the hassle of going to the video store, but you also save emissions by not driving around town!

Pretty Lazy

Get your caffeine fix with a reusable travel mug. All those cups and cardboard sleeves add up to a lot of waste. Money-saving extra: many coffee shops give a discount for reusing mugs.

Easiest on Your Wallet

Those to-go boxes you eat from in the office every day, not to mention plastic utensils, ketchup packets, and those little stirrers for your tea, create lots of trash. Pack your lunch in reusable containers and you'll also save yourself a fortune on workday food costs.

Challenging

Carry a reusable tote to the grocery store or drugstore. If you forget your bags or make an unexpected stop, use the plastic bags you get to line your trash can and save money by not purchasing trash bags. Use the savings to buy more reusable tote bags!

Bonus

Get your clean on! Donate old clothes, used cell phones, books, CDs, electronics—anything you no longer need—to charity. Get that warm, fuzzy feeling of helping someone else while decluttering your house. Then, next year you can gather up those donation receipts and deduct them from your taxes.

OUT AND ABOUT

A number of simple choices can help offset the emissions from your commute.

Laziest

Don't take receipts from ATMs, gas pumps, or any other place where there's a choice. It's only a few inches of paper, but think of how many you get in a year.

Pretty Lazy

Instead of paying your teenage neighbor to wash your car, take it to a car wash. It actually uses less water, and many car washes reuse rinse water.

Easiest on Your Wallet

Fully inflated tires ensure that your car runs more efficiently, which saves big on harmful emissions. To go a step further, after filling the gas tank, let the pump sit for an extra three seconds. This prevents those last few drops of gas from splashing out and contaminating groundwater.

Challenging

Though it takes a little bit of planning, combine errands into one trip. Go to one shopping center and walk from store to store instead of driving to each new shop. Better yet, hit a superstore or warehouse once a month and stock up on nonperishables like cereal and contact-lens solution. This will result in fewer shopping trips, saving you time, gas money, and carbon-dioxide emissions.

Bonus

Rather than going to the gym, walk, bike, or rollerblade instead. All those treadmills and televisions suck energy, those mountains of towels require hot water to wash, and harsh chemicals are used to sanitize the locker rooms. Get your exercise outside and you'll not only save all those resources, but your lungs will love the fresh air, too. Get a dog to walk and play with daily and maybe you can even cancel your gym membership!

PERSONAL CHALLENGE

A daily routine can create an enormous amount of garbage—cleansing cloths, cotton swabs, cotton pads, disposable emery boards, and razor cartridges. In addition, with so many different ingredients, packages, brands, and fibers, selecting the most ecofriendly products is a challenge. Here are some ways to wade through products and clothing to find sustainable yet indulgent options.

Laziest

Products wrapped in cellophane, stuck to a cardboard sleeve, and covered in thick plastic waste an unnecessary amount of resources. Select products with minimal packaging.

Pretty Lazy

Skim the labels on makeup, skin-care, and hair-care products. Lengthy lists mean more chemical additives, which not only harm the environment but could also be unhealthy for you. Choose products with fewer ingredients (or ingredients you can pronounce).

Easiest on Your Wallet

Wash your clothes on the cold setting of your washer. Unless you've spilled something major on yourself, cold water cleans your clothes just as well as hot. Only use warmer settings for things that need to be disinfected, like dish towels or washcloths. Cold water can also make your clothing last longer, because fibers tend to deteriorate less quickly in cold water than in hot. For brownie points, hang your clothes to dry and save big on electricity.

Challenging

Even the best skin-care routine can't get rid of the puffy, bloodshot eyes and gray, pasty skin that a night of overindulging can wreak on your gorgeous face. The party girl's solution? Drink organic champagne, wine, or beer. Legend has it that hangovers are far less severe after a night of overindulging in organic wine because of fewer added chemicals. Organic alcohol doesn't use harmful pesticides in production, which means you're ingesting fewer toxins. It's typically tougher to locate and may require more than a trip to your corner liquor store, but the Internet has lots of resources. So a toast! To you! For drinking organic booze!

Bonus

Purchase clothing made from bamboo. The fibers feel as soft as cotton, but bamboo grows more quickly, which allows for more sustainable harvests.

girls' grow guide

GROW YOUR OWN VEGGIES // Jenny Rose Ryan and Michele Flynn

From the moment you put the seeds or seedlings in the ground, growing your own produce is rewarding, good for you, and most of all, tasty. Plus, it's a lot easier than you think. Let this girls' grow guide show you how.

PREPPING AND PICKING A SITE

Whether you plan to till a section of your yard or put a few big pots on the patio, picking the right place for your garden helps ensure its success. If it's your first attempt, choose a spot that gets a ton of sun. If you're using containers and aren't sure how much light will creep in, get pots on wheels so you can move them around as the day progresses.

Raised Beds

These are a great option if you want something more permanent than pots but more protected than plain tilled soil (the height helps keep the critters out). Raised beds require less weeding, and you can completely control the quality of the soil, making sure your veggies have exactly what they need. Build your own raised beds using purchased or salvaged cedar, and they'll last for years. Just cut some 10"- or 12"-wide boards to the length you want your bed to be. Square the corners, drill holes for screws, and then screw the corners together. Decide where you want your bed to live and excavate some existing turf or soil with your trusty shovel, leveling the soil so it's even (use a level to check). Place the bed in this spot and pound in wooden stakes at the corners to hold it

in place. If you like, you can also attach the stakes to the boards, but you don't need to. The soil you add will hold everything in place, and the roots from your growing plants will help even more.

Planting in the Ground

If you're planting right in the ground, rent a rototiller from the hardware store (ask them how to use it) or get a hand tiller and go to town on your turf. Pick up some compost and garden soil to add to what's already there and till that in, too.

Don't want to use a tiller? A few weeks before you plant, follow the lasagna method of prepping your garden: Don't till, dig, or alter the existing turf in any way. Cover your chosen area with wet newspapers (five sheets per layer), overlapping the edges. Cover the paper with 1" to 2" of peat moss. Layer this with several inches of garden soil. Continue to layer until the lasagna is as thick as you want it, then water till it's as wet as a damp sponge. Once the weather is right, you're ready to plant.

CHOOSING THE RIGHT PLANTS AND PUTTING THEM IN THE GROUND

If you're just starting out, you can usually rely on these veggies to do okay in most climates, even in a bad year: basil, carrots, kale, lettuce, onions, pole beans, spinach,

© susie
GHAHREMANI

and tomatoes. You can also grow all of them from seeds fairly easily.

Tomato and basil are often available as seedlings—baby plants that have already been started for you. Choose seedlings and crowns that are perky and strong, with no yellow or falling-off leaves. Don't buy a plant you pity—it'll just die and you'll be out the cash. And if you can find them, buy plants without flowers—the plant needs to adjust to its new home before it can produce.

Starting Seeds

Talk to local gardening experts and consult local websites to find out your "frost-free" date—this is the date when, in an average year, your region is no longer at risk for frost (which will kill your baby plants and seeds, unless they like the cold). Check the seed packet to find out how long the seed should grow indoors, then back-track from the frost-free date to determine when to start your seeds.

To start your seeds, gather together small containers for the plants you want to sprout. Any container 2" or 3" deep with drainage holes will do; you can even poke a few holes in the bottom of a small plastic cup. If the containers have been used before, wash them first in hot soapy water and rinse them with diluted distilled white vinegar.

Fill the containers with seed-starter mix from the garden center and moisten the seed-starting mix. Add the seeds by dropping them onto the surface of the mix (two or three seeds per container) and spacing them evenly. Cover with a layer of soil three times the seeds' thickness. Sprinkle milled sphagnum moss over everything to protect the seeds from fungal infections. Put the

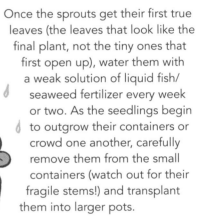

containers into trays, cover them with plastic wrap or glass to keep everything humid, and place them near a heating vent or on a heated seed mat. Keep the containers damp by pouring a bit of water into the tray so the mix pulls moisture up.

Caring for Sprouts

When things just begin to sprout, uncover the containers and move everything to a bright place, away from radiators or heating vents—a sunny windowsill is perfect.

Once the sprouts get their first true leaves (the leaves that look like the final plant, not the tiny ones that first open up), water them with a weak solution of liquid fish/seaweed fertilizer every week or two. As the seedlings begin to outgrow their containers or crowd one another, carefully remove them from the small containers (watch out for their fragile stems!) and transplant them into larger pots.

If you prefer, plant kale, lettuce, and spinach directly in the ground (or a pot or raised bed)—they like it cool, so it's fine to start them outdoors a little earlier in spring. Similar veggies (leeks, radishes, and other salad greens such as endive or watercress) can be sown outdoors in early spring, too.

As for pole beans and carrots, you actually shouldn't sow them indoors first (they do better directly seeded into the soil). But do wait until the soil is sufficiently warm (a few 55- or 60-degree days should help) before planting them outside.

Now you need to get your seedlings ready for the harsh conditions of the big, lonely world. Gardeners call this hardening off.

salad in the city

Is gardening just for people with backyards? No way, sister. Even city girls like to get their hands dirty. It's easy as pie to grow veggies in a container on a fire escape, a roof, or anywhere they'll get at least six to eight hours of sun each day. All they need is dirt, sun, water, and food.

containers Garden centers sell huge wooden half barrels as planters. If you can't manage one big pot, smaller ones will work, too. Use containers that are at least 1' deep and 1' across (tomatoes prefer 2' each way) and have drain holes. Put a 1"- to 2"-deep layer of stones in the bottom, so that your plants don't get waterlogged after a monsoonlike summer rain, and if it doesn't have drain holes, drill a few with your handy electric drill. You can reuse any container you have around, too, from stockpots to ice cream buckets.

potting soil You need enough to fill the containers. Use bagged potting soil, not dirt from a yard—that's too dense for a potted plant.

what to grow? Lettuce and basil are small plants—perfect for fire escape gardens. There are two main types of tomatoes: determinates and indeterminates. Determinates are good for midsized pots because they tend to stay compact and bushy, making them excellent plants for hanging baskets (you probably won't need stakes).

plant it Plant in the evening or on a cloudy day so the sun won't immediately beat down on your newly planted babies. Immediately douse your plants with water mixed with fertilizer until the water runs into the drainage saucer or you're sure every inch of soil has had a drink. They've had a rough day, after all.

plant food Use fish fertilizer or make a "tea" by mixing a pile of leaves in a bucket with some water and allowing them to rot for a couple weeks. Dump a little of this tasty (to plants) brew in your pots each week. Just be sure to store it outside; it's stinky.

On a nice spring day, move your containers to a protected place (a porch works great) for a few hours. Day by day, increase how long you leave them outside. After about a week, leave them outside overnight and then transplant them into your garden the next day.

Putting Them in the Ground

For all plants, check the specific instructions on the seed packet or label when setting seedlings in the ground. Plant seedlings so the roots and very bottoms of the plants are covered with soil. Mulch around the root bed and give everything a good soak.

Put stakes next to tomato plants and carefully tie the plants to the stakes with twine as they grow. As the plants get larger, pinch off the stems without flowers that pop up between branches. This will force the plant to put more effort into growing big, delicious tomatoes.

Pole beans can be staked using three bamboo or other wooden rods tethered together at the top to make a teepee. Plant the beans around the base of the teepee and watch them vine up the plant over time.

Plant carrots as densely as you want—you can thin them out as they grow (baby carrots!).

GROWING HEALTHY PLANTS

To grow healthy plants that produce big, luscious fruits and vegetables, fertilize weekly with a liquid fish/seaweed fertilizer and mulch often to control weeds and conserve water. Try to water every day in the early morning or evening. Use a soaker hose, or aim the spray from your hose at the roots (not the leaves). Run the hose at a slow soak for 15 minutes to half an hour—you want the roots to take a slow drink just like what they'd get from a misty rain. If you get a real misty rain, consider it a bonus and don't water that day.

Certain plants will welcome (or discourage) buggy visitors, so pick your plants strategically. Plants such as lavender encourage pollinators, while posting a few marigolds around the edge of your garden will discourage hungry moths. If you're in a slug-prone area, you can trap them using beer. Just fill a shallow dish with some cheap stuff and leave it in the garden overnight. The slugs will hit the brew so hard they won't even know they're dead. Keep refilling your beer traps until they all get the message.

Different diseases cause different symptoms, so if you're not sure what might be plaguing your plants, talk with a local garden center

The best part of growing your own veggies is that you get to be the crazy lady who pays for favors with kale.

about the symptoms, or pick up a copy of *The Organic Gardener's Handbook of Natural Pest and Disease Control* by Fern Marshall Bradley, Barbara W. Ellis, and Deborah L. Martin.

HARVESTING YOUR SPOILS

Enjoying the fruits of your labor is the best part of all. Here are a few tips on when to pull up or pick your veggies.

Spinach, Lettuce, and Kale

You can harvest spinach, lettuce, and kale as soon as there are a few leaves on the plants. The babies make a wonderful salad, and as soon as you get some, just snip a few leaves and eat them. Let a few plants get big and bounteous, though, and harvest them before they bolt (flower). As they get closer to bolting, the leaves will start creeping up a central stem. They'll also get bitter. If you have a burst of hot weather, spinach and lettuce will bolt fast. If you can't eat them before they bolt, peel off the lower leaves for eating, pull up the plant, and sow another round. Some years, you'll be able to get three separate harvests.

Onions

Yellow and red onions are "done" when the skin on the outside starts to crackle and look like paper. The time of year will depend on the weather where you live (so will the size). If you want them sooner, go ahead and pick them and plant some more by direct seeding. Even tiny onions pack big flavor. White onions are done whenever you want them, basically. So if you really like onions, plant a lot of them and just eat your way through the year.

Carrots

Start pulling carrots in early to midsummer. Scrub the baby ones off while crouching in your backyard and pop them in your mouth to truly taste nature's glory. Just grab a few whenever you want them, and you can eat them the rest of the year—they get even sweeter after a frost or two in fall.

Pole Beans

Pole beans will flower in midsummer, with small beans starting to form after that. Pick them when they're medium sized for best flavor and texture. Make sure you pick everything—the plant will continue to produce as long as you are harvesting, and you can have fresh green beans into September or even October if you're diligent with your picking.

Tomatoes

Depending on the type of tomatoes you got, you may be able to harvest as early as midsummer. It all depends on the weather and the light where you live. Generally, smaller tomatoes are ready sooner than larger tomatoes, and those dubbed "early" (Early Girl is a favorite) will be just that. But once you've bitten into a homegrown, vine-ripened fruit, you'll understand why it's worth the wait.

Basil

Start picking basil as soon as it has a few leaves and use it fresh; don't pull up the whole plant. If it starts to bolt, pinch off the bolted part to force the plant to grow more broadly and produce longer.

GET GOING

Now that you know the basics, it's time to get started. Experiment with different varieties and different veggies. Try strawberries in a bucket. Start your plants inside one year and outside the next. Whatever you do, the benefits of growing things yourself will far outweigh the work. Once you build one raised bed, you'll want three more all over your yard.

bring the outside in

CRAFT A CUTE TERRARIUM // Lindsay Stetson Thompson

materials

Bag of small rocks

Glass container
with a large opening

Horticultural charcoal
(available at most
gardening-supply stores)

Cactus soil

Small succulent plants
(we used 1" and 2" plants;
be sure to select ones that
require similar growing
conditions)

Landscape decorations
such as figurines and plant
markers (optional)

High-end home design magazines often feature interesting (and expensive) containers filled with artfully arranged succulents. Luckily for your pocketbook, the concept is easy to replicate at home. Even the most forgetful plant killer can keep this no-fuss terrarium alive. Just don't fight back if you get pricked.

1 Pour enough rocks into your container to make a layer approximately 2 ½" deep. Carefully pour in a 1" to 1½" layer of charcoal.

2 Add a layer of soil thick enough to reach slightly higher than the midpoint of your container.

3 Arrange the succulents to your liking. Plant them and gently pack down the soil all around them.

4 Add decorations (if you wish) to personalize the landscape. That's it!

- -

If you're giving the terrarium as a gift—or even if you just want a reminder for yourself—create a tag with care instructions specific to the succulents you've planted. Be sure to include their requirements for sun and how often they need water.

clip joint

CUT TO THE CHASE WITH HOUSEPLANT CUTTINGS // Faith Haze

materials

Plant cuttings

Clear glass jars

Potting soil

Pots

Know someone with a green thumb? Use clippings from their plants to grow your own. Once your baby plants have grown into big plants, you can populate the world with their cuttings and continue the circle of life. Now, isn't that lovely?

1 Scope out your friends' pads for plants you want to clip (and ask them for their permission before you start snipping). African violets, basil, purple passions, and coleus are all good ones to try. For all plants but African violets, clip the plant just above a leaf. For African violets, break the leaf off at the base of the plant to have enough stem. Make sure the clippings aren't too long or they will fall out of the jars.

2 At home, put your clippings in clear glass jars on a well-lit windowsill; two or three in a jar is fine. Make sure your plants have enough fresh water and change it often. In a few weeks, you'll notice little roots starting to form.

3 When the roots are really visible, you can put the cuttings into pots, place them in a spot with plenty of light, and give them a weekly watering.

Cuttings from houseplants are an easy (and free!) way to add to your lush indoor garden.

houseplant how-to

GENERAL RULES OF GREEN THUMB // Jenny Rose Ryan

Houseplants clean the air and can beautify even the most humble hovel. And while they're easier to take care of than a goldfish, they still need a little TLC now and then in order to survive. These tips will help you maintain your indoor plants—even if you're cursed with the blackest thumb—so they will reward you with their ever-changing shapes and fresh blooms for years to come.

PICK A PLANT

Plants need just three things in balance to thrive: light, heat, and water. Since each plant variety needs different combinations of these essential life givers, the first step to picking a houseplant that will succeed in your home's climate is to read the plant's label (if it has one). Or you can select one of the harder-to-kill varieties mentioned at right. But remember, no amount of top-notch organic fertilizer will make up for putting the wrong plant in the wrong spot. If your house tends to be dry but warm, pick something that does well in dry and warm climates, such as a succulent or cactus. If your house tends to be humid and cool, choose a fern. And take sunlight recommendations seriously. If your window faces north, you can't put a plant that wants all-day sun there. Pick a plant that likes lower light instead, or move the light-loving plant to a south-facing window. If you put a plant that likes a lot of light in a dim room, it'll be lanky, have less foliage, and generally look less lustrous. Think about heat as the day progresses, too. At night, a windowsill can get too cold for a plant that likes it warm. Either keep the plant elsewhere or plan to move it to a warmer place when the sun goes down.

WATCH IT GROW

Once you have that perfect plant-y friend, you have to water it and feed it. Again, heed the planting instructions—keep the little tag in the pot and you'll always have a reminder. If you're using cuttings from a green-thumbed friend (see page 99), ask her to tell you what the plant likes. If you really don't know, a good rule of thumb is to fertilize every three months and water according to leaf thickness: If the leaves are thick (like a succulent or cactus), water rarely (every month or so is fine). If they're thin, water every week (but not a lot at a time). Ferns like to get soaked, but other plants don't. Remember, it's always better for a plant to be on the dry side than overwatered. Clues that you might have used too much water include yellowing, leaf loss, and, of course, soil that's soaking wet. If you went crazy on the watering, allow your plant to dry out before you water (sparingly!) the next time. Make sure the soil is draining properly and, if it's not, transplant to fresh potting soil before the roots rot.

Now that you have your plant in the right place with the right amount of water, watch it grow. As it starts to reach the limits of its pot, transplant it to one twice as large so it has room to keep growing. Signs that a plant may need repotting include lack of growth, roots peeking out the top or bottom of the pot, or a generally cramped appearance.

To repot a plant, gently turn it on its side and roll the pot while carefully pulling at the base of the plant. If the plant won't budge, add a little water to the soil and allow it to soak in before trying again. Transfer the plant to the new pot, fill around the roots with good-quality potting soil, and fertilize with an organic plant food.

PLANTS TO TRY

African violets (shown at left) are a good starter for those new to houseplants. They're small, blossoming plants with fuzzy stems and leaves that grow from a central crown. Blooms come in dozens of colors and they bloom best when a bit pot-bound (crowded in their pot). They like average room temperatures and low light—just keep them out of direct sunlight. You can even use fluorescents, but make sure the artificial light is bright. Plant them in porous, well-drained soil and give them a home in a humid location (like a bathroom). Water the violet by setting the pot in a container of water about 2" deep and allowing the soil to absorb the water. Don't get water on the leaves because it will turn them brown.

The spider plant seems to thrive if you neglect it, so it's also great for newbies. With its long, grasslike leaves, it's perfect for hanging baskets or plant stands that allow it to cascade over the container's sides. Rotate it occasionally so all sides receive light, and keep it in average temperatures. When the plant is mature, it will send out stalks over the container's side, with a new little plant growing at the tip of each stalk. Trim these spider babies off, soak them in water, and you'll have a whole new plant. Spider plants are known for their air-cleaning ability—particularly their ability to filter out formaldehydes. Give a spider plant plenty of water during spring and summer when it is growing quickly and mist it to increase humidity. If it develops brown leaf tips, cut them off with small scissors, making a pointed leaf shape.

protect your pet

If you have a cat or dog, not every plant is right for your home. The following common houseplants are known to be toxic and should be avoided if you have pets: amaryllis, mistletoe, pothos, dieffenbachia, asparagus fern, caladium (a.k.a. elephant's ear or mother-in-law plant), jade, cyclamen, philodendron, azalea, bird-of-paradise, English ivy, Easter lily, and oleander. This is not an exhaustive list, however, so if you're unsure about your plant, look for an updated list at ASPCA.org.

scrap happy

COMPOST YOUR FOOD AND TURN IT INTO FERTILIZER // Radhika Reddy

materials

Red worms

Wood or plastic bin
with holes for aeration

Bedding material
(newspaper strips or
moistened leaves)

Rubber gloves (optional)

Who knew that food scraps could be turned into
a crumbly, nutrient-rich, soil-like substance
perfect for adding to your potted plants or garden?
Composting isn't hard to do, and if you're doing it
right, it shouldn't be all that smelly. You won't even
get very dirty. Plus, think of all that garbage you'll
be keeping out of landfills. Here's how to turn your
trash into treasure with the power of helpful, hungry
microbes and worms!

1 Assess your composting needs. A bin that can handle
two pounds of food scraps a day is a good place to
start for a two- or three-person household. Since red worms
(a.k.a. compost worms) can process half their body weight
per day, you'll need 4 pounds of 'em (go to FindWorms.com
to find a seller near you and expect to pay $15 to $30
a pound).

2 Calculate the bin size. You'll need one square foot of
space per pound of worms (4 pounds of worms = a
2'-square or 1'-by-4' rectangular bin).

3 Purchase or make your bin. It should be wood or plastic
and at least 8" to 12" deep with a lid. Drill holes in the
lid and along the top of the bin walls for aeration.

*The typical American household
generates over four pounds of garbage
daily, but almost half that can be
kept out of landfills by composting.*

composting outdoors

Got enough yard space to compost outside? That's even easier than doing it indoors, since the worms and other helpful creatures move in on their own. Hardware stores sell composting bins, but you can also just get yourself a big trash can (plastic works well), drill some 1" holes all over the sides and bottom for air and creature circulation, and start piling stuff in. Alternating green (veggie scraps, grass clippings) with brown (leaves, coffee grounds, small bits of paper) means different helpful bugs and worms will be attracted to your brew, which will help turn the scraps into compost faster. Keep the lid on when you're not adding to it and, if it gets dry, spray it down with some water. While you can turn the compost to help things move along faster, you don't have to. The natural decaying process will take hold quickly and in a few months, you'll be able to scoop out the stuff that makes your plants happy.

4 Arrange 4" of bedding material (strips of newspaper or moistened leaves) in the bin and add your worms.

5 Bury your food scraps under the bedding. If you're not keen on touching your new worm friends, wear gloves. Worms are best at processing vegetable scraps, crushed eggshells, coffee grounds, tea bags, and bread. Do not feed them meat, dairy, or oils.

6 After a few weeks, when the bedding starts to look like potting soil, move it to one side of the bin. Arrange a new pile of bedding on the other side and begin burying your food scraps deep into it. In about a month, your original batch will be ready-to-use compost. Remove it from the bin to sprinkle on your garden and repeat the process on that side. When removing the compost from your bin, be sure not to remove the worms—they aren't indigenous to your soil, so they won't last long if you accidentally put them in the garden.

A foul-smelling bin is indicative of a problem. Be sure to bury your food under the bedding, and if the worms seem overwhelmed with the scraps, lighten their load a bit.

this spud's for you

GROWING POTATOES IN A BUCKET // Jenny Rose Ryan

materials

20-gallon plastic bucket
or trash bin

Drill and drill bit

Potting soil

Potatoes that are starting
to sprout

Plant saucer large enough
to go under the bucket
(if needed)

Think you can't grow anything besides those windowsill herb kits? Think again. You can grow potatoes in a bucket! From just one medium-sized potato, you can grow three or four plants yielding 10 to 20 potatoes each. They're nature's most perfect food! (Plus, the plants are pretty, too.) All you need is a tiny bit of outdoor space—a fire escape, patio, or square of concrete will do. Plant in the spring when your soil is warmed up and you'll have fresh taters in the fall.

1 Turn the bucket over and drill 20 or 30 holes (spaced a few inches apart) along the bottom for drainage. Drill a few holes up the sides of the container, too, to help keep the soil from getting waterlogged.

2 Cut the sprouting potatoes into sections containing three eyes each (the eye is the little nub where the sprout comes from). If your potatoes are smaller than 2", just leave them whole.

3 Put 4" to 6" of potting soil into the bucket and nestle the potato chunks into the soil. Cover the potato chunks with about 2" more soil and pat it down (but not too firmly).

4 Move the bucket to its permanent location. If that's going to be a patio, put the lid from a container or a plant saucer underneath to catch the dirty water.

5 As the potatoes emerge, cover the tops of the plants with more potting soil. What you're doing here is basically forcing the plant to create one long taproot, which will grow multiple potatoes on it. Keep doing this until the bucket is half- to three-quarters full. Keep the soil moist but not soaking wet throughout the growing season.

6 When the plants have bloomed, turned yellow, and died, it's time to harvest. Depending on where you live, this could be late August to early October. Watch the plants for the above clues. You can either dump the whole bucket over (get a friend to help) and dig through the soil pile, or, if you want to keep your work area clean, carefully dig beneath each wilted plant for the goods. Potatoes toward the top will be small ("new" potatoes) and potatoes on the bottom will be big—sometimes as big as two of your fists.

7 To store the potatoes, *don't* wash them. Just leave them out to dry, dust off as much dirt as you can, put them in a paper bag with vent holes, and keep them in a cool closet or basement.

PART TWO

YOUR STYLE, YOUR WAY

hand jobs

GET IN THE KNOW—LEARN HOW TO HAND-SEW // Debbie Stoller

In this primer, you'll learn the basics of hand sewing, including how to thread a needle (no, you're not supposed to double the thread and tie a knot in it, dagnabbit!), the stitches most commonly used for small sewing projects, and even how to sew on a button.

THREAD YOUR NEEDLE

To begin a sewing project, cut a length of thread about 36" long (about as long as from the tip of your left boob to the end of your right hand with your arm sticking straight out from your body). Thread the needle by folding the thread tightly over the eye of the needle, squeezing it together, then pulling the needle out and pushing the folded bit through the eye (figure 1). Next, just pull through a tail about 6" long. Do not double your thread! Hold your needle at the top, near the needle's eye, with one finger resting on that eye so that the tail doesn't go flying out. Doubled thread is much more likely to get tangly as you're sewing, and besides, for most tasks, you just don't need the extra strength.

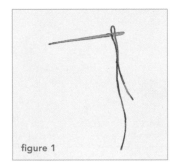
figure 1

TACK THE THREAD

Now, since you haven't made a knot, here's how to start your stitching without having the thread coming loose each time: you're going to tack the thread in place. This means making five or six very small (1⁄16" to 1⁄8") stitches on top of each other in the same spot (figure 2). Leave about a 2" tail when you start these stitches; you can trim that down to 1⁄2" later on. If you're seaming or hemming, you'll be working from right to left, so tack your thread in the rightmost spot of whatever it is you're sewing. (Or, if you're left-handed, do the opposite— here and for all the instructions that follow.) And when you come to the end of your stitch-witchery, you can finish up the same way: make another five or six tiny stitches, one on top of the other; then snip your thread, leaving a 1⁄2" tail. Look, Ma, no knots!

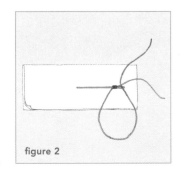
figure 2

RUNNING STITCH

If you know only one stitch, this is probably it. Unfortunately, there is hardly a sitch where it's best to use this stitch. The running stitch is great for decorative purposes, such as sewing a

patch to a T-shirt or a pair of jeans, but for sewing a seam, it ain't so hot. Even the tiniest fingernail snag in a running stitch will make your whole seam scrunch together, accordionlike. That said, here's how you can make this dang stitch that you should probably not be using anyway:

Begin by tacking your thread in place. Then, weave your needle into the fabric like so: go in about ⅛" to the left of where you tacked your thread, come back out about ⅛" to the left of that, go back in about ⅛" to the left of that, and come out about ⅛" to the left of that—like a skipping stone.

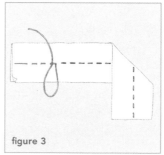

figure 3

Then pull your needle and thread all the way through, but don't let your fabric bunch up (figure 3).

BACKSTITCH

The backstitch is sturdy and damn stable (unlike the running stitch, it won't pull) and it's great for holding two pieces of fabric together. The only problem with this stitch is that although it looks nice on one side (the side you see when you're making it), it looks assy on the other. But since you'll be using this to seam two things together or close a hole in your fabric, it will usually be hidden where the sun don't shine.

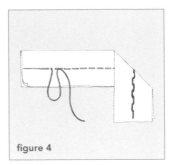

figure 4

To make it, first tack your thread in place, then insert your needle down into your fabric and come back up about ⅛" to the left of where you went in. Pull your needle and thread all the way through, then reinsert your needle where you went in the first time, and come back up about ¼" to the left of your stitch, or about ⅛" past where you came up last time. Keep repeating that last part—going back in about ⅛" to the right of where you just came out, and coming back up about ⅛" to the left of where you just came out (figure 4). See? It's called the backstitch because you keep going back before you go forward. These stitches can be very small (⅛", like we're making them here) or slightly larger (up to about ¼").

WHIPSTITCH

The whipstitch is used to join two folded or hemmed edges of fabric together or to sew an opening closed. It can also be used on the edge of a lone piece of fabric to spruce it up, like along the edge of a crocheted scarf, or around the edge of an appliqué or patch to sew it in place.

To whipstitch two fabrics together, lay the fabrics flat with their edges flush, wrong sides together. Tack your thread at the corner (or wherever you want to start) and sew a series of small slanted stitches on the very edge of the fabrics, about ⅛" from the edge. Follow the same stitch instructions on a lone piece to add a decorative edge.

HEMMING STITCH

The hemming stitch is so simple, it's hardly a stitch at all. Its whole reason for being is that it's a way to stitch two bits of fabric together without the stitches showing through (at least, not very much) on the outside of your clothing. If you're gonna hem something, start by ironing down the raw edge about ¼", then ironing it down again at the length you want it to be. Tack your thread on the top of the ironed-down part, then take your needle and grab just a couple of threads of fabric from the item (skirt, pants leg, whatevs), just below the folded edge. Next, grab a bit of fabric from the very bottom

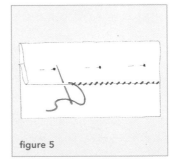

figure 5

of the folded part (this can be a bit of a bigger bite, as it won't show through on the front—figure 5). Do it again, a bit to the left, and keep stitching this way all the way around the edge to be hemmed, keeping things even-steven along the way. Pins can help you with that.

BASTE

Basting stitches are basically a loose, long running stitch that can be removed easily. These stitches are used to temporarily sew fabric together before you sew with a machine. You might do that to test the fit of a garment, to hold slippery fabrics together, or to hold a zipper in place as you sew it in permanently.

To baste, first pin the area together as you would to sew it. Thread the sewing needle. You don't need to tack it in place because it's coming out soon enough. Put the needle through the fabric where it won't be sewn over by the machine and pull through, leaving a 6" tail. Start sewing in a long running stitch and make sure the stitches are removable by tugging on the thread to see that it moves easily.

Now you're free to sew with the machine. Just make sure you don't go over your basting stitches, or they'll no longer be easily removed.

SEW BUTTONS

Ah, finally, it's time to double your thread and, sweet baby Jesus, even put a knot in the end. To sew a button on, use this doubled thread to go up through the fabric and into the button, then back down through the fabric, at least three or four times. When you're done, you may want to make a shank by tightly winding the thread once or twice around those stitches, just underneath the button, before sticking it back through to the back side of the fabric (figure 6), tacking it down, and snipping it to ½".

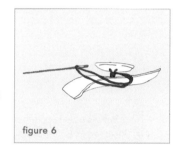

figure 6

embroidery extra credit

If your fabric is in need of extra embellishments, get fancy with these basic embroidery stitches.

satin stitch   Embroidery projects often call for the satin stitch, which is used to fill in spaces in your design (for example, to fill in the "Thank You" design on the bag on page 30). You'll be using embroidery floss to do it. To keep your work taut, use an embroidery hoop.

First, bring the needle up to the right side of the cloth on one side of the outline. Insert the needle on the opposite side of the outline, then bring the needle under the fabric to return to the starting edge. Repeat the sequence to create a smooth row of even, side-by-side stitches, changing the stitch size to reflect the outline of the pattern you're working with.

split stitch   Also used in embroidery, the split stitch is great for outlines or anywhere your design needs curves (for example, to make the outlines around the "Thank You" design on the bag on page 30). To do it, first make a small stitch with your embroidery floss. As you make your next stitch, slide the needle through the center of the previous stitch, picking it up with it. The resulting stitch will look a little like a chain and a lot like something that takes a ton more work than it does.

machine sewing 101

HOW TO USE A SEWING MACHINE // Jenny Rose Ryan

You may be the proud owner of a super-cool sewing machine, but getting started can be a daunting task—especially if you bought a vintage machine that didn't come with an owner's manual. Rather than winging it, read on to find out what all those parts are called and how to use them. In no time, you'll be ready to put your knowledge to the test, turning your fabric scraps into beautiful works of art.

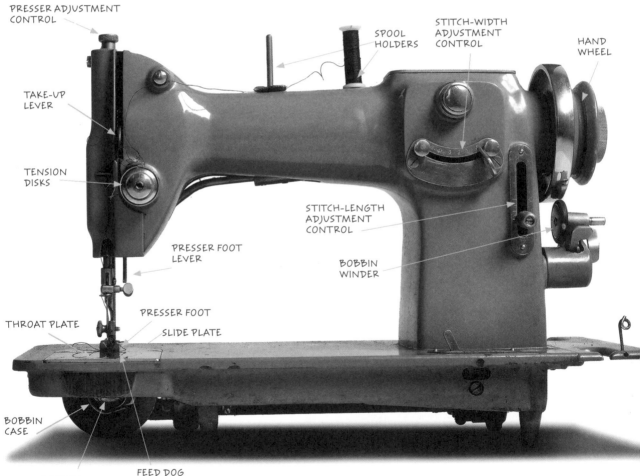

PRESSER ADJUSTMENT CONTROL

TAKE-UP LEVER

TENSION DISKS

PRESSER FOOT LEVER

THROAT PLATE

PRESSER FOOT

SLIDE PLATE

BOBBIN CASE

BOBBIN

FEED DOG

SPOOL HOLDERS

STITCH-WIDTH ADJUSTMENT CONTROL

HAND WHEEL

STITCH-LENGTH ADJUSTMENT CONTROL

BOBBIN WINDER

PARTS OF THE MACHINE

Hand Wheel

Located on the right-hand side of the machine, the hand wheel allows you to slowly control the needle by hand.

Foot Pedal

You can control the speed of your sewing based on how much pressure you apply to the foot pedal.

Presser Foot and Presser Foot Lever

The presser foot is a little part shaped like a foot that holds the fabric in place for stitching. The presser foot lever raises and lowers the presser foot. When the presser foot lever is in the upward position, the tension disks are disengaged and the fabric lies loose on the machine.

Throat Plate

The throat plate is a removable flat part right beneath the presser foot that protects the bobbin and underside of the sewing machine. It is usually screwed into place. The throat plate also has a seam guide on it—etched lines that you can use to line up your fabric so you know what seam width you're sewing. When you go to sew, you lay your fabric on the throat plate to position it.

Slide Plate

The slide plate is the plate in front of the throat plate. It protects the bobbin area from thread and fabric that could get caught in the moving parts.

Feed Dog

The feed dog feeds the fabric under the presser foot while you guide it. It regulates stitch length by determining how much fabric passes under the presser foot as the machine stitches.

Take-Up Lever

The take-up lever is a component in threading the machine and also indicates the position of the needle. Older machines require you to thread the take-up lever like a needle. Newer machines have a slot in the take-up lever that you can slide the thread into.

Stitch-Length Adjustment Control

These controls allow you to vary the length of the stitches the machine makes. Shortening the stitch length decreases the amount of fabric fed underneath the presser foot by the feed dog before the needle goes through again.

Stitch-Width Adjustment Control

These controls allow you to vary the width of the stitch.

Spool Holder

The spool holder is where you place your spool of thread when sewing. The spool holder plays an important role in keeping the stitch tension just right—from there, the thread is fed through the machine up to the needle.

Tension Disks

Tensions disks control the pressure applied to the thread to help create evenly formed stitches.

Pressure Adjustment Control

The pressure adjustment sets the pressure the presser foot will exert on the fabric. The amount of pressure you want varies depending on the heaviness of the fabric. Sheer fabrics need little pressure. Denim needs a lot.

Bobbin

This is that small spool that you wind with thread and insert into the bobbin case. The thread that comes from the bobbin becomes the underside of the stitch.

Bobbin Winder

Bobbin winders wind thread onto the bobbin. Each machine does this differently—the winders may be on the top, front, or side of the machine. Read your owner's manual to determine exactly how to use yours, or look up your machine online to figure out the trick. Generally, the bobbin is wound on the top or side of the machine using a larger spool of thread to fill it and the foot pedal to power the winding.

Bobbin Case

Some bobbin cases are removable, but some are not. They are not interchangeable among machines. The best way to learn how to thread your bobbin case is to consult your owner's manual (or look up tips for your machine online). Generally, a bobbin is put into the case so the thread and slot form an upside-down V.

THREADING THE MACHINE

Now that you know what every part is and the role it plays in the operation of your machine, it's time to thread it. The exact procedure for each machine will vary slightly, but this is the gist.

1 Turn the hand wheel toward you and raise the needle to the highest position. (Some machines require you to unlock the hand wheel by pulling it out until it clicks before you can turn it by hand.) Now use the presser foot lever to raise the presser foot (figure 1). This will allow the thread to easily pass through the threading guides.

2 Put a spool of thread on the spool holder. Slide the thread through (or around, depending on your type of guide) the thread guide (or guides) on the top of the machine. Bring the thread through the take-up lever and tension assembly on the left side (figure 2). Thread the needle, then pull a few extra inches of thread through it and to the left and rear.

3 Insert a wound bobbin into the machine and close the thread plate. Pull a few inches of thread from the bobbin, and, holding the thread from the needle, rotate the hand wheel toward you to turn the bobbin in its case. Pull the thread that's through the needle to bring up the bobbin thread (figure 3). Pull a few extra inches of bobbin thread to your left.

Congratulations! You just threaded your machine. Now you're ready to start sewin'.

SEWING TWO PIECES OF FABRIC TOGETHER

1 Gather together a few scraps of fabric and iron them. Set the tension, pressure, stitch width, and stitch length to your liking based on the fabric and your own desires. Stack two fabric pieces together, right sides facing, and pin them along one side, where you'll make your practice seam. You'll be sewing on the wrong side of the fabric (the side that wouldn't show if you were making something to wear or use). Place the pins so they're poking away from the direction you're sewing. This keeps you from stabbing yourself when you pull them out.

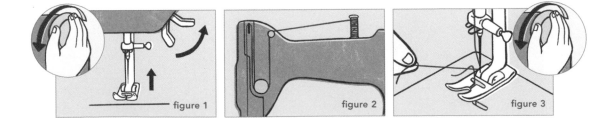

figure 1

figure 2

figure 3

2 Orient your fabric so the pinned edge is on the right, and place the upper pinned corner on the throat plate under the needle. If you've just threaded the machine, the presser foot will already be up, but if it's not, lift the lever to raise the foot before you do this. Slide the fabric under the presser foot and needle so the pins are just to the left of where the needle will land. Lower the presser foot lever. If things don't line up, raise the presser foot and adjust the fabric.

3 Before you start stitching, pull out any pins near the needle. Then, with your hands holding the fabric steady, slowly press down on the foot pedal. Don't go too fast until you feel how the machine moves and pulls. Gently stitch forward a few stitches. If you're using a straight stitch, activate the control that allows you to back up (usually a lever on the front of the machine) and go forward and back over where you started, repeating this a few times. If you're using a zigzag stitch, this step isn't necessary.

4 Continue to slowly press the foot pedal as you move down the fabric, feeding the fabric into the machine, pulling pins out before you get near them, and keeping an eye on the throat plate's guide to stay in a straight line. If you find the fabric slipping when the presser foot is down, increase the pressure on the presser foot. If the fabric is held so tightly that the feed dog is unable to move the fabric, decrease the pressure. Continue sewing all along the fabric until you get to the end and finish with the same backward-and-forward stitching you started with. Practice making seams with a few different stitch lengths and fabrics so you can get a feel for how your machine responds to adjustments.

figure 4

PRACTICE SEWING A HEM

1 Fold one edge of a piece of scrap fabric over ½" with the right side facing outward and iron along the folded edge.

2 Fold the fabric over again (so that the raw edge becomes hidden in the fold) and iron the edge one more time. Pin the folded fabric into place about ¼" from the edge (figure 4).

3 Take this practice hem to your machine and follow steps 2 through 4 in "Sewing Two Pieces of Fabric Together," using a straight stitch. Use the throat plate's seam guide to keep your stitches consistently about ¼" away from the edge.

make do and mend

MENDING YOUR CLOTHES // Kelly Rand

Wear any treasured clothing item long enough and it's bound to succumb to holes, tears, and other such maladies, but that's no reason to toss it out. Mending was second nature to our grandmothers and great-grandmothers, who knew that rips, holes, broken zippers, and even a favorite bra could all be repaired with some simple stitching and a little patience. Now, grab your pile of mending and get to work!

fix a torn seam

materials

Damaged garment

Iron and ironing board

Straight pins

Scissors

Needle and thread in a coordinating color

A torn seam is one of the most common clothing malfunctions, but luckily, it's also one of the easiest to fix. Choose a needle of appropriate size—sturdy enough to go through the fabric, but thin enough that you won't struggle.

1 Turn the item of clothing inside out. Press where the seam has come apart so the two sides of fabric line up, and pin them together.

2 Cut an arm's length of thread, insert it through the eye of the needle, and make a 6" tail on one side. Tack the thread into place (page 108). Working from one side to the other on your garment, make a small diagonal stitch up over the edge of the fabric, reinserting the needle directly under where the thread crossed over the top of the edge (this is a whipstitch). Continue making evenly spaced, diagonal stitches approximately 1/16" apart and the same length as the rest of the stitches of the seam you are repairing, usually between 1/8" and 1/4". End your stitches approximately 1/4" beyond the tear and tack the thread to finish.

3 Trim the remaining thread. Turn the garment right side out, and voilà! Good as new.

fix an underwire bra

materials

Damaged underwire bra

Needle and thread in a coordinating color

Scissors

It always seems to happen to your favorite bra, the one you wear over and over again: that sneaky underwire starts to poke right through the fabric. Well, with a few stitches, you'll be back in your favorite underthing lickety-split.

1 The first step is to put the wire back in place (figure 1). Do this by snaking it back into your bra, pulling the fabric up while pushing the wire down a small portion at a time until the wire is well below the hole it came out of (or at least far enough that you have room to close the hole).

2 Thread your needle with a matching thread color and tack the long end to secure it (see page 108). Make small, tight stitches, stacking them side by side across the hole (figure 2) until it is completely closed; one pass over the hole should secure it sufficiently (figure 3).

3 Tack off your thread, trim the ends, and the girls are back in business!

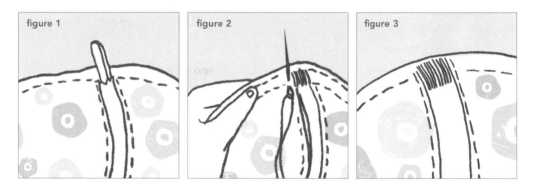

figure 1   figure 2   figure 3

Sometimes all it takes are a few little stitches to get a garment back on your bod.

patch a hole in your sock

materials

Holey sock

Scissors

Embroidery floss or wool yarn in a matching color

Darning egg

Darning needle

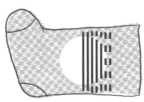

figure 1

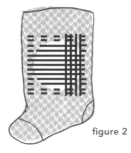

figure 2

If you don't have a darning egg, you can use a standard lightbulb instead. Your needle will glide along the glass surface, making it easier to darn; just be careful not to break the bulb.

If your sock sprouts a hole, it's a cinch to save it. Darning uses a combination of weaving and sewing to patch up holey heels.

1 To start, clean up the hole by trimming any loose threads. Thread your darning needle with a short tail, but don't knot the floss. Pull your sock onto the darning egg so that the hole is directly over it.

2 Starting ½" to the right of the hole, make a series of vertical running stitches that extend ½" above and below the hole. Keep on making stitches, working toward and then over the hole in parallel rows as close together as possible. When you reach the hole, make a long running stitch right over it and continue as before (figure 1). Continue working in this fashion until your long parallel running stitches cover the hole and extend ½" to the left of it, ending at the top left corner.

3 Turn the sock 90 degrees clockwise. Insert the needle at the bottom right-hand corner of the stitches you've just made. Use the needle to weave the floss over and under the now-horizontal running stitches and in and out of the sock (figure 2). When you reach the top of the horizontal stitches, work a new row of stitches down directly to the left of the one you just created. Continue, working toward the hole as before.

4 When you reach the hole, with the long running stitches stretching across it, just weave your floss in and out of those threads, as there is no sock to work in and out of. Continue weaving until you reach the other side of the hole, where you can again stitch in and out of the sock as you weave. End your stitches when you reach the leftmost side of the horizontal running stitches. You should now have a tightly woven patch where the hole was.

5 Trim the floss; the weave should be tight enough that a knot is unnecessary.

replace a broken zipper

materials

Damaged garment

Digital camera

Seam ripper

New zipper as close to the length and color of the old one as possible (see tip)

Straight pins

Sewing machine with zipper foot and matching thread

To change the length of a zipper, open the old zipper and lay it next to the new one. See where the slider of the old zipper rests, then use a marker to note that spot on the new zipper. Using a needle and thread, repeatedly stitch over the mark across the zipper teeth until the stitches are the same height and width as the original bottom marker. Tie off and trim the thread. Cut the zipper 1″ below the stitches.

These instructions work best for replacing a zipper on pants, dresses, or skirts in a lightweight fabric. For a long-lasting repair, a sewing machine is highly recommended.

1 Use a digital camera to take a pic of the broken zipper, so you can reference the original stitching and placement as you mend.

2 Turn your garment inside out and carefully remove the old zipper with a seam ripper, taking note of where the stitches were. Once you've removed the zipper, gently pull the broken threads out of the fabric. Inspect the seams to make sure no further mending is needed.

3 Working on the inside of your garment, with the original seam opening facing away from you, line up the right tape of the new zipper and pin it in place. Do the same with the left zipper tape. Close the zipper. Check to make sure everything lines up and looks good. If not, make adjustments by repinning to get the proper alignment or even trimming the zipper to get the right length (see tip).

4 Once the zipper looks good, carefully open it and baste both sides of the zipper tape to the garment. Close the zipper and turn the garment right side out. Inspect it again to make sure it's still aligned.

5 Working on the outside of the garment, use a zipper foot on your sewing machine to stitch along the original seams, down one side of the zipper and around to the other side (figure 1). Be careful not to break the needle on the zipper teeth when sewing over the zipper itself.

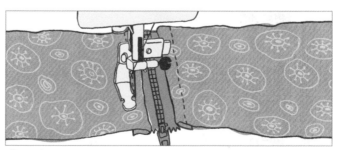

figure 1

altered states

HOW TO ALTER YOUR CLOTHING TO MAKE IT FIT // Cal Patch

We've all seen that ideal shirt at a flea market that's just not going to fit. And we each have those perfect-for-the-butt jeans that would look good with a different leg, or a sweater from Mom that we wish weren't so boxy. Each of these wardrobe alterations can be done with some quick stitchery. For best results, use a sewing machine. And when in doubt, baste before sewing—it's easily reversible and can make machine sewing much easier.

shape the waist of a boxy blouse

materials

Too-boxy shirt or blouse

Straight pins or tailor's chalk

Safety pins

Sewing machine and matching thread

Scissors

Pinking shears

Iron and ironing board

Too many shirts have unflatteringly straight side seams, causing the wearer to look like she has no waist at all. What a waste! It's easy to create a more fitted shape by changing the side seams. This one works best if the garment has plain or serged side seams, and if it fits fine through the shoulders and chest.

1 Turn the shirt inside out and try it on. Button at least two or three buttons so you can see how much room you've got to play with. Working on one side of the shirt, pinch out the excess fabric starting at your true waist— just below your rib cage—and pin or chalk where you are pinching. Your chalk markings or pins should intersect smoothly with the original side seam about 2" below the armpit. At the bottom, either blend the new seam into the existing side seam, or take your new side seam all the way down to the hem if you want.

2 Take the shirt off and transfer your marks to the other side of the shirt; just put a few pins on the other side to make sure you still have some fabric to work with when you get to it. Once you have finalized your markings, pin both sides with safety pins (they're less likely to cause injury) and put the shirt back on, right side out and buttoned. Walk, sit, stretch, dance, take a book off a high shelf—just to confirm that you haven't made it too tight. Adjust accordingly.

3 After it passes the "movement test," your shirt is ready to be resewn. Turn your shirt inside out and, starting up near the armpits, begin stitching about 1" above where your new line departs from the old side seam. Your first few stitches will be exactly on top of the old seam. Backstitch and continue sewing until you veer off onto your newly drawn line. Follow it until you've blended back into the original side seam down around your hips (overlap the old seam again for 1" and backstitch) or until you hit the bottom hem and backstitch. Try on your handiwork and confirm that it's not too tight. Don't be alarmed if there are pulls or puckers at the waist; that's because we haven't trimmed away the fabric inside yet.

4 If the fit is good, use pinking shears to trim the inside to ½" from your new seam line. Press the seams open. Finish the edges by either zigzag-stitching the seam allowances separately or folding the raw edges in toward each other and stitching them together with a straight stitch. This last method creates what is called a mock French seam; it will look the most professional.

Before   After

reshape a baggy sweater

materials

Tightly knit but too-baggy sweater

Straight pins and/or safety pins

Tailor's chalk

Sewing machine and matching thread

Scissors

Double-fold bias tape (optional)

Turn a baggy old sweater into something formfitting and flattering by redefining the side seams. This technique will work on a tightly knit cardigan or a pullover—if you can see your hand through the knit, it's not a good candidate for this alteration.

1 Turn the sweater inside out and try it on. Then pin and test the fit, just as for the boxy blouse on page 120. The entire seam that goes from your wrist up your arm to your armpit and down your side to your hip is fair game for adjustment. You may only need or want to take in some of these areas. If so, be sure to blend your new seam line into the old one. Or if the upper arms and chest are big on you, go ahead and make a completely new seam from wrist to hip. The underarm and side seams will meet at a point that should also intersect at the armhole, effectively shrinking the armhole itself. Using chalk, make a new line along the pinned fabric that is continuous and gently curving, with no kinks or bumps. The only point should be at the armpit.

2 Sew along your marked seam with a narrow zigzag stitch, so the seam will have some stretch to it. Trim the seam allowance to ¾" to allow for a little unraveling. Use a piece of double-fold bias tape to bind the seam allowances if they seem like they want to fray. Many vintage woolen sweaters—cashmere, angora, alpaca, or anything of animal origin—will be somewhat felted by the time you get your hands on them, and they won't unravel at all.

de-bell flared jeans

materials

Bell-bottom jeans with at least one plain seam per leg

Straight pins or tailor's chalk

Seam ripper (if needed)

Sewing machine with a denim needle (unless the jeans are very thin) and matching thread

Scissors

Thread to match top-stitching (if needed)

Follow these simple instructions to turn bell-bottoms into skinny jeans, or vice versa (see the box below). But keep this in mind: If there are two rows of topstitching on the outside seams, you've got flat-felled seams, which are difficult to alter. At least one seam per leg (either side seam or inseam), and ideally both, must be a plain seam.

1 Turn the pants inside out and try them on. Working only on the plain seam, pin or mark your new seam line from the knee down to the hem. Your new line should blend with the old seam at the knee. If you have two plain seams on each leg, take half the fullness out of each side. If you are adjusting only one seam, be aware that if you make too extreme a change, you will throw off the balance of the leg and it might look weird.

2 If there is topstitching on the old seam, rip it out with a seam ripper 1" above and 1" below where your new line overlaps the old. Stitch your new seam, overlapping the old one by at least 1" and backstitching at the start. Continue down to the hem and backstitch twice. Trim the seam allowance to ½", and zigzag-stitch the seam allowances together to minimize fraying.

3 If there was topstitching on the old seam, use thread that matches the stitching and continue the line of topstitching from where you ripped it out down to the hemline.

flare up skinny jeans

If you want, you can go the opposite direction and create a custom pair of bell-bottoms from skinnier jeans. Just tear out the seam (again, a plain seam) from the knee down and hem the edges or leave them frayed. Then, insert a piece of denim or twill cut to the size needed to increase the flare—it'll be a triangular shape. Contrasting colors will take you to a super-hippie place, so choose this piece wisely. Stitch it in place. Then, hem the bottom of the insert to match the bottom of the jeans.

lower the waist of an a-line skirt

materials

Tape measure

A-line skirt that is too snug
or high-waisted

Tailor's chalk or straight pins

Scissors

Single-fold bias tape in
a coordinating color

Sewing machine and
matching thread

Hook-and-eye closure
(optional)

- -

*The instructions given
here are for a high-
waisted skirt that closes
with a zipper, but you
can use this method to
work with one that has
snaps or buttons.*

Vintage skirts were often meant to sit on the "true" waist—the smallest part of your midsection, just below your rib cage. Today, we'd call such a skirt "high-waisted," since we tend to wear skirts (and jeans) much lower. Luckily, this means that if that vintage A-line skirt is too tight, you can lower the waist and have it fit perfectly. Remember: this technique only works with the A-line cut; the skirt must get bigger a few inches below the waistband.

1 Figure out where you want the top edge of the skirt to sit and use a tape measure to find out how many inches around you are at that point. Be sure the line you are measuring along is parallel to the floor. We'll call this your waist measurement (WM), even though it's not your true waist. Divide your WM in half.

2 Lay the skirt flat on a table or the floor. Hold the tape measure below the waistline of the skirt, measuring from seam to seam, and find the spot where the skirt's width is equal to your half WM. With chalk or pins, mark a line ½" above the tape measure, continuing around the front and back of the skirt. Make sure this line is parallel to the original waistband and does not cross any pockets, pleats, or other details that will interfere with your new waistline. If it does, see if you can raise or lower the line slightly and still have it fit—1" or so bigger or smaller than your WM will usually be okay. If you can't avoid such obstacles, you may want to try another skirt.

3 Open the zipper and the skirt and cut along the chalked or pinned line. You can cut right across the zipper. Since the zipper pull is down, it won't get cut off with the top of the zipper. Once you have made this cut, do not try to zip up the zipper until the skirt is finished, or you will take the pull right off and might not be able to replace it.

4 Lay the bias tape along the cut edge, starting at the zipper and working around until it meets up with the zipper's opposite side. Allow ½" of the tape to overhang at either end, where the zipper is. You will be unfolding the tape and pinning it on the right side (or outside) of the skirt, so position the tape's raw edge ¼" below the cut edge of the skirt. Sew along the upper fold line of the opened bias tape; this seam will be ½" down from the top edge of skirt. Be sure to backstitch at the beginning and end of the seam.

5 Flip the bias tape to the wrong side of the skirt and pin it all the way around. The bottom edge of the tape should be folded up inside so that it looks nice and clean. It's a good idea to trim any bulky seam allowances from darts or side seams that may keep the tape from lying flat. Wrap the ends of the tape around the zipper teeth as you flip the tape to the inside, and make sure the tape won't be in the way of the exposed teeth that will still function. You are essentially creating a new stopper for the zipper. Carefully test the zipper before sewing to make sure you can zip it all the way to the fold; check that both sides look even. If the zipper won't stay up on its own, sew on a hook-and-eye closure.

6 From inside the skirt waist, stitch along the lower edge of the bias tape so it is completely secured to the skirt. You may need a few extra stitches (by hand or machine) at each end near the zipper to tuck all your edges neatly inside.

Before   After

hem jeans

materials

Overlong jeans

Straight pins and/or tailor's chalk

Sewing machine with a denim needle (unless the jeans are very thin) and matching thread

Iron and ironing board

There are two ways to hem jeans and we cover both here. If in doubt about exactly how long to make your jeans, go a little longer—and don't do any of this before you've washed them at least once. Note that these instructions work best with straight-leg jeans—flares or pegs will lose their shape if you're hemming more than an inch or so.

METHOD #1: PRESERVATION THEORY

If you'd like to preserve the original hem but raise it higher, put your jeans on like normal. Fold up the cuffs until the bottom edge of the original hem (where the stitching is) is ½" above where you want the bottom edge to be when you're finished. Pin the fold and flip it up inside the legs so that the old hem (up to the stitching) peeks out beneath the fold. Check that the length is right, then flip the folded excess back down, and stitch exactly next to the lower edge of the old hem as close as you can. Iron your seam to flatten it out, and decide whether you want to leave the flap as is (see below) or trim it to ½" and zigzag the edges to prevent fraying.

METHOD #2: OLD FAITHFUL

This is really just your basic hem and it can be done on skirts and other pants as well, which method #1 can't. Try on the jeans and pin where you want the hemline. Now take them off and mark a line 1" below your desired hemline. Cut on the lower line. Turn up ½" to the wrong sides, then ½" again; pin. Stitch from the inside, very close to the upper fold line. A few wearings and washings will soon make your new hem look worn the old-fashioned way.

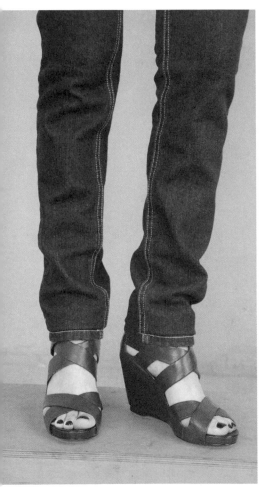

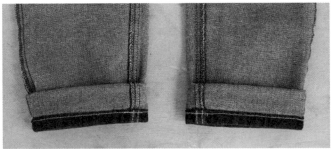

hey shorty

HIGH-WAISTED SHORTS MADE FROM JEANS // Sara Graham

materials

Scissors

Oversized jeans

Straight pins

Tailor's chalk

Sewing machine with denim needle and matching thread

Pinking shears

Iron and ironing board

Ever snag a pair of secondhand jeans with killer details only to realize they'd fit your Pop-Pop better than you? Don't despair—just whip 'em into a cute pair of sassy high-waisted shorts. For best results, get a pair of jeans at least three sizes too big with a low-hanging crotch and a zipper at least 6" long.

1 With scissors, cut the jeans off at the knees. Put them on inside out and hike them up so the crotch of the pants meets your own and the waist is high. Use pins to pinch the excess fabric equally at each side of the waistband. Continue down the legs, pinning the shorts as tight or loose as you like.

2 Using tailor's chalk, trace along the pins before removing them and the shorts. Re-pin along your chalk line. If the actual seam of the jeans interferes and you have enough excess fabric to allow it, cut out the seam.

3 Using a zigzag stitch, sew up the new side seams by following along your pencil lines, making sure the waistband's front and back line up exactly. Backstitch for strength. Cut the excess fabric from the side seams and waistband using pinking shears to prevent fraying. Leave at least a ½" seam allowance. Iron flat. Turn the shorts right side out and try them on.

4 If the crotch is still saggy, turn the shorts inside out and put them back on. Pin the crotch area while you are wearing them, pinching the excess fabric (and taking care not to stick yourself). Remove the shorts and realign the pins to create a small semicircle, which spans from the center of the crotch to about 4" down the inseam of each leg. Cut away the excess crotch fabric before sewing, as it can be tough to maneuver your machine around the original construction. Sew from one inseam to the other, following the semicircle and backstitching at the beginning and end of your seam.

diy skivvies

GIVE YOUR OLD T-SHIRT NEW LIFE—ON YOUR BOOTY! // Amy Karol

materials

Knit-jersey camisole and pair of underwear to copy

Old T-shirt, the bigger the better (you may need two)

6 ½ yards stretch lace ⅜"–½" wide

Sewing machine

Sewing-machine needle for knits (optional but helpful)

Matching thread

Scissors

Scrap paper

Tape

Pencil

figure 1

What do you do with old T-shirts that you just can't get rid of—like the one from that Rush concert you never want to forget, or the tee you wore as a camp counselor all those summers ago? Save them from the Salvation Army by turning them into the cutest undies ever.

1 Grab your camisole and undies, and lay them on top of an old T-shirt to make sure you have enough fabric. (Tip: Using a T-shirt that is similar in weight and stretch to the camisole and undies you are copying will give you the best results.) If you can't fit both onto one T-shirt, use two. Trace around the body of the camisole (do not trace the straps; you'll be making straps out of lace), adding ¼" to the side seams, and cut through both layers of the T-shirt, so you have a front and a back (figure 1). With the camisole pieces' right sides together, use a straight stitch to sew up the side seams with a ¼" seam allowance. Set aside.

2 Before cutting out the undies, make a paper pattern. Lay two sheets of scrap paper side by side and tape them together. Center your existing undies face up on the paper and trace, adding ¼" at the side seams and crotch seam (figure 2). Repeat this step, tracing the flip side of your undies. Draw a crotch pattern on a piece of paper, mimicking the crotch piece of your existing undies as much as possible, and cut out the pattern. Adjust the shape as needed so it will fit your pair when it's sewn on.

3 Fold the undies paper patterns in half to make the two sides symmetrical, and cut out (figure 3). Lay these paper pieces, still folded in half, with the fold aligned on the fold of T-shirt fabric. Make sure the grain of the T-shirt is still going up and down. Trace and cut out.

4 Trace the crotch-piece pattern on the T-shirt and cut it out. Use a zigzag stitch on the raw edges.

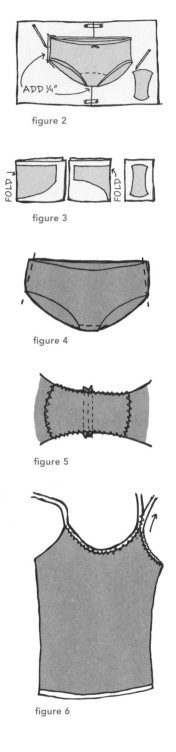

figure 2

figure 3

figure 4

figure 5

figure 6

5 With right sides together, sew the side seams and crotch seam of the underwear, using a ¼" seam allowance (figure 4).

6 Lay the crotch piece on top of the crotch, centered over the exposed seam, and zigzag over the outer edges (figure 5). Try the underwear on. If they fit, proceed. If they're too big, take the seams in a bit, and if they're too small, remove stitches with a seam ripper and use a smaller seam allowance.

7 On the right side of the fabric, lay stretch lace over the raw edges of the leg openings and the waistband, extending it a bit over the edge. Stitch it down with a wide zigzag. (Tip: When sewing the lace, thread the needle with thread to match your lace and the bobbin with thread to match the T-shirt.) Do not pull the lace or the fabric while you stitch. Make a sassy, decorative bow by stitching the middle of a 3" piece of lace to the front of the undies, right below the center of the waistband. Tie in a double knot and trim.

8 On the camisole, stitch stretch lace to the hem and the back neckline in the same manner as above.

9 Finish the remaining raw edges of the camisole, extending enough lace from the front neckline and armpits of the body to create the straps (you'll secure the two pieces of the strap together with a zigzag stitch up the middle) (figure 6). To do this, first measure the length of your existing camisole's straps. Now, using a long piece of lace, leave enough tail for one strap (approximately 13") extending beyond one side of the front neckline, and stitch the lace across the edge as above, leaving enough lace extending beyond the other side of the front neckline to create the second strap (another 13" approximately). To create the double strap, stitch another piece of lace over the raw edge of one armpit, starting at the back of the camisole and extending the lace in the front, making it long enough to match the strap from the neckline. Repeat on the raw edge of the second underarm. Stitch both tails of one strap together down the middle, and repeat to create the second strap. Attach the straps to the back, stitching straight across, right sides together.

mock jacobs

KICK UP YOUR CARDIGAN // Callie Watts

materials

Forty-five ½" buttons

Cardigan

Needle and matching thread

Scissors

Can't shell out enough sand dollars to hit the Marc? Save your clams and push your own buttons by embellishing an old cardigan.

1 Begin by laying down 45 buttons on your sweater in nine rows of five, radiating out from the neck. (If your sweater can't fit five buttons between the neckline and shoulder seam, use smaller buttons.)

2 Attach the row of buttons that goes down the center front first. Remove any original buttons that interfere with your pattern and replace them with the new ones. These replacement buttons will have to be sewed on so they're positioned to go through the buttonholes—they won't be right next to the other buttons in their row, but when you fasten your sweater, they will all line up.

3 Next, sew on the rows that are flush against the shoulder seams. The buttons at either end of these rows should sit against either the neck or sleeve seams.

4 Space out the other six rows of buttons based on these first three rows, and sew the buttons around the neck first, so you know where each row starts.

Whether you want to look refined and demure or over-the-top, add toppings to your smock to take it from then to now.

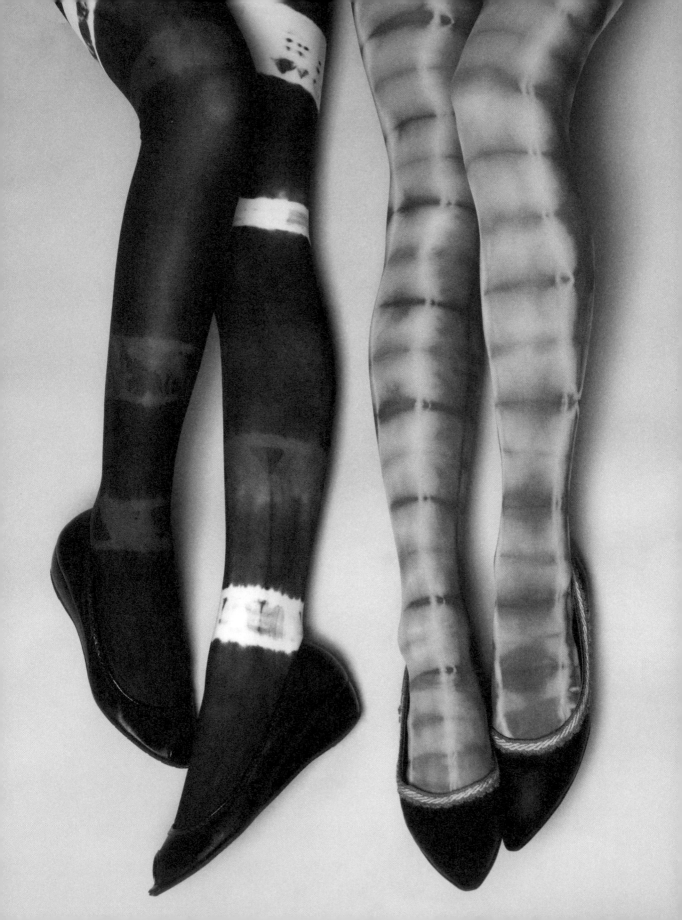

dyer straights

REVAMP TIRED TIGHTS WITH TIE-DYE // Callie Watts

materials

White tights (no more than 50 percent polyester)

Rubber bands

Black fabric dye, such as Rit

Fuchsia fabric dye, such as Rit (for the option on the left)

Old, large pot (you won't want to use it for cooking again)

Old tongs or a wire hanger

Have some cheap tights that need updating, or did you dirty up the toes of your white hose? Give your old tights new life with a DIY dye job.

OPTION 1

To create the design on the right in the photo, fold each leg of your tights accordion-style from the toe to the crotch. Pinch the folded material and secure both sides of each stack with rubber bands. In your pot, mix the black dye according to the package instructions and bring it almost to a boil. Submerge your tights for about 15 minutes, stirring constantly with your tongs or hanger to ensure even coverage. Rinse with water (start with warm and finish with cool) until it runs clear. Remove the bands and lay the tights flat to dry.

OPTION 2

To make the design on the left in the photo, knot your tights wherever you want a stripe. Make the knots on each leg match up if you want the stripes to be even. In your pot, mix the black dye and bring it almost to a boil. Submerge your tights for 30 to 60 minutes, stirring constantly, and rinse clean, as above. Untie any knots where you want a colored stripe. Empty, clean, and rinse in your pot, then mix the fuchsia dye and bring it almost to a boil. Submerge the tights for 30 minutes, stirring constantly, and rinse clean as above. Undo the remaining knots and lay the tights flat to dry.

no mean feet

TURN HOLEY SOCKS INTO HANDY GLOVES // **Maresa Ponitch**

materials

**1 pair of style-y socks
(no anklets, though)**

Scissors

**Needle and matching
thread**

Don't be devastated by the first signs of a hole in the toe or heel of your favorite socks. Turn this tragedy into treasure with a few cuts and little stitches.

1 Cut off the entire foot of the sock, just above the ankle, and set the foot aside. You will be using the hollow tube.

2 Paying attention to the length and width of your fingers, make three lengthwise slits through both layers of the sock at the raw (foot) edge.

3 Turn the sock inside out and sew the cut edges of the slits together to create tubes for your fingers. Be sure to sew the full length of the slits, or the gloves will split at the base of your fingers. Do not sew the slits' open ends—your fingers are supposed to stick out there! If you like the finger openings frayed, leave them the way they are. Otherwise, do a quick whipstitch around the openings to help keep everything together.

4 Turn the sock right side out. Lay it over your hand, note where your thumb will go, remove your hand, and cut a slit about ½" long for your thumb.

5 Put the glove on to stretch out the thumb hole. The edges will be frayed—which enhances the charm—or you can whipstitch those, too.

save your sweater

MAKE A SCARF OUT OF FELTED WOOL // Jennifer Knapp

It's the worst thing that can happen to your favorite wool sweaters: shrinkage. But now you don't have to say good-bye. Just slice them up into a cool new scarf (or head to the thrift store and find alpaca someone else has rejected).

Grab three or four jumbo-sized, 100 percent wool sweaters in complementary colors. Throw them in the washing machine, wash with hot water, and dry them on high heat. This process—commonly known as "felting"—will shrink them and make the fibers dense and fuzzy. If you've already shrunk your sweaters, skip this step. Cut the sweaters into 6"-wide strips in a variety of lengths. Don't worry, the edges won't unravel. Overlap the strips by ½" and pin together, alternating colors and lengths and making the scarf as long as you want. Sew along each overlap using a zigzag or running stitch. Remove the pins and trim the excess material right to the seam.

makin' change

TURN A CASSETTE INTO A COIN PURSE // Rachel Benefiel

materials

X-ACTO knife

Old cassette tape

Pliers

Dremel tool or sandpaper

About ½ yard fleece

3¾"-by-5" piece of cardboard

Needle and matching thread

4"-by-2" coin-purse frame

Extra-strong craft adhesive, such as E-6000

Wondering what to do with that crate of cassettes you just can't seem to part with? Repurpose your fave music flashback into something you can appreciate without the help of a Walkman: a DIY coin purse. Even if you got rid of your tapes with the advent of the iPod, they're a dime a dozen at thrift stores everywhere, so scope your local Goodwill for one that tickles your fancy. Then follow these steps to carry your change in cheeky, nostalgic style.

1 Use the X-ACTO knife to crack open the cassette shell so you have two separate sides (be careful—they can break quite easily). Discard the spool of tape and use pliers to break off any parts that stick out on the inside of the plastic shell. Use a Dremel tool or sandpaper to grind these areas smooth.

2 To create the inside of the coin purse, cut two pieces of fleece slightly bigger than your cardboard piece and two triangles of fleece measuring 3" on each side. Lay the rectangular fleece pieces together, wrong sides facing, with the long edges at the top and bottom. Place one triangle on top, wrong side up, with its bottom edge flush to the bottom of the rectangle and the bottom left point of the triangle aligned with the bottom left corner of the rectangle (figure 1).

3 Using a needle and thread, sew these three pieces together along the bottom edge of the triangle. Now fold the material so the bottom right corner of the rectangle matches up to the top unsewn point of the triangle, creating a V. Sew the pieces together along the edge of the triangle, creating one side of your coin purse (figure 2).

4 To make your coin purse sturdy, fold the cardboard in half crosswise, and slip it between the rectangular pieces of fleece. Then flatten out the fabric and sew the second triangle onto the other side of the V in the same manner.

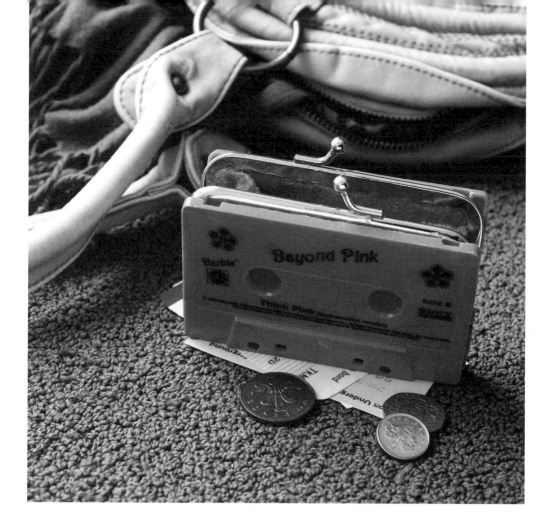

5 Now it's time to add the closure. Apply craft adhesive inside the top of one of the purse frame pieces (do not apply it to the sides). Take the fleece liner and push the corresponding part of it into the coin-purse frame. If you have difficulty getting the fleece into the frame, use your X-ACTO blade to ease it in (carefully, though—you don't want to cut the fabric). Use your pliers to crimp down the frame. Repeat this process on the other side.

6 To add the cassette covers, apply a decent amount of adhesive to the inside of both cassette pieces, right up to the edges. Position these pieces onto the sides of the coin purse and squish them down, making sure they adhere well. Hold everything together like this for a few minutes to allow the adhesive to set. Let dry.

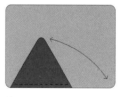

figure 1

figure 2

beau chapeau

CRAFT A HAT FOR A LASS // Callie Watts

Headgear is back in a big way, especially small early-twentieth-century fascinators, and classy '60s pillbox hats. Luckily for fashionistas on a budget, these two toppers are easy and inexpensive to make. Use vintage fabric and you can trick everyone into thinking yours took ages to find.

hat-shaped box

materials

Pillbox hat frame (available at most millinery- or wedding-supply stores)

1 yard thick fabric

Tailor's chalk

Scissors

Needle and matching thread

Magna-Tac 809 or other fabric glue

Binder clips

Feathers

Flexible appliqué

1 Trace the top of the hat frame on the wrong side of your fabric and add 1" all the way around. Cut out the circle and make ¾"-deep snips at 1" intervals around the perimeter. Using fabric glue, secure the fabric to the top of your frame, gluing and smoothing each tab down, overlapping as you go. Let dry.

2 Cut a piece of fabric that is long enough to wrap all the way around the frame plus 1" and that is the height of the frame's side plus 2". Cut the strip in half crosswise (you'll get a better fit around the frame using the separate pieces). Sew a ½" hem along one long side of each piece. Make three equidistant 1½" snips along the unhemmed long sides. Carefully glue the first piece of fabric around the frame, with the hemmed edge matching the top edge of the hat frame. Fold in the short edges of the second piece of fabric ¼" and press. Then wrap the second piece of fabric carefully around the other side of the hat frame so that the folded edges overlap the edges of the first piece by ¼" on each side.

3 Fold the snipped edges to the inside of the hat frame and glue them so the fabric showing is smooth. Use binder clips to secure the fabric; let dry.

4 Glue feathers over one of the seams on the frame, secure them with a binder clip; let dry. Glue a flexible appliqué over the base of the feathers; let the hat dry completely and remove all binder clips.

fascinator street

materials

3 yards 2"-wide velvet ribbon (found at most fabric/trimming stores)

2 yards 4"-wide buckram (found at most fabric/trimming stores)

Scissors

Straight pins

Needle and thread in a color that matches the ribbon

Safety pin

2 fan feathers

1 feather bunch

Magna-Tac 809 or other fabric glue

Piece of heavy paper cut into a 2" circle

Piece of cotton fabric cut into a 2" circle

Bobby pins or hat pin

1 The main element of your fascinator will be velvet-ribbon-covered buckram. Cut the buckram to 1⅛" wide. Cut the ribbon into two 1½-yard pieces and lay them one on top of the other, right sides facing. Pin the sides and pin one end of the buckram to one end of the ribbon. Sew a ¼" seam along both sides of the ribbon and across the end to where the buckram is pinned. Turn the tube right side out by rolling the ribbon over the buckram—attaching a safety pin to the other end of the buckram to make this easier—pushing it down, and smoothing it out. Trim any excess buckram and whipstitch the open end shut.

2 To begin shaping the hat, take the whipstitched end, fold 6" of the ribbon up to make a loop, and pin. Continue making loops, molding them in a circle, and pinning them in the center. When you have about 15" of ribbon left, make one larger loop, leaving a 5" tail. Pin this loop into itself, creating two loops that lie somewhat flat; then pin these evenly onto the tail, creating the side band of your fascinator. Then flatten a bottom loop that is in line with the tail, creating a headband-like shape. Arrange the decorative loops to your liking.

3 Take the two fan feathers and decide on their placement for the side embellishment—you will be attaching them inside the flattened loop so that one protrudes on each side. Don't glue them down yet. Also take the feather bunch and decide how it will be positioned on the center of the hat. After noting the placements, set the feathers aside.

4 Flip the hat over, stitch the center of the loops together, and sew down the bottom of every loop. Remove the pins. Stitch the sides of the loops together anywhere they touch, to maintain the shape.

5 Apply fabric glue to both sides of each fan feather's base and attach it according to your plan (see step 3). Let dry. Glue on the feather bunch as planned and let it dry.

6 To create the base, glue the heavy paper and cotton fabric circles together, let dry, then glue the paper side of the circle to the underside of the fascinator. To wear, attach the fascinator to your hair with bobby pins or a hat pin.

put yo hood up

MAKE A BOYFRIEND HOODIE // Tara Marks

How many times have you seen the ultimate sweatshirt, only to realize a men's small fits you like a circus tent? With this pattern and a sewing machine, you can craft your own custom zip-up, guaranteed to fit like a dream.

materials

Large sheet of lightweight paper, such as newsprint or tracing paper

Scissors

2 yards main color sweatshirt fleece

1 yard accent fabric (something with a little stretch, like cotton jersey, works best)

Straight pins

Sewing machine with regular foot and zipper foot and matching thread

18" closed-end zipper

1 Using the pattern on the bottom of page 144, transfer the pattern for your size to the lightweight paper. Note that pattern measurements are given for size small with medium, large, and extra-large in parentheses. Cut out the paper pattern pieces and use them to cut out the fabric, leaving a ½" seam allowance around each piece. You'll need two sleeves, two torsos, two hoods, and two cuffs from the main fabric, as well as two hoods and one waistband from the accent fabric.

2 Pin your torso and sleeve pieces together, with the fabric's right sides facing, along the lines highlighted in red (see figure 1) and stitch, using the regular foot on your sewing machine. Then fold everything in half along the dashed line in the diagram, right sides together, so the blue lines match up. Starting at the bottom of the torso, pin the edges together along the sides and sleeves and stitch.

3 Take a cuff piece and fold in half widthwise, right sides together, so the short edges line up, and stitch to form a ring. Then fold it in half lengthwise, wrong sides together, by folding the top half of the ring you just made to the outside. Pin the cuff to the bottom of the sleeve, with right sides together, and sew. Repeat for the other sleeve. Do the exact same thing you did with the cuffs to the waistband, and then sew it to the bottom of the sweatshirt, making sure the seams line up.

4 Sew the two main-fabric hood pieces, right sides together, along the curved edge. Repeat with the accent fabric. Put the main-fabric hood inside the liner hood, right sides facing, and sew together at the face opening. Then flip the main-fabric hood out so the liner is inside and the right side of the main fabric is facing out. Pin the bottom of the hood to the neck hole, right sides of the outer fabric together as if the hood were down, making sure the opening of the hood is centered on the sweatshirt, and stitch.

5 For the zipper, cut a diagonal line the length of the zipper from the front neck, starting at one front edge of the hood. Put the zipper foot on your machine and sew in the zipper, making sure to topstitch your seams once the zipper is sewn in.

figure 1

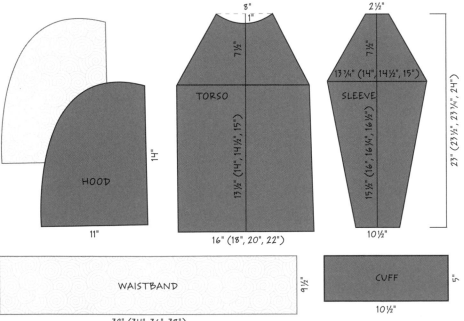

Pattern pieces for Small (Medium, Large, Extra-Large)

sew simple

MAKE YOUR OWN DAMNED SKIRT // Katrina Blodgett

materials

Enough fabric to wrap around your hips plus 3", at whatever length you like

Scissors

Straight pins

Sewing machine and matching thread

⅝"- or ¾"-wide elastic

Fabric marker (optional)

Iron and ironing board

Rickrack, pom-poms, or ribbon (optional)

Here's a formula for sewing a skirt that's so easy you can knock it out in about an hour. Use polyester or rayon fabric for a swingy look or use a breathable fabric like cotton for a cool summer skirt. Now take some measurements and sew your own damned skirt.

1 Okay, here we go. Once you've cut the fabric into a rectangle as wide as the circumference of your hips plus 3" and as long as you like (knee length or above works best), fold it so that the right sides are together, pin, and sew the side edges together.

2 Take the elastic and wrap it around your waist kind of snugly (it will stretch as you sew and if you make it comfortable or loose now, your skirt will be too big). Allow about an extra ½" to ¾", then cut the elastic and sew the ends together to make a circle.

3 Divide the skirt and the elastic into fourths by folding them in half and in half again. Mark the fourths of the skirt along the top edge with pins and use either pins or a fabric marker to mark the fourths of the elastic.

4 Turn your skirt wrong side out and pin the elastic to the skirt at your marked quarters on the outside (the wrong side) of the fabric. Align the seams on the elastic and the skirt when you pin.

5 Starting at the seam, use a zigzag stitch to attach the elastic securely. To do so, pinch the fabric and elastic together at the next pin, stretching the elastic so that it is the same length as the skirt while you zigzag-stitch to the quarter mark. Keep going this way until the entire waistband is attached. Turn the elastic under and iron it in place. Turn the skirt right side out and then, stretching while you sew, zigzag again on top of the elastic to keep it folded under.

6 Hem the skirt and leave it plain or sew on fancy stuff like rickrack or pom-poms. You made a skirt!

musical muffs

MAKE FUZZY HEADPHONES // Callie Watts

Make your muffs do double duty by keeping you warm and pumping the tunes. They're the perfect accessory for that chilly time of year, and in the summertime you can detach your muffs and rock solid gold headphones.

materials

Scissors

Faux fur fabric scraps

1" thick foam (available in most trimming stores)

1 or 2 sheets of felt that matches your fur

Needle and matching thread

Safety pin

Straight pins

2 hook-and-eye closures

Headphones

Masking tape

Gold spray paint

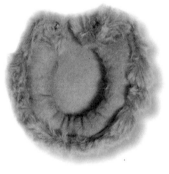

1 Cut two 6" circles from the faux fur. On each one, make a ½" slit every inch around the perimeter of the circle (this prevents bunching when you sew the fur). Set them aside.

2 Cut two 4" circles from the foam. Cut out and discard a 2½" circle from the middle of each 4" circle. Then slice each 4" foam circle open, making two C shapes.

3 Cut two 3½"-by-13½" strips of felt. Fold each piece of felt in half lengthwise and sew the sides together. Turn each felt tube right side out and pull a piece of foam through it. It helps to fasten a safety pin onto the end of the foam strip; you can grip it as you feed the foam through the tube. Trim each stuffed felt piece so it is just slightly longer than the foam and stitch the ends shut.

4 Fold one of the stuffed felt tubes into a circle and pin it onto the wrong side of a fur circle, positioning the opening of the felt piece so that it lines up with one of the slits in the fur. Extend this ½" slit in the fur to 1" and fold the fur over the edges of the felt tube so that they overlap slightly. Sew the fur to the felt, making sure to tuck under the rough edges of the fur (as shown in the close-up) to hide any unsightly seams. Sew a hook and eye to each end of the stuffed felt tube, on the inside of the muffs.

5 To turn your headphones gold, remove the original foam covering from the headphones and tape up the speaker holes. Spray the headphones with gold spray paint. Let dry.

6 Reattach the original foam to the gold headphones and cover it with your handmade muffs. Secure the muffs with the hook-and-eye closure.

Bump to the beat while trapping the heat with these detachable faux-fur earmuffs.

fair leather friend

GET TOUGH WITH A HEADBAND AND CUFF // Sara Brownell and Nici Williams

materials

Tape measure

Pencil

2 square feet vegetable-
tanned lightweight
tooling leather, 2- to 3-
ounce thickness (1 ounce
equals 1/64")

Utility knife

Rotary leather hole punch
(includes several hole sizes)

Rawhide, polymer,
or hickory mallet

Sponge

Leather stamping tools
(get an alphabet set for
stamping words or design
stamps for embellishing
your leather)

Light-brown leather dye

Small bowl

Soft cloth or paper towels

Water-based acrylic paint or
black leather dye (optional)

Paintbrush (optional)

Clear leather topcoat

1 line 20 snap with 3/16"
post and snap setter

Two 5" pieces suede string

Leather is a key badass accessory: you can add it to any getup for some rock-'n'-roll hoochie cool. Bring out your inner easy rider and make a real fashion statement with these custom headbands and cuffs, sure to make you the belle of the headbanger's ball. Try your local craft or leather supply store for materials or order them online.

1 For the cuff, measure your wrist and add 1". For the headband, measure your head; you'll want the band to wrap from ear to ear (approximately 13"). Decide how wide you want your headband and cuff to be and, with a pencil, mark these dimensions on the leather. On a cutting board or work table, cut out the two strips of leather with a utility knife.

2 Use the leather punch and mallet to stamp a hole in one end of each strip, 1/8" from the edge (figure 1). The hole should be big enough to accommodate suede string for the headband and a snap for the cuff. Test on a scrap piece if needed.

3 Wet the leather lightly with a damp sponge. Using the stamping tools and mallet, create your design by setting each stamp against the leather and hitting it with the mallet at a 90-degree angle against a hard surface (ideally, marble). When your design is done (figure 2), let the leather dry (about 20 minutes).

4 Pour some brown dye in a small bowl. Dip a soft cloth or paper towel into the dye, wipe off the excess, and apply it gently to the leather with smooth diagonal strokes. Be conservative—it's easy to add another coat but impossible to revert if you've used too much. You can apply water-based acrylic paint or black leather dye with a paintbrush to highlight your stamped design (figure 3). Let your leather sit for a few hours until completely dry.

figure 1

figure 2

figure 3

5 Apply the clear topcoat, using the same method as above, and let it dry for 30 minutes.

6 To finish the cuff, use the mallet and a snap setter to add a snap to the holes. A snap comes in four pieces: two of them will fit together in each hole. Make sure the smooth-faced piece is visible on the outside of your cuff. Use the snap setter and mallet to fuse the snap pieces together on each end of the strip, hitting at 90 degrees. Your snap setter will come with a detailed how-to. Take a look at a snap on another item to get a clear sense of how the pieces fit together, and experiment on a scrap.

7 To finish the headband, slip one of the suede strings through the first hole and tie an end knot inside the headband large enough so it doesn't slip through. Do the same thing on the other side.

sew faux

STITCH UP A FAUX-FUR WRAP OR COLLAR // Callie Watts

materials

Wrap and collar pattern (see facing page)

Large sheet of paper, at least 19" by 10" for the wrap or 10" by 17" for the collar

Pencil

Straightedge

½ yard fake fur fabric

½ yard satin lining fabric

Scissors

Sewing machine or needle and matching thread

Safety pin

Iron and ironing board

Straight pins

As any '40s dame worth her blood-red lipstick can tell you, nothing says glamour like a furry pelt draped around your shoulders. But if you're the kind of broad who thinks that the only thing uglier than killing an animal for fashion is shelling out big bucks for something you can make yourself, then get out your sewing machine and start stitching. Both versions can be made out of the half-yard of fabric called for, with some left to spare.

MAKE THE WRAP

1 You'll begin by transferring and enlarging the pattern onto your paper using a 1"-by-1" grid. To do this, draw the grid shown at right on the paper, then copy over the pattern piece freehand, block by block, following the chart.

2 Fold your piece of fur fabric in half, hairy sides together, and pin your pattern to it, with the pattern aligned on the fold as indicated; cut out the shape. Cut another piece from the satin in the same way. Set the pieces aside.

3 To make the ribbon, cut two strips of satin about 1" longer than you want your ribbon to be and twice as wide. Fold the satin in half lengthwise, with the shiny side facing in, and sew up the side and across one end. Put a safety pin on the sewn end and use it to turn the ribbon right side out. Iron the ribbon flat.

4 Place the fur and satin pieces so that their right sides are together (the furry side facing the shiny side). Attach the ribbon tie by laying it between the two pieces of fabric, with about 1" sticking out at the corners of the wrap and the rest folded in the middle so it won't get caught up when you sew around the edges. Pin the layers all the way around to hold.

5 Sew about ¼" in from the edge, leaving a 6" opening at the center of the wrap where the neck would be. Be sure to sew over the ribbon a couple of times to reinforce it—this is going to get tugged on a lot, so it needs to be strong. Turn the wrap right side out through the hole in the neck and sew the opening shut using a hidden stitch (start your stitches on the fur side so you cannot see the knot, and make the satin side stitches as tiny as possible, with bigger stitches on the fur side).

MAKE THE COLLAR

To make the smaller collar, follow the above directions, omitting the parts about the ribbon—use a rhinestone pin to hold the collar together. Get out on the town, Ms. Fancy!

WRAP

PLACE ON FOLD

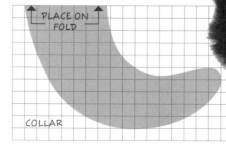

PLACE ON FOLD

COLLAR

Enlarge grid so squares are 1" by 1".

she's got a nude attitude

BE A FRAME-PROTECTING DAME // Tracie Egan Morrissey and Callie Watts

materials

Chart photocopied onto
40-pound (or thicker) paper

Acrylic paints in the
necessary colors (see tip)

Small, thin paintbrush

1 piece lining fabric
cut to 7 ½" by 8"

Scissors

Sewing machine and
matching thread

2 pieces vinyl cut to
6 ½" by 7 ¼"

Needle and matching thread

Guys don't make passes at girls with scuffed glasses,
so make some protection for your vision correction!
Whip up this porny paint-by-numbers glasses case in
clear vinyl and you'll surely draw some attention.

1 Fill in the spaces on the photocopied chart with the
corresponding paint colors using the paintbrush. Once
you've colored in your naked lady, choose a background
color, and fill the rest of the page.

2 To assemble the case, position the lining right side
down and sew a ½" hem all the way around. Fold
the fabric in half lengthwise, right side facing out. Sew the
bottom and the open long side shut, then turn the lining
pouch inside out.

3 Trim the painting so that it is about ½" smaller all
around than the vinyl, and keep your naked lady on
one side of the sheet (don't center her). Place your image
between the vinyl sheets and stitch around all four edges.
Keep your stitching off the paper—if you have to take a
stitch out of the paper, it will leave a mark.

4 Fold the stitched vinyl piece in half lengthwise, right
side out, and stitch the open long side and bottom
closed. Slip the lining pouch into the case and hand-sew the
lining to the top of the case, stitching through the holes that
are already there. Trim the vinyl as close to the stitch line as
you can.

- -

*Buying every color you need for paint-by-numbers can
get expensive. If you don't already have a good supply of
acrylic paints, get a few basic colors and blend them to
build your palette.*

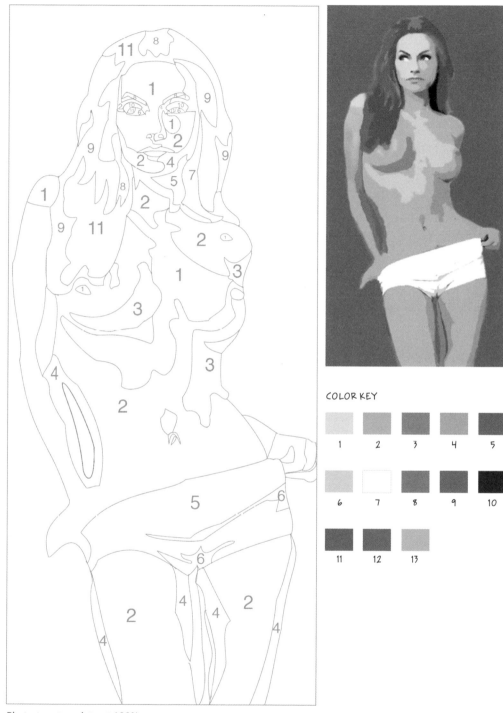

COLOR KEY

| 1 | 2 | 3 | 4 | 5 |

| 6 | 7 | 8 | 9 | 10 |

| 11 | 12 | 13 |

Photocopy template at 100%.

charmed, i'm sure

MAKE A CHARM BRACELET // **Djenn Hayes**

Beads have been around since the earliest days of *Homo sapiens*, and the basic concept of beaded jewelry is the same as it was when bronto burgers were king: pass some form of string or rod through a pretty or otherwise significant bauble with a hole in it and make it wearable—simple. With this in mind, anyone with a couple of pairs of pliers and about three hours can make a charming charm bracelet.

materials

White plate

Clasp (if needed)

Package of medium-gauge open jump rings

Needle-nose pliers with wire cutters

Length of chain with links big enough to pass a headpin through (look for cable, figaro, or rolo chains) and long enough to fit around your wrist loosely but without sliding off

Beads and charms in all shapes and sizes

50 to 75 headpins in a color to match the chain (see tip below)

Round-nose pliers (available at craft-supply stores)

It's a good idea to buy extra headpins. They're cheap, and you'll burn through them until you get the hang of making loops.

1 Set the plate on your table (it will provide a white background to work against, making it easier to see as you attach the pins to the chain—plus the lip keeps the beads from rolling away).

2 To attach a clasp to your chain, you'll use jump rings (you'll also use them to attach the baubles). Open a ring by sliding it over your needle-nose pliers and spreading the pliers slightly. Hook the ring plus one half of the clasp onto the end of your chain. To close it, gently squeeze using your pliers until the ends of the wire just touch. Don't close it more than that, because you'll end up with one end awry. It'll scratch up your skin and snag your clothes! Repeat to attach the other part of the clasp to the other end of the chain.

3 To make the baubles, thread up to four beads and/or charms onto a headpin. If the pin is too small, thread a seed bead onto the end to help hold your desired bead. Leave at least ¼" at the top for the loop and trim off any excess wire with the wire cutters. Then use the round-nose pliers to bend the wire 90 degrees away from the beads. Next, roll the end of the wire toward the bead to make the loop. The loop does not have to be perfectly round or anything, but you'll want to make sure it's big enough that the bauble will be able to move when hooked onto the chain.

4 Hook the bauble onto a link on the chain using a jump ring and taking care to hang it on the "bottom" so it will fall toward your elbow as opposed to your hand. The charms will flip around as you move and can be really uncomfortable if they aren't facing away from your hand. Close the jump ring *gently* with needle-nose pliers, again taking care to just touch the wire back onto itself.

5 Repeat the bauble-making-and-attaching process until the chain is filled up or you like the way it looks—as few as seven charms (one per inch or so) will still look good. It might help to lay out your chain and charms before you attach them to make sure you like the balance. Keep trying the bracelet on and shaking it a little to ensure that the charms won't fly off and that the clasp will hold under the pressure.

big bling

MAKE A COCKTAIL RING // Jennifer Knapp

materials

Needle-nose pliers with wire cutter

3½ feet of 24- or 26-gauge sterling silver wire (available at craft- and beading-supply stores)

At least 12 crystal beads

Inspired by swinging-'60s cocktail style, these big candy-colored crystal rings have enough sparkle for any party. Or pop your ring on for a casual night out and hypnotize your crush. It's easy to make and easy to wear, so don't be afraid to rock its ruling powers.

1 Using the wire cutters, cut 14 pieces of silver wire, each 3" long. Set two wire lengths aside. With the remaining 12, hold one end of a wire piece with the needle-nose pliers and fold over ⅛" to form a tiny loop. Thread a crystal bead or beads onto the wire and set it aside—the loop will hold the crystal in place when the ring is assembled (figure 1). Repeat with the remaining wire pieces and beads.

2 Wrap the first of the two unadorned wires around your ring finger twice (figure 2). Remove the loop from your finger and wrap the second length of wire in a tight spiral around the first ring (figure 3). Leave ¼" of space unwrapped.

3 Using needle-nose pliers, open out the doubled wires in the unwrapped area of the ring so that they form a circle (figure 4).

4 When your ring is complete, take each crystal-bejeweled wire, form a loop with your pliers on the other end, hook it into the circular section of your ring, then twist the end around itself to keep it in place (figure 5). Be sure to leave the loop loose enough that the crystals will move freely. Trim off the excess wire. Cheers!

figure 1

figure 2

figure 3

figure 4

figure 5

flower power

MAKE A FABRIC PIN OR HAIR CLIP // Jennifer Knapp

materials

Scissors

Kerchief (silk and rayon are great)

Needle and matching thread

Epoxy craft glue

Pin back or hair clip

A brightly hued scarf adds a blast of color to the drabbest wardrobe, but how often can you loop one of those things around your neck before the look grows tired? Mix it up by twisting an old silky kerchief or some airy fabric into a big, blooming-flower brooch or hair accessory.

1 Using scissors, cut the scarf into a strip 4½" wide and 24" long. Fold the material lengthwise, right sides facing, and stitch ¼" in along the long edge. Turn the fabric right side out. Fold the ends in and stitch them closed.

2 Make a loose running stitch along one of the long sides. Pull the ends of the thread to gather the fabric as you stitch. Begin to wrap the fabric in a spiral, making a stitch every few inches through all the layers of fabric to hold the bundle together. When the spiral is complete, push the needle through the center of the spiral and make a few stitches through all the layers of fabric. Knot the end of the thread.

3 Fluff the flower and fold the petals outward to shape them. Using epoxy craft glue, attach the flower to a pin back or a hair clip and allow the glue to dry.

Give your old kerchief new life by transforming it into a big, blooming flower.

chains of love

NECKLACE SUCCESS IN A FEW EASY STEPS // Susan Beal

Does your wardrobe need a little sparkle? Use basic wire-wrapping techniques to create some bangin' new baubles. Add colorful beads to a chain for a set of complementary necklaces you can wear one at a time or layered together. All of these necklaces are made using double-wrapped loops.

basic double-wrapped loop technique

materials

Wire clippers

24-gauge craft wire

Round-nose and flat-nose jewelry pliers

Beads in different colors and sizes

1 Cut a 4" piece of wire. Use your round-nose pliers to bend the wire so it forms a right angle 1½" from one end (figure 1). Grip the wire at the bend with your pliers, then use your flat-nose pliers to pull the tail all the way around the round-nose pliers, creating a neat circle with a tail of wire extending beyond it (figure 2). Using the flat-nose pliers to hold the circle, grip the end of the wire tail with the round-nose pliers, slowly wrapping the tail around the wire above the circle to create a coil (figure 3). After wrapping two or three times, clip the end of the wire flush with the coil.

2 Put a seed bead on the wire, then your main bead, then another seed bead—a bead sandwich. Finish with another wrapped loop on top of the beads. Bend the wire about ⅛" above the top bead to leave space for the wire coil and repeat the coiling process, clipping the tail when the wrap meets the bead (figure 4).

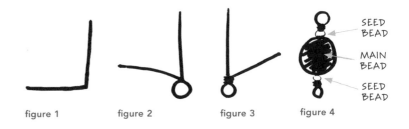

figure 1   figure 2   figure 3   figure 4

SEED BEAD

MAIN BEAD

SEED BEAD

swingy necklace with spaced beads

materials

11 featured beads in different colors and sizes

Eleven 4" pieces 24-gauge craft wire

Seed beads or other small beads

Eleven 2" lengths sterling silver or base metal chain

1 Arrange the featured beads on your work table in the order you want them to appear. Form a double-wrapped loop around a bead sandwich (see facing page). Attach a piece of chain to each loop before closing it. Now you have one bead sandwich between two pieces of chain.

2 Make a second double-wrapped loop with a bead sandwich featuring the next bead. Attach one side to one of the first pieces of chain and the other side to a new piece of chain.

3 Continue adding a bead sandwich at a time until you have used all the featured beads. Attach the last loop to the first loop's chain to complete the circle. This necklace goes on right over your head, so you won't need a clasp!

choker with three beads

materials

Three 4" pieces 24-gauge
craft wire

Seed beads or other
small beads

1 main bead for the center
of the choker

2 secondary beads

Two 6 ½" lengths sterling
silver or base metal chain

2 small jump rings

1 clasp

1 Following the instructions on page 160, make a double-wrapped loop with a bead sandwich, featuring the bead you want to be the center of your choker design.

2 Add a double-wrapped bead sandwich on one side, linking it to the featured bead section with one loop and to a piece of chain with the other before you start coiling them. Repeat with another bead sandwich and the second piece of chain on the other side. Now you have three linked beads in the middle of a longer chain.

3 Using the jump rings, attach the clasp to the chain.

pendant necklace

materials

Two 4" pieces 24-gauge
craft wire

Seed beads or other
small beads

1 secondary bead

1 main bead for the pendant

16 ½" length sterling silver
or base metal chain

1 clasp

2 small jump rings

1 Create a double-wrapped loop with a bead sandwich on it (see page 160) for the bottom half of the pendant, using the secondary bead.

2 Make a second double-wrapped loop, linking it to the first wrapped loop before you coil the wire for the top half. Place a bead sandwich on the wire, with your featured bead in the center of the sandwich. Make a final wrapped loop on top to finish it off.

3 Slip the chain through the top loop of the pendant. Attach the clasp to the chain using the jump rings.

she bang

DECOUPAGE A BANGLE // Betsy Lowther

materials

Scissors

1 sheet patterned paper

Bangle bracelet (wood bangles are available at most craft-supply stores, or use a plastic one from a cheap accessories store)

Paintbrush

Mod Podge or decoupage glue

Turning a bracelet from beastly to bangin' couldn't be easier. All you need is a little glue and some purty paper to decoupage your way to a most stylin' gift. Reuse an ugly old bracelet you already have and you'll be the most earth-friendly girl on the block.

1 Cut the paper into strips about ¼" wide and long enough to wrap around the width of your bracelet. You'll need about 30 to 40 strips to cover the entire exterior.

2 Brush a light layer of glue on the inside and outside of a strip of paper and position it on the bracelet, smoothing out any wrinkles. Repeat with each strip, slightly overlapping them as you work your way around.

3 Cover half of the bracelet, then prop it upright on its nonpapered side to dry for 3 or 4 hours. Finish the other half and let it dry again.

4 Coat the covered bangle with glue for extra protection.

bracelets for your besties

FRIENDSHIP BRACELETS TWO WAYS // Meredith Jenks

Friendship bracelets are the perfect craft: They're easy to create, the materials are crazy-cheap, and they're totally portable crafting-wise. But the best part is handing them out to all your homies. All you need to start knotting is embroidery floss in four colors.

the basic "v" friendship bracelet

1 Cut a piece from each floss that is twice your arm length. Gather the four pieces and fold in half, tying a knot about 4" from the doubled end. Tape the end of your bracelet to a surface.

2 To make your bracelet symmetrical, split the colors in half so the set on the left mirrors the set on the right. The following instructions are specific to the color choices shown here, so make a note of how your colors correspond to these: Two purple strings on the far left and far right, two blue strings on the inside of the purple strings, then two orange strings, and two red strings in the middle (figure 1).

3 Friendship bracelets are primarily made by two knots: the forward knot and the backward knot. For the "V" bracelet, start with a forward knot: Take the far left string (purple) and make a "4" shape over the string to the right of it (blue). Wrap the purple string under the blue string, pulling the tail through the "4" shape (figure 2) and sliding the knot up until it's taut against your main knot. Repeat to make a second knot. The string that was originally farthest left (purple) should now be to the right of the farthest left string (blue). Use the string that was originally farthest left (purple) to make two forward knots on the string to its right (orange). Now the string that was originally farthest left (purple) is the third string from the left. Use it to make two forward knots on the string to its right (red). The string that was originally farthest left (purple) should now be the fourth string from the left (between the two red strings).

figure 1

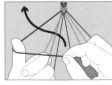

figure 2

figure 3

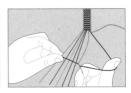

figure 4

4 Take the far right string (purple) and make a backward knot over the string to the left of it (blue). A backward knot is basically the same as a forward knot, but the "4" shape is reversed (figure 3). Repeat to make a second knot. The string that was originally farthest right (purple) is now second farthest right. Use it to make two backward knots on the string to its left (orange). Now it should be the third string from the right. Use it to make two backward knots on the string to its left (red). The strings that were originally on the farthest

left (purple) and farthest right (purple) should be next to each other in the middle. Knot them together with either two forward knots or two backward knots. Your first row is complete!

5 Repeat steps 3 and 4 until you've reached your desired length, then tie the loose strings in a knot. Split the threads in half and make two braids (knotting the end of each). Cut the doubled strings at the other end and braid those the same way to finish off the bracelet.

the woven friendship bracelet

1 Repeat step 1 from "The Basic 'V'" bracelet, then arrange the strings in any order (they do not need to be symmetrical).

2 Take the far left string and make a forward knot on the string to its right. Use the same string to make a second backward knot. This will return the strings to their original position.

3 Now take the second string from the left and make a forward knot and backward knot on the string to its right. Repeat this step with each string across the row.

4 Once you have completed the row, take the far right string and make a backward knot with the string to its left. Then use the same string to make a forward knot. Continue this step with each string moving left across the row (figure 4).

5 Continue knotting rows, repeating steps 2 through 4. Remember, working left to right tie a forward knot first, then a backward knot. Working right to left, tie a backward knot first, then a forward knot. When you've reached your desired length, finish off as in step 5 of the other bracelet.

PART THREE

HEALTH & BEAUTY

give your hair the finger

HOW TO DO A FINGER WAVE // Rachel Weeks

materials

Hard comb with both fine and coarse teeth

Setting lotion or curling fluid (available at beauty-supply stores; see tip)

Hair wave clamps (if needed; available at beauty-supply stores)

A friend

Curling iron (if needed)

Bobby pins

Hairnet

Hair dryer

Hair spray

Vintage hair comb or barrette

Setting lotion plasticizes hair. To kick it real old school, try this recipe for flaxseed setting gel, straight from the '20s: In a small pan, mix ¼ cup flaxseed oil with 1 cup water. Boil until thickened, then strain the liquid into a jar. Add 3 drops rosemary oil and refrigerate.

The passage of the Nineteenth Amendment and the good times of the Roaring Twenties helped create a new kind of American woman—the flapper. Because not everyone could rock a flat and sleek bob, curls and finger waves were incorporated into the popular style. Modern ladies, if you like the look shown on the previous page, just follow these directions and finger yourself—flapper style!

1 If you have naturally wavy hair, before you get started, note the direction your hair waves when it's air-dried. You may even want to write this down, because hair must be thoroughly wet to produce good finger waves, and it's difficult to follow the natural wave if you're not familiar with it. Now get your tresses good and wet and part your hair as you normally would. Choose a section of hair on the side of your part where there's more hair, dip your comb in setting lotion, and comb from scalp to end in that section, ensuring an even but not excessive application. (Working in sections as you saturate and style keeps the lotion from drying before the hair is shaped.)

2 Making sure your hair is combed flat against the head on each side of your part, comb down from the part about 2", pulling the hair tight along the way. Hold the comb so the teeth face upward, toward your part (figure 1).

3 Place your index finger above and parallel to the comb, over what will be the center of the wave you are shaping (figure 2). Pull the comb down about ½" away from your finger, following the natural wave of the hair, keeping the comb straight and the teeth facing your planted index finger. As you move the comb, penetrate every layer of hair down to the scalp.

4 With your index finger still firmly in place, move the comb straight up to meet it (again, penetrating all the layers), making a slight ridge in the hair. Direct the comb slightly forward along your index finger (toward your face) to lock the hair in place (figure 3). This will also secure the ridge and allow room between the comb and the ridge so you can create another wave. After you've secured the ridge, draw the comb through the rest of the hair.

figure 1

5 Still holding the first ridges between your middle and ring fingers, create another ridge below, following the same steps, only this time, direct the comb backward along your index finger away from your face.

6 Continue to wave the hair, letting go of set waves and using wave clamps, if necessary. (Wave clamps make this process easier for difficult-to-style hair. The drawbacks are that the lines will not be as clean and your waves may not last as long, so if you can avoid them, do.) Repeat steps 1 through 5 to wave all the way around the head, matching the direction of each wave as you go (figure 4). Enlist the aid of your friend for hard-to-reach sections. (You can create attractive finger waves around your face going solo, but a whole head of waves will require a pair of helping hands.)

figure 2

7 Loose pieces of hair in front of the ear can be curled and pinned into a flat ringlet with a little setting lotion. For short hair, the ends can be wound around your finger and pinned flat against the head, creating a pin curl. You can also use a curling iron to give the curls a little flip once the waves have completely dried. To hold longer, nonfingerwaved hair in the back, fashion yourself a bun (see page 179) and secure it with bobby pins.

figure 3

8 Place a hairnet over your head and blow-dry your hair thoroughly. While your hair is drying, press in the waves more deeply. Once it's dry, comb hair back from the face, pushing upward into the waves.

9 Spritz lightly with hair spray and adorn your Betty boop-oop-a-do with a vintage comb or barrette.

10 Finger waves ain't easy. If at the end of this process you find that you're a beauty school dropout, you can always sell out and buy yourself a professional waver.

figure 4

the do in doo-wop

A BOUFFANT YOU'LL WANT TO FLAUNT // Rachel Weeks

materials

Fine-toothed comb

Hairpiece (optional)

Bobby pins

Hair spray

Curling iron (optional)

Back in the '60s, harmonizing soulstresses like the Ronettes and the Shangri-Las were among the first to model the decade's famous bouffant. To really defy gravity, you might want to invest in a hairpiece. Look for something easy to secure on your head that's as close to your hair color as possible. Then bust out the hair spray and get your very own retro-punk bouffant.

1 Using the comb, divide your hair into three sections: a layer lining your face, running 1" or 2" deep from ear to ear; a layer 1" or 2" deep underneath the bulk of your hair, also running from ear to ear; and a middle section of the remaining hair. Clip the ear-to-ear sections to the side so you can concentrate on the middle one.

2 If you have a hairpiece, secure it at the crown and go to step 3. Otherwise, take small chunks of hair from the crown of your head one at a time and tease, tease, tease the roots with your fine-toothed comb, holding the hair straight up and hair-spraying the teased pieces as you go. Build your rat's nest as high as you dare, leaving a bit of hair underneath for step 3.

3 Still working in the middle section of hair, start taking chunks from the bottom-right side of your head, and wrap them around your hairpiece or your homemade rat's nest to create a smooth outer appearance. Wrap the pieces upward with a twisting, beehive-like effect in mind,

bobby-pinning the whole way around. When you have wrapped all the portions from the right side and reached the center of the back of your head, start grabbing from the left side, still circling upward and pinning along the way. Don't aim for perfection—this is rock 'n' roll, not a beauty pageant!

4 Once the bulk of your 'hive is in place, you have some freedom with the front section you set aside at the beginning. If you have bangs, you can style them as usual. If you don't, you can tuck a portion of hair from the left side behind your right ear, sweeping across your forehead for a banglike effect. Whichever way, you will want to use the rest of this layer to give the front of your 'ffant a smoother appearance, either by continuing the twisted-beehive look or smoothing it straight back over your rat's nest and securing with a bobby pin.

5 Finally, do what you want with the bottom layer—you can leave it loose, but you can also use a curling iron to give it a more coiffed, Ronette-worthy touch.

bee fabulous

GIVE YOUR DO A BEEHIVE // Rachel Weeks

materials

Dippity-do

Hot rollers

Hair clip

Hairpiece or "wiglet" close to your natural hair color

Fine-toothed comb

Hair spray (choose something that will be stiff for a long time, baby)

Hairbrush

Bobby pins (45 to 60 to take your hair to final altitude)

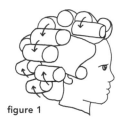

figure 1

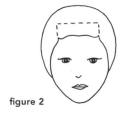

figure 2

Invented around 1960 by Illinois hairdresser Margaret Vinci Heldt, the beehive inspired fashionable young women to make standing Friday appointments at their local salons so they'd have big-hair flair all weekend long. Wanna try doing the do for yourself? Follow these directions, and you'll be reaching new heights in no time!

1 Clean hair is difficult to style, so plan ahead. Work with hair that was washed the day before and has accumulated some oils, and avoid conditioner altogether. Right after you wash your hair, apply a small amount of Dippity-do to the roots, work it through, then blow-dry.

2 The following evening, when it's time to style your hair, plug in your hot rollers and let them heat for at least 15 minutes. Next, you're going to roll with the homies—but, bitch, be careful! The layer of hair closest to your neck should be rolled over, not under like you normally would (figure 1). Remove the curlers after 15 to 20 minutes and run your fingers through the curls, separating them slightly. Lightly spray your hair.

3 Grab a fairly thick section of hair at the center of your forehead that's 3" or 4" wide and goes back a bit (figure 2). Clip it to the side of your face. You will deal with this part at the very end.

4 Plop that hairpiece on the very top of your head with the rest of your hair curled and still down (figure 3). Tease the hairpiece to high heaven, and smooth the outside so it will blend with your real hair.

5 Honey, comb. Tease the roots with a backcomb if you have thin hair. You want the length of your hair to be as smooth as possible while achieving the fullness you need. The underside of your hair is what will actually show, so teasing on top is fly. Spray the roots lightly for hold.

6 Lightly brush the underside of your hair. Then start taking chunks from the right side of the separated chunk in front, and wrap them around the wiglet on top, pinning with bobby pins the whole way around. Beehives rose to fame with a twisting appearance, but eventually evolved into styles with twisting foundations that didn't necessarily twist on the outside. If you don't get a perfect, soft-serve-cone-like result, don't lose faith.

figure 3

7 Continue taking chunks of hair from the right side of your head with the twisting effect in mind. When you get to the center of the back of your head, start grabbing from the left side, circling upward until the hair from the left completely covers the hair you've already pinned from the right side (figure 4). Leave all the hair along your face on the left side until the very end, then use it to cover any rough spots along the back.

figure 4

8 For the finishing touch, take the chunk you set aside at the beginning from your forehead and tease it up at the roots. Pin yourself a tiny pompadour a few inches back from your forehead with a bobby pin, take the end and roll it in a tiny hot roller, then find a creative place to glue that curl flat on your hive. Hurricane-proof that bodacious do with the rest of your hair spray, apologize to the environment, and go party with a fabulous style that's retro-riffic and straight sexy!

A few more items you may want:

Adornments   *Beehives of the '60s were often accented with small bows or flowers. If you're prepping for a special occasion, think ahead and get crafty!*

Toilet paper   *Your hive will stay flush all weekend if you wrap it in TP before bed. And if you're really a diva, get a silk pillowcase to avoid hive-crunching while you sleep.*

Small toothbrush   *For teasing touch-ups, a toothbrush won't get caught on other pieces of hair like a comb will when inserted in the hive.*

flip your lid

PUT YOUR HAIR DOWN, FLIP IT, AND REVERSE IT // Rachel Weeks

materials

Volumizing lotion or foam

Round hairbrush, preferably a vented version

Hair dryer

Hair clip

Fine-toothed comb

8 to 12 hot rollers (see tip)

Hair spray

Although many hair historians credit Katharine Hepburn with popularizing the flip in one of its earliest forms, you'll probably remember it best on '60s sirens Doris Day, Marlo Thomas, and Mary Tyler Moore. These days, you can still spot toned-down versions on lady politicians and Southern beauty queens, but hair-oines will always have a soft spot for the hardheaded hipsters of yore who knew how to swing a flip so stiff you could store cigs in it. Unskilled stylists, fear not: just follow these easy steps and you'll be singing flippity-do-da in no time.

1 Flips will be harder to maintain on longer tresses and work best on chin- to shoulder-length cuts. But if your hair is longer, you can still get a nice toned-down version following these instructions. Begin by washing your hair. While the locks are still wet, apply the volumizing lotion from roots to tips to make your hair more manageable.

2 Using your hairbrush, begin pinching sections of hair from the top of your head and laying them over the arch of the brush (figure 1). Apply heat from your hair dryer about 3" away from the brush. This should create some top volume while slightly curling the ends under. As you move down your head with the hair dryer, begin lifting the top sections away and brushing out the bottom layers so that the hair is moving underneath rather than on top of the brush. Turning the brush in your hand during this process will begin curling out the ends.

3 To get the hardheaded height of '60s flips, separate the very top layer and clip it out of the way—you're going to start teasing and you want this part to stay smooth to cover up the backcombing. Use your comb to tease hair at the roots of the middle and bottom layers. Keep the teasing at the roots, not farther down the length of your hair, to keep it from interfering with the hot rollers.

figure 1

figure 2

figure 3

4 Using the largest rollers, place the top two layers of your hair over a roller (so the ends will come out curled under). Then use the smaller rollers and wrap the remaining hair under them (so that the ends will be curled up—i.e., flipped) (figure 2).

5 Take the rollers out and lightly brush the volume of the crown and the sides of your head into the flip shape around the nape and sides. Reinforce the flip by holding it down between the index and middle fingers of one hand while lightly backcombing in an upward motion in the other hand (figure 3). Hold the flip shape close to your head while lightly lifting hair at the crown with the comb to add volume.

6 Spray heavily with hair spray and go show your friends—they'll flip their shit!

Hot rollers will ensure the best staying power for your flip, and they are strongly recommended for extremely straight hair. However, a curling iron or hot-air brush will work in their place. Just follow the blow-drying directions in step 2 using the curling iron or hot-air brush to create the flip shape.

twisted sister

DOING A FRENCH TWIST // Rachel Weeks

materials

Mousse (optional)

Hair dryer (optional)

French twist comb, bobby pins, or a sturdy long clip

Hair spray

The French twist dates back to the days of hoopskirts and bustles in nineteenth-century France, but you're more likely to remember it as the signature hairstyle of Miss Holly Golightly in the 1961 classic, *Breakfast at Tiffany's*. Since that film, Hollywood actresses and middle-school dance-goers alike have rocked this clean, classy do that feels cool and looks *très chic*! To try it out for yourself, just follow these eight easy steps.

1 The French twist works best on shoulder-length hair or longer, but variations are possible for shorter hair. Let your hair collect some natural oils before doing the twist. If you must work with it clean, apply mousse from roots to ends before you blow it dry. You can do a little light teasing all around the front of the hair just after blow drying to make sure it still has volume when it's in the twist, but Holly, go lightly—this is not the beehive!

2 Gather your hair at the nape of the neck, as though you are going to make a low ponytail. Don't secure it.

3 Holding the base of the ponytail, start twisting the hair upward, either clockwise or counter clockwise. Twist all the way to the ends without allowing the rope of hair to coil. As you twist, a roll should form against your head (figure 1).

4 Place your middle or ring finger on your crown, creating an anchor point above the place where the roll stopped forming, and fold the hair downward over the anchor point (figure 2).

5 If you still have significant length left after folding the hair over once, use your thumb as a lower anchor point and fold upward again. Repeat folding up and down over your fingers while keeping them at the same distance from each other until you reach the ends of your hair. The hair from the left side of your head will be rolled over to cover these coiled ropes, so keep them close to the head (figure 3).

6 Tuck the coiled ends into the roll either on the bottom or the top, depending on where you ended when you were folding.

7 Roll the hair from the left side of your head over the folded rope and tuck everything under (figure 4).

8 If you're using a French twist comb (a short, decorative comb with broad teeth), insert it in the direction of the twist, snagging only a small portion of the roll as you pass over it and making sure that the comb is not hugging the head. Lift the comb 180 degrees and then push it gently into the roll, hiding it in the groove, close to the scalp. If you're using bobby pins, place them along the side of the tuck as close to the center as you can get to secure the style. A long, sturdy clip will hold the do in place, too. Spritz on a little hair spray for hold, and *oui, oui, c'est fini!*

figure 1

figure 2

figure 3

figure 4

sticky bun

GIVE THIS EASY TWIRL A WHIRL // Rachel Weeks

materials

Flat iron (optional)

Mousse or texturizing balm
(if needed)

A pair of hair sticks or
chopsticks (see tip)

Hair spray

The bun has been popping up in Asian hair history since ancient times. In the third century, Japanese royalty wore ornately decorated buns right at the crown, while farmers, who carried goods atop their heads, sported chignons at the nape of the neck. Before bobby pins, women used special, handcrafted hair sticks to hold their buns in place. In a pinch, plain old chopsticks will do—just follow these five simple steps for one crazy-easy, Asian-inspired style.

1 This style works best on hair that is shoulder-length or longer and not freshly washed. For a sleeker look, prep by straightening your hair with a flat iron. Style the front of your hair however you like—if you've got layers, use mousse or a texturizing balm to separate them out around your face.

2 Take the length of your hair and pull it into a ponytail, holding it wherever you want the bun to be—this might be at the nape of the neck, the top of your head, or somewhere in between. Begin coiling the length of your hair by twisting it clockwise or counterclockwise until it begins forming a bun on your head. Once you have wrapped the length of your hair in a circle around the base, hold it firmly in place using one hand.

3 Hold a hair stick behind your head and insert it in the center of the bun. Pick up about half the depth of the hair in your bun with the stick, and push the stick down and to the left until the pointed end is forced to stick out. Then, rotate the stick in the direction of the twist so that the bun tightens up, and push the stick along the scalp, guiding it upward until the pointed end is sticking out of the front of your bun.

4 Repeat step 3 to insert the second stick from the opposite direction. Lightly hair-spray, and your bun is done!

- -

If hair sticks alone won't hold your bun, try securing it with an elastic hair band or bobby pins, then insert the hair sticks as accessories.

go gibson girl

TURN HEADS WITH A NINETEENTH-CENTURY DO // Rachel Weeks

materials

Comb

Hairbrush, preferably
a natural-bristle brush

8 jumbo hot rollers
(if needed)

Hair spray

Long roll-style hairpiece
(or "rat") that matches
your hair color, the bigger
the better

Bobby pins

Small curling iron

The Gibson Girl epitomized beauty, independence, and American optimism in the pre–World War I era. Spunky, romantic, aloof, and accessible—despite one killer corset—the Edwardian "ideal woman" exuded a modern femininity as she (gasp!) hit the greens with her newfangled golf clubs and played tennis with the boys. Her signature hairstyle, since featured on a U.S. postage stamp, was a soft pompadour made by waving the hair with hot tongs and piling it high on the head. Bring back this vintage do in just a few easy steps.

1 To get the wispy, voluminous look of a true Edwardian, it's best to work with underconditioned hair. If your hair texture tends to 'fro sans blow-drying, go ahead and let it. With your hair down and combed out, create a part from ear to ear across the crown of your head, so that you've gathered about a third of your hair above your forehead (figure 1).

2 The Gibson works best with long, naturally wavy or curly hair, but straight girls can rock it with some heated help. If straight is what you're working with, use the hot rollers. (Otherwise, skip this step.) Be careful to roll the hair you've separated above your crown under the curlers, while the remainder can be rolled up and over as you usually would (figure 2). Remove the curlers, lightly mist with hairspray, and separate the front third portion of hair once again.

3 Smooth the front, separated portion of the hair forward over the face, and secure the rat about 1" back from your hairline. Use several bobby pins to make sure it doesn't budge (figure 3).

4 Holding the ends of the front, separated portion, loosely twist the hair, leaving at least 4" or 5" untwisted at the roots.

figure 1

figure 2

figure 3

5 Once the hair is twisted, lightly pull the front section over the rat so that the false hair is completely covered by your natural hair. Keeping the hair loose, coil the twisted hair into a loose bun behind the rat, and secure it with bobby pins.

6 Take the remaining length of your hair and loosely coil it around the bun, securing it with bobby pins.

7 If you have stray strands, give your look a nice finishing touch by pulling them forward and using the curling iron to create wispy tendrils around your face and along your neck. The same can be done with any full-length pieces you may want to pluck from your bun to create a customized Gibson all your own.

go go kahlo

YOU'LL BE MADE IN THE SHADE WITH THIS MEXICAN BRAID   //   Rachel Weeks

materials

Smoothing cream (optional)

Hair dryer (optional)

Bobby pins

Fake flowers (optional; most dollar stores have a great selection)

Frida Kahlo's trademark "native" style featured colorful, traditional Mexican clothing, exotic jewelry, and her famous braids and knots—among them the French-braided coronet that frames the face. Now we can join the braid-y bunch, too, by doing our own plaited locks, just like Mexico's favorite daughter of the revolution. (Do note, however, that the coronet, or "boho braid," can be difficult to perform on yourself, so you may need a plaiting pal.)

1 It's best to work with unwashed hair, which makes it more manageable to style. If you do wash your hair, use a smoothing cream before you blow it dry.

2 Part your hair down the middle and start out with three even locks of hair on one side of the part (we'll call them A, B, and C) (figure 1). You can make these as thick or thin as you want, but to achieve Frida's look, the chunkier the braid, the better. The idea in the following steps is to make two French braids from the part to each ear.

3 Grab a new lock of hair from beneath lock C, and combine the two. Cross C over the top of B, making it the center lock (figure 2).

4 Pick up A, and combine it with a new lock of hair from that side, lifting it over the top of C and making it the center lock (figure 3).

5 Pick up B along with new hair from that side and cross it over the top of A into the center (figure 4).

6 Continue picking up new locks of hair every time you move the outside lock to the center. Doing so will secure the plait to your head (figure 5). Secure the end of the braid. Repeat steps 2 through 6 to create the braid on the other side of the part.

7 With the rest of your hair, you can achieve a number of different styles (figure 6). If you have especially long hair and want to go for a Frida updo, form two more long, loose regular braids with the rest of your hair. Take the end of each braid, pull it toward the top of your head, and pin it under your braided headband. Or, get knotty by twisting portions of your hair around your finger until they bend over, then pin them to your scalp. Or you can always go for Frida's *Self-Portrait with Loose Hair* and let it all hang down.

8 Finally, cover up any bobby pins or stray hairs with bright fake flowers.

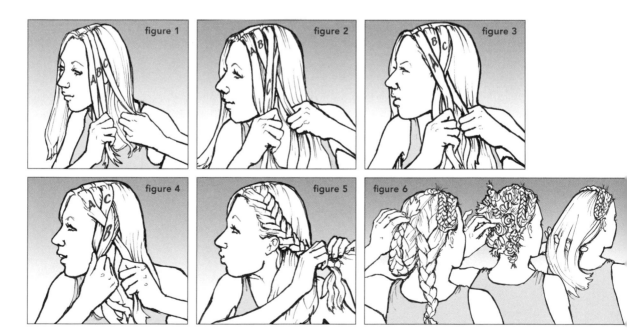

let the good times roll

SWIRL YOUR OWN '40S CURLS // Rachel Weeks

materials

Fine-toothed comb

Pin-curl clips (you can use bobby pins in a pinch)

Bobby pins

Hairbrush (optional)

Hair spray

While their husbands were off fighting in World War II, American women kept the home fires burning—and the good hair rolling—back in the States. Hairstyles of the 1940s were all about Hollywood glamour—even Rosie the Riveter had a little pin curl peeping out from beneath her polka-dot bandanna, proving that we could "do" it, too. Follow these four easy steps, and soon you'll be rollin' '40s in no time.

1 Working with damp hair, separate it into 1" sections. Thoroughly comb each section.

2 Take the end of your first 1" section of hair and start winding it clockwise around the index finger of your opposite hand (as if you are wrapping it around a spool of thread). Make sure not to twist the hair as you wind. Gently allow the curl to slide off your finger, tuck the ends inside the curl, and secure it to your scalp with a pin-curl clip. Repeat to create pin curls all over your head.

3 If your hair is longer than chin-length, it's important to give yourself time—most likely overnight—to allow your curled hair to air-dry completely. Once the curls are dry, remove the pins. Part your hair in the middle, take hold of the front section on one side (from ear to part), and run your fingers through it, creating a semismooth chunk. Roll the hair under itself until the top of the roll is perched near your scalp. Secure the roll to your scalp with bobby pins. Repeat on the other side.

4 Gently brush out the bottom pin curls, either with your fingers or a hairbrush, and lightly spritz with hair spray.

let's get this straight

STRAIGHTENING TIPS FOR KINKY CHICKS // Rachel Weeks

materials

Pick or wide-toothed comb

4 to 6 jaw hair clips

Straightening balm or spray, or relaxing cream

Paddle-style hairbrush

Hair dryer

Ceramic straightening brush or iron (if needed)

Hair shine solution

In the days before the ceramic straightener, curly girls used to lay their heads on ironing boards and have Mom give their hair a good rub with the iron to get it pin-straight. Thanks to the geniuses at Conair, however, you can leave the iron in the closet. (There are cheaper options available, but the ceramic-plated models are less damaging to hair.)

1 Working with freshly washed and conditioned, towel-dried hair, detangle it with your comb, beginning at the ends and working your way to the roots. Separate the hair into four to six sections, using clips to keep the chunks in place.

2 Apply straightening-solution. For curlier hair, go with a balm or cream. Straight-to-wavy-headed ladies should be fine with a spray. With balms or creams, dispense a quarter-size amount into the palm of your hand. Work it through each section of the hair, combing to distribute it evenly. When you finish a section, wind the hair tightly into a twist before putting the jaw clip back in place—this will prevent the hair from air-drying before you can apply heat. To use a spray, spritz lightly to moderately, depending on how curly your hair is.

3 Take one section and lay it on top of the paddle brush, directly at the roots. Direct the hair dryer's airflow downward on the hair in the brush, and follow the brush out to the ends with the dryer, repeating until the section is completely dry. Do this with all sections.

4 If the blow-out doesn't do the trick on its own, bring in your ceramic hair-straightener. Curlier hair types may need to straighten it in layers, while gals with straighter locks may only need a few swipes through on a low heat setting. Top off your style with a tiny amount of shine serum—don't give your hair a lube job.

lighten up

HIGHLIGHT YOUR TRESSES TO GO WITH YOUR DRESSES // Rachel Weeks

materials

Store-bought hair color kit
or 1 packet BW2 powder
and 1 bottle 40- or
20-volume developer
(see tip below)

Towel

Hair clip that will hold
all your hair

Toothbrush

An assistant

Deep conditioner

Color toner (if needed)

----

*You don't need a special
highlighting kit—regular
old hair color will do. If
you have naturally dark
hair, opt for something
just a few shades lighter
than your natural color
to avoid orangey results,
and do a strand test first.
For bleach and peroxide,
head to the beauty-supply
store for BW2 powder and
developer. The higher the
volume number for the
developer, the stronger
the bleach, so try the
20-volume if you don't
want to go too light.*

Women have been highlighting their hair for centuries using techniques that range from washing with alkaline soap and baking in the sun to powdering with pollen and crushed yellow flowers. These days, you don't have to risk burning your scalp to punch up your color—you don't even have to visit a salon.

These DIY instructions are based on the baliage (or "hair painting") method. Use a store-bought color kit if you've never dyed your hair before or want subtle results. Only use bleach and peroxide if you're serious about streaks and/or have dyed your hair before. If you are naturally blond and just want to boost your color, forget the whole thing! Lemon juice plus sunlight is the way to go.

1 Begin with dry, unwashed, thoroughly combed hair free of product (which prevents the color from penetrating).

2 Prepare the hair color mixture according to the kit's directions or mix the BW2 powder with the developer until you get a thick paste. To avoid highlighting your clothes, drape a towel over your shoulders.

3 You will want to apply the color in layers, the number of which depends on how heavy you want your highlights to be. Begin with your hair piled on your head and clipped; release it layer by layer from the bottom to the top (the final layer will be the crown of your head).

4 Apply a dollop of color to the toothbrush (highlighting kits—if you're using one—come with a small plastic comb, but using a toothbrush will give you a more even application). Beginning at the roots, brush it onto selected strands all the way to the tips. For thinner, subtler highlights, use less color on the brush and paint it on by skimming the surface of the hair. For bolder highlights, use more color per swipe and go deeper into the hair sections.

5 Repeat step 4 all the way around your head until you've completed the layer, having your assistant do the back. Don't worry too much about keeping the highlighted portions from touching nonhighlighted hair—whatever rub-off occurs gives more natural-looking results. Lightly release the hair and start another layer.

6 For from-the-box color, leave it in as long as the directions advise. For bleach and peroxide, wait 10 to 20 minutes, depending on how light you want to go.

7 Thoroughly rinse out the color in the shower. Then use a deep conditioner (this process strips hair of natural oils, so the conditioner is needed to restore moisture). Do not shampoo.

8 If you have dark hair, you may wish to follow up with a toner to even out the color on your streaks. Style as usual.

Mess up? It happens to the best of us. Try buying another kit and adding back some of your natural color. Or call your stylist!

bangin' bangs

TACKLE A TRIM YOURSELF // Susan Juvet

Though it seems intimidating, cutting your own bangs is actually really easy. All you need is a careful hand, a pair of sharp scissors, and these simple steps.

1 Start with clean, product-free, dry hair. Never cut your bangs wet. Take a comb and part your hair the way you plan on wearing it. Then comb a layer of hair—a section that reaches from the outer edge of one eyebrow to the outer edge of the other—forward over your face. For wispy bangs, keep the layer near your hairline; for dense bangs, start the layer closer to the top of your head. Tie back the rest of your hair (figure 1).

2 If the hair covering your face is very long, begin snipping as straight as possible, from one side to the other, cutting no more than ½-inch at a time. Snip slowly and steadily—you can always cut more, but you can't put it back! Stop when your bangs just cover your eyes (figure 2).

3 From this point forward, trim with your scissors pointed vertically. This will make your bangs look less severe and leaves room for error. Let your hair lay flat against your forehead, then start by snipping in between your eyebrows using only the tips of your scissors (figure 3). Take just a little bit off with each cut until you've reached your desired length (take a step back every three to four snips to assess).

4 Use this same technique to trim the sides of your bangs, beginning from the outer edges and snipping your way in (figure 4). Use the center point as a length marker for the hair above your eyes—this trick will keep your bangs even. Stop snipping when your bangs have reached the top of your eyebrow arches. Brush or comb them out and style as you please.

figure 1

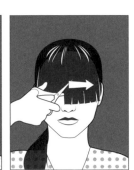
figure 2

figure 3

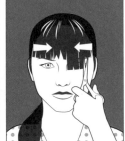
figure 4

no-shampoo do

CUT OUT THE CHEMICALS FOR TERRIFIC TRESSES // Jenny Rose Ryan

If your limp, tired hair is in need of rejuvenation, maybe the answer isn't deep conditioners and fancy shampoos. Most commercial shampoos are made with a bevy of ingredients, many of which, like sodium lauryl/laureth sulfate, strip hair of natural oils, creating the need to replace them with conditioner, making you dependent on even more products. So, if you want to restore your hair's natural fabulousness, try the no-shampoo challenge!

TOSS THE SHAMPOO

Replace shampoo and conditioner with a combo that cleans without stripping: baking soda and apple cider vinegar. In the shower, make a watery paste of baking soda and massage it into your hair and scalp. Some people, especially those with long hair, find this easier to do before they get in the shower, or while lounging in the bath. The paste should be watery, not gritty; you want particles of baking soda small enough to rinse away easily. After rubbing in the baking soda, rinse your hair in the hottest water you can stand to ensure that it all washes out. Next, rinse with apple cider vinegar—make a solution of four parts water to one part vinegar so you don't smell like a pickle. Or rinse with diluted beer or lime or lemon juice, all of which will make your hair shine.

BRUSH DAILY

In addition to replacing your hair-care products, it's important to gently brush your hair daily using a natural bristle brush. This will evenly distribute the oils and leave you with the lustrous mane you've always wanted. For extra sass, rub small amounts of essential oil, like lavender, on the ends to moisturize and leave a pleasant scent.

IF YOUR HAIR IS GREASY

Some people experience greasy hair during the first few weeks. Greasy, though, does not mean dirty. Your scalp is just adjusting to its new shampoo-free reality. Wear a scarf or hat, or put a bit of oil-absorbent cornstarch at your roots and comb through. But don't sprinkle on too much or you'll look like a member of Parliament (the governing body, not the Funkadelic). If you're patient as things adjust, you may discover that your usually fine, wispy locks are wavy and voluminous and that your itchy scalp is itchy no more. All the more reason to wash those chemical prods right outta your hair.

IF YOUR HAIR IS DULL

To add some extra shine to your tresses, bring 2 cups of water to a boil with a cup of dried chamomile flowers or chamomile tea. Simmer for a half hour. Cool, strain, and use the tea as a final hair rinse the next time you shower.

IF YOUR HAIR IS DRY

If your mane needs moisture, mash an avocado, rub it through your locks, and leave for about 15 minutes. Rinse thoroughly so you don't smell like a bowl of guac.

learn your lines

1960s EYELINER TIPS // Gabriela Hernandez

Even though eyeliner has been around since ancient Egypt, the 1960s took it to a new level. Here are some DIY tricks to get Sophia Loren's sultry Egyptian-style lines, Twiggy's banana-shaped liner and flashy lower lashes, and the classy, doe-eyed look of Audrey Hepburn.

FOR SOPHIA

Apply a charcoal-gray matte shadow on the whole lid to the lash line. Trace the upper lash line with a black pencil, increasing the thickness of the line as you move toward the outer corner of the eye. Use a black pencil on the lower lash line, which should meet the top line at the outer corner of the eye and flick upward. Apply full top false lashes and two coats of black mascara.

FOR TWIGGY

Apply a beige or white shimmer shadow from the brow bone to the lash line and in the inside corner of the eye. Define the crease of the eyelid with a black or brown powder shadow. The crease line should be drawn just slightly above your natural crease. Apply liquid liner on the upper lash line, making a thick banana-like shape and extending it slightly beyond the edge. (Practice makes perfect; if you don't get it right the first time, try, try again. You can also practice on your hand.) Use thick false lashes on the top lid and apply black mascara. Draw in lashes on the bottom of the eye with liquid liner and apply single false lashes spaced about ⅛" apart. Rim the inside lower lids and bottom of the eyes with a dark beige pencil and merge this line with the light shadow on the inner eye.

FOR AUDREY

Use a neutral beige base shadow on the entire lid. Define the crease with a dark brown shadow. Then use black liquid eyeliner on the upper lash line, thickening the line from the middle of the eyelid and extending the line slightly upward at the outer corner of the eye. Use a black pencil to fill in any spaces on the lash line. Line the lower lid with the black pencil from the middle to the outer corner and connect it to the top line. Put on full false lashes and use liquid liner to cover glue spots. Apply black mascara on top and bottom lashes.

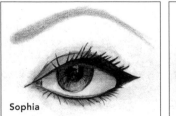
Sophia

Twiggy

Audrey

natural beauty

1940s TIPS FOR EYES, CHEEKS, AND LIPS // Gabriela Hernandez

materials

Tweezers

Foundation in a shade matching your skin tone

Light moisturizer or primer to match your skin tone

Concealer

Cream blush or rouge powder

Translucent loose face powder

Brown or taupe eyebrow pencil

Eyebrow brush

Eyelash curler

Black mascara

Vaseline

Single false lashes, lower-lid lash strips, or upper-lid lash strips (if needed)

Dark brown or black eyeliner pencil

Lip liner in a shade to match your lipstick

Satin-finish lipstick in bright red or soft raspberry (day) or darker red or crimson (night)

Soft brown or gray eye shadow (nighttime only)

The concept of the natural beauty has been around since the 1940s—a time of rationing, when women all across America believed they could achieve finished looks with limited resources. Here's how you can look like a '40s natural beauty, with instructions for both the more minimal daytime and heavier nighttime looks.

FOR A DAYTIME LOOK

1 In a well-lit area, use tweezers to clean stray hairs from your eyebrows and define the arch. Pluck in the direction of hair growth and when in doubt, don't pluck. Follow the natural curve of the eyebrows and shape (figure 1).

2 Apply foundation to the face and neck and blend well. Use a light moisturizer or primer under foundation for a more even application. You're using foundation only to even out your skin color, so keep the application light.

3 Use concealer on darker areas of the face—under the eyes, around the nose, on the inner corner of the eyes, and over any blemishes. Blend well.

4 If you're using a cream blush rather than a powder, apply it to the high area of the cheek and blend it up toward the temples. The color should disappear as you feather toward the temples.

5 Apply translucent powder to your face and neck to set your foundation. If you're using rouge powder, apply it now.

6 With the eyebrow pencil, fill in the eyebrows and define the curved shape. Gently stipple the color as if making individual hairs. Don't go too dark. Brush it through the brows to blend.

7 Curl the lashes and apply two coats of mascara. Use Vaseline to make the lids shine. If you have very sparse lashes, glue single lashes (a small cluster of five or six hairs) at the outer corners, or apply a strip of false lashes meant for lower lashes on the top, from corner to corner. (They're shorter than traditional falsies, so they'll thicken the lash line without elongating it too much.) Emphasize the lashes by drawing a thin line with eyeliner pencil at the base of the lashes, and smudge it slightly.

8 Using your lip liner, exaggerate the top lip by drawing a line slightly outside your natural lip line, creating two mound shapes. Complete the look by filling in the lines with bright red or soft raspberry lipstick.

FOR A NIGHTTIME LOOK

For evening, follow steps 1 through 7 above. Then add shadow to the outer edge of the top lid. Blend the edges, but keep the shadow confined to the crease. Apply longer false lashes for a more dramatic look. Use a darker pencil for eyeliner, and apply the mascara so that you emphasize the outer lashes. Instead of the brighter daytime-red lipsticks, use a darker red or crimson.

For longer-lasting lipstick color, fill in the lips entirely with lip liner before smoothing over it with lipstick. Set the lips with a light dusting of translucent powder for longer wear and a matte finish (figure 2).

figure 1

figure 2

silent treatment

SEE WHAT IT TOOK TO GET THE CLARA BOW LOOK // Gabriela Hernandez

materials

Light moisturizer or primer to match your skin tone

Foundation in a shade matching your skin tone

Dark eyebrow pencil

Black eyeliner (optional)

Black mascara

Dark red lip liner

2 red lipsticks, 1 in a lighter shade and 1 in a more intense shade, suited to your skin tone (see tip)

- - - - - - - - - - - - - - - - - -

When choosing red lipsticks, ladies with medium-toned warm skin should go for a red, wine, or crimson shade. Lighter-skinned ladies should use raspberry, plum, or cherry.

No one epitomized the Roaring Twenties more than silent-film star and original "it" girl Clara Bow. She plucked her eyebrows thin, rimmed her eyes with kohl and shadow, and coated her skin with vanishing creams and powder. But it was her heart-shaped lips that made the boldest statement. They were painted heavy and dark and styled to form a round, plump pout. Use these simple steps to create the bow yourself, collagen injections not necessary.

1 Begin with a light moisturizer or primer for an even application. Apply foundation to the face and neck and blend well. To emphasize the lips, keep face makeup to a minimum—do not use blush.

2 Keep the eyebrows clean and arched and fill in with a dark pencil. Clara Bow darkened her eyes with black liner and gobs of mascara, but you can always skip the black liner and apply only a light coat of mascara to keep the focus on the lips.

3 Blend foundation into your lips to create a neutral surface on which to draw a new lip shape. Use a dark red liner to outline the shape of the Cupid's bow (the small indentation in the middle of the top lip). Make sure to extend the line slightly above the top lip, creating two mounded shapes. Continue drawing downward to the bottom lip, creating a half circle that dips just below the centerline of the lips.

4 Fill in with lipstick, using a lighter shade in the corners and a more intense shade in the center. Repeat the lipstick application for more intense color. The top lip can be shaped either with a more pronounced peak or a softer round shape.

you've got nail

GET DIGGABLE DIGITS WITH A DIY MANICURE // Jackie Zenone

materials

All-purpose base/top coat

A bunch of sweet colors

Nail glue

Tiny Swarovski crystals
(available at most craft-
supply stores)

At least two skinny nail-art
bottles in complementary
colors (Star-Crossed) or
one in a contrasting color
(Zebra Print)

Tweezers

Star-Crossed

Regular trips to the nail salon might not figure into a working girl's budget. With a bit of practice and patience, and a stop at your local beauty-supply store, you can do your own nails and still look fresh to death. The next time you've got a couple of hours to kill, gather your girls together, crank the jams, and get ready to turn heads with the hottest DIY nails this side of South Beach.

STAR-CROSSED

Cool down your hot summer nights with some ice. Switch up the colors to match your bathing suit and out-floss everyone at the pool. First, apply a clear base coat. Then apply a bottom color coat. Using a skinny nail art brush, paint three thin lines of accent color diagonally, starting from top left corner of nail and extending toward the bottom right corner. Using a different nail art color, paint three diagonal lines of a complementary accent color from top right corner toward the bottom left corner. Cover with a clear top coat. Apply dots of nail glue wherever you want to throw on a crystal. Using tweezers or a finger, place the crystals in the desired spots over the glue. Apply one final clear top coat to seal the crystals.

Nothing makes you feel supa-dupa fly like a fresh mani.

ZEBRA PRINT

This one takes some practice, but it's freestyle, so any mistakes can usually be worked into the design—you'll be ready for that urban safari in 15 minutes flat. It helps to sketch the zebra pattern first, so you can get a feel for how to make good stripes: try drawing stretched-out wishbone shapes that loosely fit together. First, apply a clear base coat and bottom color coat. With a skinny nail art brush, paint on your zebra pattern, line by line, in a contrasting color. Cover with a clear top coat.

Zebra Print

Frosty Frenchie

FROSTY FRENCHIE

Tiny crystals put a poppin' twist on a French mani's classic chic. Play around with base colors—neon gives an '80s feel, gold looks totally regal, and black is surprisingly sophisticated. First, apply a clear base coat and a color coat. Once dry, draw a line of nail glue across the top of the nail. Place crystals in a line over the glue, as with a French manicure. Cover with a clear top coat.

helpful hints

Before you get started, be sure you have enough time to do it right. Just keep these tips in mind, and you'll be sure to nail it.

- Always paint a base coat and a top coat—it means the difference between nails that last a day and nails that last a week.

- Don't skimp on polish quality unless you want to rock rubber gloves every time you get your hands dirty.

- When layering or doing accents, let each color dry for at least 5 minutes to prevent blending. To make your lines as thin as possible, be sure to wipe excess polish off on the edge of the bottle before beginning to paint.

- For an easy way to clean brushes, fill a shot glass with nail-polish remover, dip the brush in and wipe it on a cotton pad until all the polish is gone.

- After your nails are done, stay put for at least 30 minutes! Nothing sucks more than creating the perfect set only to ruin it two seconds later while fishing something from your purse.

pour some sugar on me

DIY EXFOLIATORS ARE SMOOTH OPERATORS // Yael Grauer

materials

1 cup raw sugar

About 1 ounce sweet almond or avocado oil (available at most health-food stores)

½ teaspoon vitamin E oil

Pure cocoa butter (optional; available at most health-food stores and some drugstores)

Up to 6 drops essential oil of your choice

12-ounce jar with tight-fitting lid

Sure, you can buy prepackaged scrubs made up of essential oils and preservatives, or you can craft your own from super-simple ingredients that are easy to find, easy on the wallet, and don't need chemicals to keep. Here's an all-natural scrub that will leave your skin smooth as buttah. Mix some up for gifts, too, and help all your friends shine.

1 Pour the sugar into a mixing bowl and add about an ounce of oil (more if you have very dry skin and less if you want the scrub on the dry side).

2 Mix in the vitamin E oil (it'll act as a preservative) and a dab of cocoa butter, if you like (it's great for scent and nourishes the skin).

3 Add a few drops of essential oil, but don't overdo it! Six drops an ounce is plenty. Make sure to mix thoroughly. Lavender is soothing, orange and lemon are invigorating, and ylang-ylang is quite romantic. Vanilla is also yummy.

4 Mix all of the ingredients together and pour your homemade scrub into a pretty, clean jar with a tight-fitting lid.

- -

Natural-foods stores and bath shops stock oils specifically designed for skincare, but the cold-pressed oils in grocery stores, such as apricot kernel, grapeseed, sunflower, safflower, or extra-virgin olive oil are all safe bets, as well.

SUGAR SCRUB

scent of a woman

GIVE BO A TKO WITH DIY DEODORANT // Amy Karol

materials

Double boiler

3 tablespoons unrefined shea butter, preferably organic

3 tablespoons baking soda

2 tablespoons arrowroot powder or cornstarch

2 tablespoons organic unrefined cocoa butter

2 vitamin E oil gel caps (optional)

4-ounce jar, with lid

10 to 20 drops of your favorite essential oil

Conventional deodorants contain none-too-natural ingredients like parabens, artificial colors and fragrances, sodium lauryl sulfate, and aluminum. To keep your stink at bay and enjoy that fun stick-it-to-the-Man feeling, make your own. The best part is that you know exactly what you're putting on your body. Keep in mind, this isn't an antiperspirant, so you'll still sweat. But at least it'll smell like roses (or whatever essential oil you choose).

1 In a double boiler, combine the shea butter, baking soda, arrowroot powder or cornstarch, and cocoa butter. Puncture and squeeze the oil from the vitamin E oil capsules into the pot—this serves as a natural preservative, so it's worthwhile. Give the mixture a good stir.

2 When the mixture is liquefied, remove it from the heat, pour it into the jar, and stir in the essential oil. Place the deodorant in the fridge for a few hours until it's solid.

3 Let the mixture come to room temperature (you don't have to store it in the fridge)—the texture will be somewhere between a firm cream and a soft solid.

4 To use it, scoop out a pea-size amount with your fingers and apply it to your armpit. Be gentle, especially after shaving. A slightly wet armpit makes for easier spreading. This little jar will give you at least three odor-free months.

splish splash

MAKE YOUR OWN FIZZY BATH BOMBS // Emy Flint

materials

2 plastic mixing bowls

1½ cups baking soda

¾ cup citric acid (available online and where canning supplies are sold)

½ cup cornstarch

2 tablespoons light oil such as olive, jojoba, or sweet almond

2 teaspoons of your favorite essential or fragrance oil

¾ teaspoon water (boil and strain berries for tinted water; optional)

½ teaspoon borax (optional; used to soften water)

A few drops of food coloring (optional)

Small cup

Spoon

Witch hazel in a spray bottle

Molds of your choice (see tip)

Cellophane wrapping or a waterproof container

> Makes 4 to 8 bath bombs, depending on mold size

Take your long soak in the tub from ordinary to extraordinary with DIY bath bombs. These great balls of fizz release moisturizing oil and divine scent when they hit the water. Feeling creative? Add dried flowers, glitter, herbs, or softening agents like epsom salts, powdered milk, or oatmeal flour. The dry-ingredient amounts will not vary with these additions, but you may need more oil and water.

1 Make sure your work area is well ventilated so you don't have to breathe in a bunch of powders (not toxic, but irritating all the same), and make these on a day with low humidity, if possible. In one of the bowls, make up an emergency mixture of ½ cup baking soda and ¼ cup citric acid in case things start to react as you begin combining ingredients. If they do, add a bit of this mixture to the "batter" to stop the fizz.

2 Mix 1 cup baking soda, ½ cup citric acid, and the cornstarch in another bowl, stirring to break up any clumps. Combine the oils, water, borax, and food coloring in the cup. Be sparing with the coloring—if you put too much in, it may stain your tub.

3 This step can be tricky: Slowly pour the wet ingredients into the dry ones, stirring as you go (figure 1). You want to create a mixture that has a grainy texture and feels only slightly moist. Test this often: when you squeeze it in your hand, it should stay clumped together. If it falls apart, add a little more of the wet mixture. If you mix too much liquid in, the ingredients will start to fizz; just add some of the emergency mixture until the texture is right. Don't worry if you have wet mixture left over in the end; the amount you need will depend on the humidity in the air.

4 Pack the mixture very tightly into your mold, then tip the mold over and tap it out (figure 2). Spray the bomb lightly (too much will make it fizz) with witch hazel; this forms a crust to keep it from crumbling. If you mess up, just refill your mold, making sure that you pack it well, and tap it out again. To attach two parts together, spray the flat surfaces of two half-spheres with witch hazel until they fizz slightly, then press them together until they hold.

5 Let your bath bombs dry overnight, then wrap them tightly with cellophane or store them in waterproof containers until you're ready to use. Note that if you've got sensitive skin, you should test the ingredients on your skin before you soak. Bombs away!

For molds, we used a tablespoon to make mini bombs and an ice-cream scoop for bigger ones. Plastic Easter eggs, measuring cups with round bottoms, and soap or candy molds can be used, too. There are also molds made specifically for bath bombs that form a sphere when snapped together. Or you can use your hands—just remember to squeeze very tightly.

figure 1

figure 2

so fresh, so clean

MAKE SOAP THE OLD-FASHIONED WAY // Kaia Wong

materials

Latex gloves

Goggles

4 cups very cold distilled or filtered water

1 large stainless steel, enamel, or hard plastic container with a lid

13 ounces (1⅓ cup + 1 teaspoon) sodium hydroxide (NaOH), a.k.a. lye (try Roebic Crystal Drain Opener or Red Devil Lye—do not use Drano, which contains other chemicals)

1 small stainless steel, enamel, or hard plastic container

Large stainless steel spoon or whisk

48 ounces palm oil, 14 ounces coconut oil, and 1 liter olive oil (available at health-food stores)

Large stainless steel or enamel pot

2 tablespoons or more of ground spice such as cinnamon, cocoa, turmeric, paprika, curry, ginger, or seaweed (optional)

(continued on facing page)

Make yourself some good old-fashioned lye soap, which is gentle enough for your privates and strong enough for your dishes. Lye is the key ingredient in the chemical process (called "saponification") that transforms oil and water into glycerin-rich soap. Lye must be handled with caution since it's caustic in its pure form, but it's safe for your skin once it's in a soapy state.

Warning: Lye dissolves aluminum, tin, cast iron, wood, copper, Teflon, and human flesh. To be safe, wear latex gloves and goggles, including during cleanup. If it gets on your skin, rinse with water and neutralize with vinegar or lemon juice.

1 Working outdoors and wearing gloves and goggles, add the cold water to your large container and measure the lye into the smaller container. Slowly pour the lye into the water (never add water to lye—this could cause dangerous splattering) while stirring briskly with a spoon or whisk (figure 1). As you stir, the solution will become cloudy, heat up to between 150° and 200°, and emit fumes (do not breathe them!). Keep stirring for a couple more minutes until the lye is completely dissolved and the solution is clear again. Cover the container and allow it to cool for at least 1 hour or even overnight.

2 Heat the palm oil, coconut oil, and olive oil together in a large pot over medium heat. If you'd like to have coloring, add the ground spice of your choice. Cool the mixture until it is slightly warm to the touch.

3 Line each soap mold with plastic wrap or a plastic bag. (Silicone bakeware can be used without a lining and plastic molds can be greased with one of the oils.)

4 Slowly pour the lye water into the oils while stirring with the stick blender, if you have one—otherwise use the spoon or whisk. Use a rubber spatula to get into the crevices of the pot. Stir just until the soap mixture reaches "trace"—a term used to describe an appearance like watery pudding. At this point, if you drizzle the soap back into itself, the surface of the liquid holds the pattern. This will take about 1 hour whisking vigorously or about 10 minutes using a stick blender on low speed (with pauses to rest the motor).

5 If you want, stir in 1½ to 2 ounces essential oil, an exfoliant (such as coffee grounds, cornmeal, almonds, wheat germ, or poppy seeds), and/or vitamin E. Pour the soap into your mold (figure 2). For swirled soap, pour the colors alternately into the mold and swirl with a spoon. Cover the mold with plastic, then wrap it in a bath towel for insulation. Let the soap sit for 24 to 36 hours to solidify—but don't let your equipment sit around. Wash it by scraping and wiping out as much soap as possible. Then either scrub it with very hot water and detergent or put it in the dishwasher.

6 Remove the soap from your mold and cut it into bars using the knife. Place the bars in a cardboard box so that they do not touch and let them cure, uncovered, for 3 or 4 weeks. Wash or cut off any ashy bits on the surface of the soap. It's ready to use! It has a shelf life of several years.

materials (continued)

Soap mold (you can use a cardboard box, plastic containers, or bakeware)

Plastic wrap or plastic grocery bags

Stick blender (recommended), or spoon or whisk

Rubber spatula

1½ to 2 ounces essential oil, exfoliant, and/or vitamin E

Bath towel

Large, sharp knife

Large cardboard box

> Makes 2 dozen 4-ounce bars

figure 1

figure 2

herbal soak

DIY TEA BAGS IN THE TUB // Erika Bardot

Soaking in a warm bath is a great way to relax, rejuvenate, and rewind, and it won't break the bank like a massage. To take your bath to the next level, load up on some all-natural goodies from health-food stores. Shove these restorative treats into an old sock or stocking, tie it off, throw it in the tub, and jump in. Here are some tried and true "tea bag" recipes, though if you're pregnant (or trying to be) avoid using ginger and rosemary.

GO GIRL
To get you moving and grooving, mix up fenugreek seeds, loganberries, astragalus, peppermint, ginseng, ginkgo leaves, alfalfa, rosemary, ginger, and cloves.

WHOA, NELLIE
For nervous tension, throw together lavender, lemon balm, spearmint, and honeysuckle flowers.

SLEEPLESS NIGHTS
For insomnia, stir up some kava kava, rose hips, chamomile, catnip, and skullcap.

BRAIN PAIN
For your poor, pounding head, shake together peppermint, rosemary, chamomile, linden flowers, and sage.

BODY ACHES
For working out the kinks, pour in some lemon balm, ginger, echinacea, and alfalfa.

OH, BLOODY HELL
A discreet blend for womanly discomfort includes echinacea, linden flowers, raspberry leaves, false unicorn, and cramp bark or black haw.

GOLDEN GIRL
Make a purifier for healthy skin by including astragalus, echinacea, red clover, sassafras, sarsaparilla, and burdock.

DITCH THAT ITCH
To calm itchy, irritated skin, soak in some steel-cut oatmeal. Its soothing qualities are also great for kids with chicken pox.

BOOGIE NIGHTS
Craft his-'n'-hers aphrodisiacs with this basic formula: fenugreek seeds, damiana, and burdock. For her, add loganberries. For him, add epimedium (a.k.a. "lusty goat herb"—for real).

sole food

KICK CALLUSES TO THE CURB WITH A DIY FOOT SCRUB // Jessica George Firger

materials

1⅔ cups Dead Sea salt

1 tablespoon dry coffee grounds

1 drop vitamin E oil

6 or 7 drops bergamot mint oil

1 ounce grapeseed oil

1 ounce jojoba oil, plus more for longer storage

1 ounce avocado oil, plus more for longer storage

16-ounce jar

If your new sneaks are wreaking havoc on your feet, use this crunchy foot scrub. Beehive Beauty Boutique & Spa in Brooklyn invented this 100-percent au naturel elixir and shared it with us, and now we're sharing it with you. The Dead Sea salt exfoliates; grapeseed, jojoba, and avocado oils moisturize; and the natural stimulants in coffee and mint put some spring in your step. All oils can be purchased at your local health-food store or fancier pharmacy. Dead Sea salt is available at online specialty shops, but you can also substitute coarse-ground sugar or regular granulated sugar.

Mix the ingredients in a blender, pulsing four or five times. Store the foot scrub in the refrigerator, and if you don't use it all up in a month, add 1 or 2 tablespoons of jojoba or avocado oil to maintain the consistency. To use your foot scrub, apply two quarter-size dollops to each foot. Using your hands, massage it into your feet and calves, then rinse with warm water.

Sure, you might like it rough and hard sometimes—but not when it comes to your feet.

face off

DIY BEAUTY PARLOR // Jennifer Knapp, Jean Railla, and Jenny Rose Ryan

Has your skin seen dewier days? Is your smile not so pearly today? With just a few dollars and a little time, you can give yourself an at-home makeover, sure to refresh your complexion and brighten your teeth.

need a steam?

materials

1 tablespoon dried nettle

1 tablespoon dried chamomile flowers

1 tablespoon dried sage leaves

Large bowl

3 to 5 cups boiling water

Large towel

Gentle facial cleanser

Moisturizer

Two spoons

Place herbs in a large bowl and pour the water over them. Place your face about 6" over the bowl and cover both your head and the bowl with a large towel. The towel should create a tent so that the steam does not escape. Breathe deeply into the steam for five 3-minute intervals, resting in between, for a total of 15 minutes. Follow with a gentle cleanser and apply moisturizer. You glow, girl!

Still look like you had a night? Depuff your peepers by sticking a couple of spoons in the fridge, then place the cool, curved sides on top of your closed eyes for a minute or so.

skin a little oily?

materials

2 tablespoons old-fashioned steel-cut oats

1 cup water

Small saucepan

Cook the oatmeal and water in a pan for about 5 minutes. When the oatmeal is tender and well-cooked, drain the excess water and cool the oatmeal to room temperature. Place the cooled oatmeal on your face and relax for 25 minutes. Rinse with warm water and pat skin dry.

skin a little dry?

materials

Small bowl

Fork

¼ medium avocado

1 tablespoon honey

1 tablespoon aloe vera gel

1 tablespoon green clay

Moisturizer

In a small bowl, use a fork to mash the avocado. Stir in the honey, aloe vera gel, and green clay (available at most health-food and beauty supply stores). Spread an even layer of the mixture over your face, avoiding the eye area. Leave the mask on for 15 minutes, then rinse off with warm water, pat dry, and moisturize as usual. Leftovers will store in the refrigerator for a day or two.

do your teeth resemble café con leche?

materials

2 tablespoons fresh sage leaves

2 tablespoons sea salt

Small bowl

Pestle or wooden spoon

Cookie sheet

Toothbrush

Put the sage and salt into a small bowl. With a pestle or some other heavy, smooth tool (such as a wooden spoon), crush the sage and salt into a paste. Next, spread the mixture onto a cookie sheet and place it in a 250° oven for 15 minutes, or until the mixture has hardened. Return the mixture to the bowl and crush it into a finely ground powder with the pestle. Apply this powder to a wet toothbrush and scrub away. Store your homemade tooth powder in an air-tight container and use it once a week for 6 weeks, or whenever you need a little shine.

pain and simple

AN A TO Z LIST OF EASY REMEDIES TO MAKE AT HOME

// Tuline Baykal, Dina Botozolli, Scarlett Fever, Molly Kincaid,
Jessica Lloyd, Jenny Rose Ryan, and Janis Wildly

If you're tired of turning your body into a mobile toxic waste dump of prescriptions and drug cocktails, aim for the gentle healing of home cures, botanicals, herbs, and homeopathic remedies. Before there were doctors aplenty, these tricks were what folks used to treat everything from skin issues to sleepy-time troubles, tummy upsets, and nights of too much ale. For most of these cures to work, you need to notice the problem early, so if the itch or pain has been sticking around for days, head to the doc. And as with any herbal supplements, it's a good idea to check with your doctor or herbalist before you add them to your regular routine—especially if you're on other meds or if you're preggers.

ACHES AND PAINS

If you're feeling achy, whether from the flu or the daily grind, a few tricks can help you shake out the funk. First, stand up, stretch, and breathe. Concentrate on the part that hurts and imagine the pain dissipating as you exhale. If yoga's your thing, do a few slow sun salutations (basically a good, long stretch) to ease your aches. Move into the sun or in front of a fire. Rub on some warming salve like Tiger Balm. Use a hot water bottle or heating pad, or add 1 tablespoon dry ground ginger to a hot bath and soak away in delight.

BLISTERS

Back in the day, lavender was brought into battle for minor boo-boos. That's right—when the ancient Romans were kicking ass and taking names, they smelled like your grandma. And guess what? You can too. Blisters from those sassy new sandals? Blend a few drops of lavender essential oil in your

hand with equal drops of vitamin E oil, and a little dab'll do ya.

For a blister fix that you can store and keep for up to two months, mix the following together in a 4-ounce wide-mouth jar: 3 ounces vegetable carrier oil (sweet almond, jojoba, etc.) or aloe vera gel, 30 drops lavender essential oil, and 30 drops tea tree essential oil. Blend the ingredients and apply directly as necessary to help blisters. This one works on bug bites and mild burns too.

BUG BITE PREVENTION

If you're not heading deep into the wilderness during prime bug season, there's no need to smother yourself in DEET—especially when nature already has so many substances to repel those creepy crawlies.

Spray Two Ways

Lemongrass, which contains citronella, is a known foe to bugs and is available at

© susie GHAHREMani

many markets. Make a spray-on tincture by chopping up enough to make ¼ cup and pouring on ½ cup of either isopropyl alcohol or apple cider vinegar (depending on whether you'd rather dry out your skin or smell vaguely like a pickle). Allow this mixture to soak and mingle for a week or so, shaking it a couple of times each day, then strain and pour it into a spray bottle. Spray this concoction on your skin.

You can also go big and combine 60 drops citronella essential oil with 2 ounces witch hazel in a spray bottle. Shake and use. For those particularly buggy days, make it even stronger by using 120 drops of citronella oil. To tone down citronella's pungent scent, add about 5 drops of your favorite essential oil to the mixture. But don't go too crazy or you may attract what you seek to repel.

Oil Blends
A variety of essential oils can help stave off the little buggers. Combine 20 drops eucalyptus oil, 20 drops cedarwood oil, 10 drops tea tree oil, and 10 drops geranium oil with ¼ cup of a carrier oil like jojoba or sweet almond. Blend together and pour into a reusable container—small vanilla-extract bottles or other brown glass bottles are the perfect size and the dark glass protects essential oils, which can be light-sensitive. Rub this mixture all over your exposed skin and watch the bloodsuckers flee!

BUG BITES
When bloodthirsty jerks do get to you, lean on lavender and comfrey to make you feel comfortable. Their calming qualities are the perfect remedy for reddened, angry, bug-bitten skin.

For an easy, soothing skin spray, mix 15 to 20 drops of lavender essential oil with ¼ cup water. For a bug bite soother that you can store for up to two months, try the same lavender-and-tea-tree-oil combo that you would use on blisters (see page 208).

Comfrey is another herb that's great for bug bites. It contains allantoin compounds, which studies suggest may promote cell regrowth while helping to relieve inflammation. Applied topically, this powerhouse root seeps right into the deepest layers of tissue and begins to heal the wound by helping the blood coagulate, relieving immediate pain, and speeding up overall recovery.

To use comfrey, you can either buy the root powder or get it in dry-leaf form. The powder can be applied as is to any wound. To use the leaves, it's best to brew a strong tea, soak a clean cloth in it, and then apply it. (This is called a poultice.) A word of caution: while there is such a thing as comfrey tea, what we're suggesting is meant for topical use only—unmeasured internal use can be toxic to the liver. It's also not for use by pregnant women.

BURNS
Zap your wrist with a curling iron? Heal the burn with these tips straight from grandma's back pocket.

Immediate Actions
Immerse the affected area immediately in cold water for about 10 minutes to cool the skin. Smear it with honey, grated potato, or the juicy part of an aloe vera plant to encourage healing. Or blend a few drops of lavender essential oil in your hand with equal drops of vitamin E oil and dab the mixture onto the burn.

Planning Ahead
For a mixture to keep on hand for these types of owies, try the same lavender-and-tea-tree-oil combo that you would use on blisters (see page 208). Comfrey is also great for burns. See instructions for how to apply it topically under Bug Bites.

CHILLS

Have a chill you just can't shake? Add some ginger to your diet to get your blood moving. Along with the ability to soothe an aching stomach, ginger also stimulates digestion and boosts circulation, respiration, and nervous-system function by helping to reduce platelet "stickiness" and thus improving the health of the whole cardiovascular system. A steaming cup of fresh ginger tea will help you get super toasty. To make it, add 2 tablespoons grated ginger and a pinch or two of cayenne pepper to 1 quart boiling water. Mix well and let steep for about 10 minutes, then strain some into a mug. Add your favorite sweetener (maple syrup is great), if you want. You'll heat up in no time.

CONTUSIONS (A.K.A. BRUISES)

If you bash your leg into the coffee table while running for your phone, grab an ice pack or bag of frozen peas and hold it to your gam for about 10 minutes to reduce swelling. You can also keep it from swelling up with a witch hazel compress—just soak a rag in some witch hazel and hold to the skin for a few minutes. To reduce pain and discoloration, rub the inside of a banana skin on the bruise.

COUGHS AND COLDS

When winter rolls around, quit your coughing with these herbal remedies.

Steam It

For a soothing congestion remedy, add 10 to 15 drops of tea tree oil to a shallow bowl of just-boiled water, hold your head just above the mixture, drape a towel over your head, and inhale the steam.

Gargle It

Stop cold and flu germies in their tracks with the antiseptic action of a warm-water gargle infused with 10 to 20 drops of tea tree oil.

Drink It

If it's your throat that's killing you, try this spin on the traditional hot toddy: Steep 2 tablespoons chopped fresh sage in 8 ounces boiling water for 10 to 15 minutes, then strain into a mug. Stir in a shot of Jim Beam and 2 teaspoons honey. Squeeze in the juice from 2 lemon wedges, then add them to the mug for garnish. In addition to giving this drink a delicious flavor, sage packs major healing power—its antiseptic qualities are excellent for a sore throat. Sage is also very aromatic, and breathing the steam from the brew helps clear the sinuses.

If you're all stuffy, indulge in this soothing herbal toddy variation (the smell alone makes it worth mixing): Steep 2 tablespoons chopped fresh thyme, 1 tablespoon chopped fresh mint, and a peppermint tea bag in 8 ounces boiling water for 15 minutes. Strain, then stir in a shot of gin and 2 teaspoons honey. Garnish with a sprig of fresh mint. Simply breathing in the aroma gives ravaged nostrils some instant relief. Thyme is a powerful and versatile herb, known for its ability to soothe headaches, coughing, and bronchial inflammation, and peppermint relieves allergy symptoms.

You can, of course, make any of these toddies without liquor; you'll still have a soothing tea. The ancient healing root of ginger can also be used to treat colds by easing congestion in the throat and lungs—see Chills on page 211 for instructions on how to brew it into tea.

CRAMPS

Aunt Flo cramping your style? Push the pain away with a little reflexology. With bare feet, rest one foot on the opposite knee. Using the tip of your thumb (not the pad, the surface is too broad), find the tender uterus pressure point on the flat, hard surface of the inner heel, just under the anklebone. Push in a rotating motion with firm pressure for 30 seconds, four times on each foot, alternating left and right. You probably won't have period pain if you're pregnant, but we've got to warn you: don't use this pressure point if you've got a bun in the oven. After you've worked out the pressure point, rub some ginger essential oil over the area where your cramps ache most. Ginger has antispasmodic properties that can help relax and soothe muscles.

CUTS

Whether you cut yourself chopping veggies in the kitchen or knick your knee shaving in the shower, you can help speed healing with herbs. Clean the wound under cold running water for about 5 minutes. If deeply cut, you may need stitches. Otherwise, sprinkle the area with witch hazel or lemon juice. Both honey and calendula are antiseptic, so they can be used topically to fight infection—honey will keep skin moisturized and calendula promotes quick healing.

Comfrey also has an amazing ability to heal topical wounds. See instructions for how to apply comfrey under Bug Bites on page 210. Once you've applied your salve, bandage it.

DETOX

For centuries, health practitioners across the world have claimed to heal many ailments by detoxing excess chemicals from the body. If you want to give your body a break from ingested toxins, or strengthen its ability to filter them out, here are a couple of things to try.

The Gentle Cleansing Diet

For a gentle two-week cleanse, try the following diet. The first couple of days may be hard, but by the end of two weeks, you will feel lighter and have more energy than you ever imagined.

- Eat only seasonal, organic fruits and vegetables.
- Limit yourself to whole grains such as brown rice, quinoa, millet, and amaranth.
- For protein, keep it low fat with legumes, lean meat, and fish.

- Eliminate sugar, refined foods, coffee, booze, and cigarettes.
- Drink 2 to 3 cups of nettle tea per day as a tonic, to help move the toxins through the liver.
- Drink at least 8 glasses of water a day.
- Get active and sweat for at least 15 minutes a day.
- Meditate by sitting quietly and focusing on your breath for 15 minutes a day.

Cleanse the Liver

As our body's filter, the liver is in charge of cleansing toxins from the entire blood stream—everything from booze to drugs to pesticides to fats and sugars. It's strong, it's tough, it regenerates itself, but doing all that dirty work can leave your liver overworked and put you at the mercy of all sorts of ailments and diseases.

Milk thistle has been used to help the liver since the middle of the first century. Silymarin, the active ingredient, is believed to defend the liver against free radicals, environmental pollution, and various other toxins that can lead to signs of aging and degeneration. So, if you love your liver, try supplementing your daily diet with a bit of the stuff. Available at most health-food stores, the best milk thistle contains 70 to 80 percent silymarin. Capsules range in dosage from 140 to 300 mg and can be taken two to three times a day. As with any supplements, talk to your doctor or herbalist before taking it, especially if you are on any medications.

DRY SKIN

To get rid of dry patches on your elbows and knees, all you need is baking soda. Take a couple of big pinches and make a paste in your palm with a few drops of water. Rub gently on scaly areas and rinse away. This works great as a face scrub, too.

If you're itchy or scaly, tea tree oil is your friend. Just dab a small amount on a cotton ball, drip a little water on it to dilute, and swab it around your face. Apply it directly to athlete's foot and scaly scalps and watch your poor skin heal. Or, add it to basic castile soaps (like Dr. Bronner's) and use it in the shower for an all-over clean feeling.

EYE STRAIN

Working long hours on a deadline doesn't just do a number on your social life. It's also a strain on your eyes, especially if you're spending most of that time on a computer. When you go to bed, use a lavender eye pillow to help relax and depuff your peepers. Or try placing a warm chamomile tea bag or cool cucumber compress on your eyelids.

HEADACHES

Whether your head hurts from a hangover or plain ol' tension, you can use your thumb to numb a headache. Press the length of your thumb against the base of the adjacent forefinger to form a ridge of muscle. Find the point in the center of the crease created by your thumb and forefinger. Using your other thumb as a placeholder, relax your hand, then find the tender spot on the lower (almost under) side of the forefinger bone and press on it firmly with the tip of your thumb (you might have to dig around until you find it). Do this on both hands for 30 seconds at a time until the headache is gone.

To keep the headache gone for good, rub some ginger essential oil on the affected area—its antispasmodic properties can help relax and soothe.

HERPES

While there's no cure for them, herpes outbreaks are mostly brought on by stress, so avoid that at all costs. When you can't, try to counteract it with yoga, echinacea and goldenseal supplements (to support immunity), and plenty of rest. If that doesn't head it off, and you find yourself with an outbreak, keep it as clean and dry as possible and wear cotton underwear, if any at all.

Vinegar sitz baths can work well for herpes outbreaks. To make a sitz bath, throw some vinegar in your tub and fill it with warm to hot water. Sit in the tub with your knees up and your legs wide apart and let the water rush in and out of you. Follow up by patting yourself dry with a clean towel. Next, you want to dry it out, moisturize it, and heal it. Hydrogen peroxide dabbed on sores during the day dries things out and aloe before you go to bed will help heal it.

IMMUNITY

If you feel a cold coming on, don't just wait for the bug to hit. Take the fate of your immunity into your own hands.

Astragalus is widely revered among Chinese practitioners as "the Great Protector." Chock-full of zinc and selenium, this immune-boosting herb also contains polysaccharides, which stimulate the body's "fight back" mechanism, and research indicates that the herb can increase the function of T-cells. Astragalus works similarly to echinacea, but you won't build up immunity to it, as you would with echinacea. It's safe for men and women of all ages, though it's always a good idea to check with your doctor or herbalist before taking. (And if you are bean sensitive, you may get a bit windy.) Astragalus should not be used by people with autoimmune disorders.

You can also supplement your diet with this powerful herb even before cold and flu season hits; 20 to 30 drops of tincture in a glass of water two to three times a day

should do it. (On-the-run types can just take it in capsule form, as directed.) Or begin dosing when you feel the itch in your throat and the sniff in your nose; then keep on it until you're in the clear, plus a few days extra.

Another thing to try is a daily dose of vitamin B complex. These vitamins help convert carbohydrates into glucose, which gives the body energy. They are found in many foods, including whole grains, nuts, milk, eggs, meats, fish, fruit, and leafy greens. But they are also depleted by some common behaviors, like drinking and leading a stressful life. Supplementing with a good vitamin complex that includes B-1 (thiamine), B-2 (riboflavin), B-3 (niacin), B-6, B-9 (folic acid), and B-12 is probably a good idea. Be sure to take it with a meal to avoid the yucky vitamin-tummy feeling. Most B vitamins are water soluble, so whatever your body doesn't need will get peed out. Don't take more than the recommended dosage, though. It is possible to overdo it, and with vitamin B-6 especially, the results can be unpleasant.

INDIGESTION AND STOMACHACHES

Who didn't grow up sipping ginger ale to soothe a bellyache? If you've ever wondered if it was the ginger or the bubbles that did the trick, let's clear things up: it's the ginger. Ginger has been used medicinally throughout India and China for centuries. Brew up some ginger tea for nausea or to settle the stomach (see Chills on page 211 for details on how to do it). Peppermint tea has a similar effect because of the menthol contained in the plant. It also calms the muscles lining your stomach and intestines to help ease digestion.

INSOMNIA

Lavender and chamomile are strong calming agents, so drink this concoction when you're ready for a snooze. Steep 2 tablespoons chopped fresh lavender and a chamomile tea bag in 8 ounces boiling water for 15 minutes. Strain, then stir in a shot of St-Germain elderflower liqueur and 1 teaspoon honey.

Or, instead of giving in to grandma's favorite sleep tonic, Valium, try a nonaddictive option: valerian root.

First hailed by the Greek physician Galen, valerian root has been used through the centuries in Europe as a sleep promoter and stress buster. Native to Europe, North America, and the northern part of Asia, this herb has proved effective on people with stress-related insomnia. In fact, studies show that valerian functions in a similar manner to such drugs as Halcion and Valium: it sedates by stimulating activity of the nerve transmitter GABA, which dampens the brain's arousal system.

Begin with a small dose to judge its effects on you, then increase the dose as needed. For use as a sleeping pill, take 300 to 500 mg of valerian in capsules or tablets 30 to 60 minutes before bed. In the proper dosage,

valerian has no side effects like the groggy hung-over feeling offered by other sleep meds. There are no known contraindications for valerian root, but it's always a good idea to consult your doctor or herbalist before taking it—especially if you are pregnant or breastfeeding.

LIBIDO HELP

Passion and lust come and go, and let's face it, sometimes we all need a bit of help to get in the mood. Since ancient Mayan times, damiana—a small shrub that produces an oil that smells like chamomile—has been used to jump-start the libido. This pleasure-enhancing herb is said to increase sensitivity, desire, and fulfillment; it works by increasing blood flow to the sex organs, giving you the extra oomph that you may need to have a super-hot night with that special someone.

The easiest way to introduce damiana into your life is to drink it in tea form. Steep 1 teaspoon of dried leaves in 1 cup boiling water. Let sit for 5 to 10 minutes, strain, then sip away while you daydream about the adventures to come. For optimum sexual response, it is recommended that you drink the tea 30 minutes to 1 hour before sex. As always, remember that herbs work gently, so be patient and don't overdo the dose. Enjoy the subtleties and have fun!

MORNING OR MOTION SICKNESS

Struggling with morning sickness or motion sickness? Try a cup of ginger tea (see the instructions in Chills on page 211). There are no known side effects from using this righteous root, so sip away. (Note: As always, if pregnant, use in moderation.)

PMS

To stop that hurricane of premenstrual rage, take these daily doses of vitamins in the week leading up to your period: 400 mg dry vitamin E; 1000 mg calcium (a mood stabilizer); 500 mg magnesium (helps prevent depression); vitamins A and D (needed to process the calcium); a multimineral supplement; B complex with B-6. If you can handle it, try to omit caffeine and/or sugar, too.

From mid-cycle to end, take evening primrose oil six times a day or black currant oil two times a day. Black currant has the same effect as evening primrose; you just need to take less, and it costs much less.

RASHES AND HIVES

If your skin got too close to something it hates, don't head straight for the hydrocortisone cream. Look to black tea, which has tannic acid to soothe itchy, red skin. Use a squeezed-out tea bag as a compress or you can pour cooled, strongly brewed tea into a spray bottle to mist on your rashes. Using a squeezed-out chamomile tea bag on your skin can also soothe the irritation of a rash. For a rash soother that you can store and keep for up to two months, use the same lavender-and-tea-tree-oil combo that you would use on blisters (see page 208).

SUNBURNS

Keep aloe vera in the fridge to soothe your burn on a sunny day. You can also mix 15 to 20 drops of lavender essential oil with ¼ cup water for a soothing skin spray. Or place a squeezed-out chamomile tea bag on your skin to ease the burn.

TOOTHACHES

If your tooth is aching and there's no dentist in sight, use clove oil to numb the pain. Clove oil can be bought in any health-food store. Put a few drops on a Q-tip and apply it to the gum line where it hurts. If you can't get to the health-food store, you can make

your own by crushing 3 to 5 cloves and mixing with a teaspoon of olive oil. Warning: Do not leave the Q-tip between your gum and cheek all night, or you'll end up with a fun burn.

URINARY TRACT INFECTIONS

If your pee pee hurts to wee wee, you might have a UTI coming on. Try these tips, but if they don't work, get thee to a clinic. Otherwise, you can wind up with a kidney infection (and the medical bills to prove it).

Use Reflexology

Find the bladder pressure point by running your thumb along the inside ridge of your bare foot and dig in just before the heel bone. Locate the most sensitive spot. Push as hard and as long as you can bear on the whole area and also diagonally up into the center of the foot. This covers the bladder, urethra, and ureters. You'll need to apply intensive, extremely firm, broad, deep, and lengthy pressure to fully relieve symptoms. Try for 10 minutes on each foot. Drink loads of water before, during, and after to flush out germs.

Drink real cranberry juice, not Ocean Spray. You'll know it's the real thing if it's really tart. Avoid caffeine, sugar, alcohol, chocolate, and citrus, but drink lots of water and pee whenever you feel you have to, even if you just did. When you get tired of drinking water and cranberry juice, try dandelion tea, watermelon juice, or celery juice—they're natural diuretics.

Take Sitz Baths

Try taking sitz baths, alternating vinegar with garlic (use two cloves of crushed garlic). Fill the tub with warm water and sit in it with your knees up and your legs wide apart, letting the water rush in and out of you.

YEAST INFECTIONS

If you keep winding up with a case of the yeasties, here are some ideas for what to do. Every woman is different, so if one of these remedies doesn't work, try another. Some people swear by one, others by another. It all depends on what your girl wants.

Regardless of which tactic you try, wear cotton underwear—or none at all if you can get away with it. Your cooch needs air. If none of these work, you may need to get some over-the-counter help. And if that doesn't work, talk to your doc.

The Sitz Bath Cure

If you feel the dreaded yeast coming on, swallow acidophilus and take sitz baths often. First, throw some vinegar, garlic, or acidophilus in your tub. Then, fill the tub with warm to hot water, and sit, with your knees up and your legs wide apart, and let the water rush in and out of you. The point is to flush the yeast out of your hole.

The Garlic Cure

Garlic, too, can put things back in order. Just peel a clove and stick it in your lady bits. If you're worried about it getting lost, you can tie a string around it, but bearing down and pushing will usually move it low enough to remove. You won't smell like garlic bread all day, either, if you're worried about that.

Cooling Relief

If you want a cooling sensation as you treat your yeast infection, freeze plain unsweetened yogurt in the fingers of a latex (plastic if you're sensitive) glove and snip off "doses" (fingers) when you need relief. Then, just peel off the latex and insert the tube into your hoo-ha. (You may experience a brief moment of brain freeze as the cooch-cube warms in your region.) Alternatively, coat an o.b.-style tampon with yogurt and change it as you normally would for Aunt Flo. You might want to throw down a pantyliner to catch the residue.

Preventative Measures

You're more susceptible to yeast infections when you're on antibiotics, so if your doc prescribes them, take acidophilus capsules or eat yogurt to maintain the proper bacterial balance.

ZITS

To halt brewing zit eruptions, steep a few teaspoons dried or fresh basil leaves in a cup of boiling water for 20 minutes. Strain and refrigerate the soothing concoction (it'll keep for a few months), then blot as needed.

If your skin is oily, one solution is . . . more oil! Every day, dab a cotton ball in extra-virgin olive oil or coconut oil, swipe it all over your face, and rinse with a hot washcloth. In a few weeks, your skin will be grease-free and glowing.

PART FOUR

EAT, DRINK & BE MERRY

get it going

STARTERS AND SALADS // Chef Rossi

Need some munchies to get the party started? Look no further than these epic appetizers and fresh salads.

HEAVENLY HUMMUS

In a food processor, puree a few cloves of **garlic** and four heaping handfuls of canned **chickpeas**, four good plops of **tahini**, and a few drizzles of fresh **lemon juice**. Add a good drizzle of **olive oil** and then a few drizzles of water until the mixture has the pastelike consistency of hummus. Season with **salt**, **pepper**, and ground **cumin**.

HOLY MOLY GUACAMOLE

Mash four ripe **avocados** with one finely chopped **onion**, one minced **jalapeño**, two cloves of minced **garlic**, a couple squeezes of fresh **lime juice**, and **salt** to taste. Mix super-well, or do as I do and run the whole batch in the food processor for a second or two. Season with ground **cumin** if you want.

SIMPLE SHRIMP COCKTAIL

Peel and devein the **shrimp** yourself or buy it that way, like princesses do. Boil up a pot of water and season the water with **salt**. Throw in some fresh **lemon juice** (and a peeled and halved **white onion**, too, if you want it to be super special). Drop your shrimpies in the boiling water and cook until they turn orange. Drain and run cold water over them to cool. Refrigerate until ready to serve. For the sauce, mix one bottle of **ketchup** with two big plops of **horseradish**, a dollop of **spicy mustard**, a couple dashes of **Worcestershire sauce**,

and a nice shot of your fave **hot sauce** (I like Tabasco, myself). To serve, pour the sauce into a dip bowl and surround with the shrimp. To be ultra-fancy, squeeze a little **lemon juice** on the shrimp or surround them with **lemon wedges**.

THREE-JUICE CEVICHE

Start with about a pound (455 g) of **fish**, such as salmon, tuna, mahi-mahi, snapper, or whatever fish looks good in the store. Cut the fish into the smallest dice you can; likewise for half of a **red onion** and half of a **red bell pepper.** Mince up one **jalapeño**, chop a handful of **cilantro**, and mix the whole shebang together with the juice of one nice big **lime** or two measly ones. **Salt** to taste. Let this sit for about an hour and serve. I like this one on top of plantain chips, tortillas, cucumber slices, and even plain ol' crackers.

FUNKY GREEK SALAD

Use any kind of **salad greens** you want; a combo of baby arugula and baby spinach is divine. If you use a large-leaf lettuce, you'll need to tear it up into bite-sized pieces. Put your greens in a bowl, top with a heaping handful of halved **cherry tomatoes**, a heaping handful of chopped pitted **kalamata olives**, and a heaping handful of peeled **cucumber** (sliced into circles or half-moon shapes, or just diced). Throw in about half a thinly sliced **red onion**, then drizzle **All-Purpose Greek-Style Yogurt Dressing** (recipe follows) all over your funky salad and top with a few sprigs of fresh **mint**. Some folks like to add **feta cheese** here, being Greek and all, but since this is a yogurt dressing you don't really need it. But you're a big girl, so do as you please.

All-Purpose Greek-Style Yogurt Dressing

Pick up some **plain Greek-style yogurt** (kinda like regular yogurt drained of water). Dollop four heaping plops of yogurt into a bowl, then whisk in a shot of **champagne vinegar**, a good plop of **Dijon mustard**, a smidgen of minced **garlic**, a pinch of **chili powder**, two shots of **olive oil**, and then **salt**, **pepper**, and **oregano** to taste. You can play around with this to your heart's content.

Three-Juice Ceviche

The more yogurt, the thicker it will be; the more oil and vinegar, the creamier. Whatever floats your tuchus.

GRILLED PEAR SALAD

Cut slightly under-ripe **pears** into quarters and cut out the cores. If you're not gonna cook your pears right away, leave them in water mixed up with a few good drizzles of **lemon juice** to keep things from turning brown. When you're ready to cook, drain your pears (if you had them soaking) and toss them in some **olive oil**—just enough to coat them lightly—and season generously with **salt** and **pepper**. Grill the pears until they're nice and marked on each side, or, if you don't have a grill, just stick them under the broiler for about eight minutes.

Meanwhile, tear **Boston or Bibb lettuce** (or whatever kind you prefer) into bite-sized pieces. Toss with just enough olive oil to lightly coat the greens, then season with salt and pepper. Drizzle with fresh lemon juice (one lemon or two, depending on how much salad you have) and toss again.

Mound the salad high on a plate, then top with your pears. Throw on some **cherry tomatoes**. A heaping handful of crumbled **blue cheese** on top is killer too.

CELERY ROOT SALAD

Buy three or four **celery roots**—these suckers are ugly, but they sure taste good! Using a mandolin or a sharp knife, cut into quarter-inch slices, then julienne (cut into thin slices about matchstick size). Blanch the roots in **well-salted boiling water** for just a few minutes, then drain and run under cold water. For the dressing, mix three heaping plops of **mayonnaise**, two good drizzles of fresh **lemon juice**, one drizzle of **champagne vinegar**, one super-small plop of **Dijon mustard**, and salt and freshly ground **pepper** to taste. Toss the celery root in the dressing and let sit for at least an hour, if not several hours, before serving over a bed of **watercress**. European traditionalists will demand you garnish with toasted **walnuts** and sliced **apples** (think Waldorf salad), but you can decide for yourself.

CUCUMBER-MINT SOUP

This recipe is so easy you'll wonder why you don't make it every week. Just peel, seed, and chop about six **cucumbers**. Don't worry about how nicely you chop; you're gonna puree anyway. Then throw your cucumbers in a food processor or blender with a few heaping plops each of **sour cream** and **plain yogurt**. Add a smidgen of fresh **mint**, **salt** and **pepper** to taste, a pinch of **cayenne**, a drizzle of fresh **lemon juice**, and a pinch of ground **cumin**. Puree and chill. When it's time to serve, garnish with fresh **mint sprigs**.

SWEET 'N' GREASY CHICKEN FRITTERS

Empty any box of dry **corn muffin mix** or **cornbread mix**, such as Jiffy, into a large bowl. Cut up a few pounds of **boneless, skinless chicken** into bite-sized chunks.

Sprinkle your chicken with a few nice pinches each of **garlic powder**, **salt**, freshly ground **pepper**, and **paprika**. Drizzle just enough **Worcestershire sauce** over the chicken to season it and give it a little wetness—a shot or two should do it. Mix up the whole shebang, then toss the chicken into the dry mix (a few pieces at a time, so the dry mix doesn't get too gunked up) and toss until they're totally coated. Put at least an inch of **vegetable oil** in a deep skillet and get it nice and hot. Deep-fry your chickadees until they're brown and crunchy. Drain 'em on paper towels. Serve with **Down-Home Remoulade** (recipe follows). It's also excellent with **barbecue sauce** or **honey mustard** and a pitcher of **margaritas**.

Down-Home Remoulade

Mix a stalk of finely chopped **celery**, a handful of chopped fresh **parsley**, half an **onion** (finely chopped), a splash of **Worcestershire sauce**, a splash of **cider vinegar**, two plops of **spicy mustard**, and three times what this mixture adds up to in **mayonnaise**. Season with **salt**, **pepper**, **paprika**, and **Tabasco sauce**. This is good with everything from the chicken fritters to shrimp cocktail to onion rings to fish sticks to old shoes.

You don't need a lot of tools or time to rock these recipes— just gusto for a good meal and a willingness to try.

fruits de mer

FISH AND SEAFOOD // Chef Rossi

Fried, seared, stewed, or baked, get friendly with the fishies by following these mouthwatering recipes.

FISH IN CHILE-TAHINI SAUCE

This dish will feed at least 10 people, as it's more fun to serve a whole side of **salmon** and let everyone dig in for themselves. If you're only having two for dinner, then just buy two pieces of salmon fillet. Throw a few cloves of **garlic** into your food processor if you have one, or just mince to hell by hand if you don't. Mix in a good plop of **Chinese chile paste**, a couple plops of **tahini**, a half coffee cup of **water**, and the **juice of two lemons**, and season to your liking with ground **cumin**, ground **coriander**, **salt**, and **pepper**. Drizzle in a little **olive oil** and mix well. Place your fish in an oiled baking pan and cover completely with the tahini sauce—I like to let it sit out at room temperature for 30 minutes to get it nice and marinated—then stick it in a 375°F (190°C) oven and cook until done. A big piece of fish may take 15 minutes, smaller pieces less time. Check doneness by peeking into the center of the fish to see if it's opaque (then you can mush the tahini sauce over where you checked and nobody will ever know). Garnish your creation with sliced **lemon** and **cilantro**.

CAJUN FISH FINGERS

Cut fillets of your favorite **fish** into strips. Cod and halibut work great, but Cajun folks might just need their catfish. Season the fish with a nice amount of **Cajun spice mix**. Take out two bowls. In one, mix three **eggs** with **salt**, **pepper**, and **Tabasco sauce**. In the other, mix a coffee cup of **flour** with the same amount of **cornmeal**, and throw in some **paprika** for color. Dredge the fish fingers in the egg goop, then in the dry mix,

Cajun Fish Fingers

and put on a baking sheet until you're ready to fry. Get a deep skillet super-hot with about an inch and a half (4 cm) of **oil** in it, then carefully drop in your fish fingers. When they turn gold and smell fattening, they're done. Serve with **honey mustard**, **tartar sauce**, or **tartar sauce mixed with Cajun spice**.

FISH TACOS

For about four tacos, take one pound (455 g) of any **fish fillets**: cod, halibut, snapper, or whatever. Cut into ½"-by-1" (1 cm-by-2½ cm) strips. They should look like big squared-off fingers. Season with **salt** and **pepper**, dredge in a mixture of half **cornmeal** and half **flour**, and fry in a hot skillet with at least a quarter inch (4 mm) of **vegetable oil** sizzling in it. Fry until they look golden and crisp, then drizzle with fresh **lime juice** and place two "fingers" in the base of a warmed **flour tortilla**. Serve with shredded **lettuce**, **salsa**, and **guacamole** (page 220). You can also grill whole fillets of fish instead of frying strips.

BRAZILIAN SHRIMP STEW

Sauté one chopped **onion** and one diced **bell pepper** in some **olive oil**. Add a small can of peeled **tomatoes and their juice**, stir, and simmer for a few minutes. Throw in a pinch each of **cayenne** and fresh **cilantro**, and **salt** and **pepper** to taste. Simmer for a few more minutes, then add a coffee cup of **unsweetened coconut milk** (not the piña colada kind). Stir and simmer for a few more minutes, then add a nice plop of minced **garlic** and as much peeled and deveined **shrimp** as you want to eat. Since this is a stew, you might prefer the cheapo baby shrimp, which come ready to cook and don't need cleaning. You can throw a pound to a pound and a half (455 to 680 g) of them in and still have plenty of sauce. Cook until your shrimp are cooked through and the stew starts to thicken, about another 15

minutes. Serve over **steamed rice**. Garnish with **chopped peanuts** or **toasted coconut**.

WASABI-CRUSTED TUNA

Get some nice **tuna steaks**—something around a half inch (1 cm) thick. Season the tuna with **salt**, freshly ground **pepper**, and a healthy amount of **wasabi powder**. Sear the tuna by throwing it down in a hot skillet with a little **vegetable oil** in it. For sashimi-style tuna, sear quickly on the outside and leave it raw on the inside. If you like your fish a little more dead, cook for a few minutes on each side—but no more, or you'll have tuna leather. Just before serving, drizzle with a bit of **soy sauce** and garnish with sliced **scallions**. Serve with steamed **jasmine rice**.

MOUTHWATERING MEDITERRANEAN FISH

Take any fab **fish fillet**—such as cod, salmon, halibut, or trout—and season well with **salt** and **pepper**. Sear the fillet on both sides in a hot skillet with a good drizzle of **olive oil**. Meanwhile, chop up a heaping handful of pitted **kalamata olives** and some fresh **rosemary**. Mix them together in a food processor with a little bit of olive oil until nice and pasty, then generously spoon over your fish when it's done.

SALMON WITH MINT CHUTNEY

Season a **salmon fillet** well with **salt**, **pepper**, and a nice drizzle of **olive oil**. Put on a baking sheet and bake at 350°F (175°C) until done, about 15 minutes. To make the chutney, mix a plop of minced **garlic**, a plop of minced fresh **ginger**, two drizzles of fresh **lemon juice**, a handful each of minced fresh **mint** and **cilantro**, and a pinch each of ground **coriander**, ground **cumin**, **salt**, and **sugar**. When the salmon is done, dollop the chutney over it and serve.

fine young carnivores

MEAT & POULTRY // Chef Rossi (unless otherwise noted)

From Turkish chicken to Jamaican jerk to the Best Little Chili in Texas, here are some meaty recipes you can sink your teeth into.

MARTHA WAINWRIGHT'S ROAST CHICKEN AND VEGETABLES

Start with a nice whole **chicken**, preferably organic. Pat it dry. Put it in a large roasting pan. Cut an **onion** in half and stick it inside the chicken along with some fresh **thyme** or **tarragon** (not too much; fresh herbs can be quite strong) and put a clove of **garlic** in between each drumstick and thigh. Evenly distribute around the chicken an assortment of any or all of the following vegetables, cut into large bite-sized pieces: two large **red potatoes**, about four peeled **shallots**, a large **sweet potato**, a stick of **celery**, a few **carrots**, and a **summer squash**. Then add five whole cloves of **garlic** (peeled or unpeeled), several sprigs of fresh **thyme** and **oregano** (or a quarter teaspoon each of dried), and **salt** and **pepper**. Drizzle the whole thing (including the chicken) with **olive oil** and top the chicken with a couple of pats of **butter**. To give the chicken a little

Martha Wainwright's Roast Chicken and Vegetables

glaze, rub one tablespoon of **honey** all over it with the back of a spoon. Cover loosely with a sheet of aluminum foil and roast in a 350°F (175°C) oven for an hour to an hour and a half, basting three times after about 40 minutes and removing the foil after about 45 minutes. When the chicken is almost done, boil water and cook **whole-wheat pasta** or **egg noodles** in it. Serve the vegetables over a small pile of pasta tossed with some of the cooking liquid, with the chicken alongside.

JERKING OFF, CHICKEN STYLE

Mix up half a coffee cup of **malt vinegar** or **balsamic vinegar**, a heaping handful of chopped **onion**, a regular handful of chopped **garlic**, a smidgen of dried **thyme** and dried **oregano**, and a giant plop of your fave minced **chiles** (for serious jerk, use habaneros and add a little honey). Remember to wash your hands after chopping those suckers. Add a pinch each of ground **cloves**, **cinnamon**, and **nutmeg**, a healthy dose of **salt** and **pepper**, two good splashes of **Worcestershire sauce**, and a couple of splashes of **vegetable oil** or **olive oil**. Toss with a whole **chicken** cut into eight pieces and marinate overnight. Grill or broil until cooked through, then garnish with a whole mess of chopped **scallions**.

TURKISH SALAD OVER CHICKEN (OR TOFU)

Turkish salad works as a topping for almost any fish or meat. In its country of origin, this condiment—basically a simple parsley and onion salad—is king. Or shall I say queen? Thinly slice up four white **onions** and mix with four heaping plops of chopped fresh **Italian parsley**. Mix in four good drizzles each of fresh **lemon juice** and **olive oil**, then season with **salt** and **pepper**.

For the chicken, mix a couple glugs of olive oil with a few drizzles of fresh lemon juice,

a couple pinches of chopped fresh **oregano**, a plop of minced **garlic**, and a good dash or two of freshly ground **pepper**. Even if you're eating solo, drop in four boneless **chicken breasts** (the leftovers are yummy) and put in the refrigerator to marinate for a couple of hours or overnight if you have time. To cook, pan-sear your chicklets on both sides in a hot skillet until well browned, then throw them in the oven at 350°F (175°C) for 10 or 15 minutes until they're cooked through. Top with Turkish salad. For a veggie version, use **firm or extra-firm tofu** instead of chicken, simply searing it in a skillet post-marination.

LAMB AND APRICOT BASMATI RICE PILAF

Put a pot of water on to boil and season it with a smidgen of **saffron** if you have it, or a pinch of ground **turmeric** if you don't. Season well with salt.

Meanwhile, sauté one chopped **onion** in few plops of **butter**. When the onion is soft, add small chunks of **lamb** and brown thoroughly. (Two pounds [910 g] of lamb should make a great pilaf for six people.) Add a pinch of ground **cumin** and ground **coriander**, some **paprika**, **salt**, and **pepper**, and a drizzle of fresh **lemon juice**. When the meat is brown, toss it in a bowl with about half as much **basmati rice** as you have lamb. Add a handful of **golden raisins** and sliced **dried apricots**. Scrape it all into a well-greased baking pan and cover by one inch with the boiling water. Cover the pan with aluminum foil and bake at 350°F (175°C) for about 40 minutes or until the rice is tender. To serve, put in a large serving bowl or platter and garnish with toasted **pine nuts**, **almonds**, or **cashews**, and chopped fresh **parsley**.

BEEF BRISKET

Start with a large **beef brisket** trimmed of excess fat. Rub the brisket all over with pureed **garlic** (you'll need about three cloves). Season the brisket with **salt** and freshly ground **pepper**. Brown both sides of the brisket in a lightly **oiled** heavy skillet. Lay the brisket in a deep roasting pan and cover with sliced **onion**, chopped **celery**, and a few **bay leaves**. Mix a bottle of **ketchup** with a cup of **barbecue sauce**, a splash of **Worcestershire sauce**, and a few dashes of **Liquid Smoke**. Pour over the brisket. Add a cup of water to the pan. Bake at 400°F (205°C) for 30 minutes, then lower the oven temp to 300°F (150°C), cover with aluminum foil, and bake for two hours. Add a generous amount of cut peeled **carrots**, quartered peeled **potatoes**, and quartered **tomatoes**, and a coffee cup of **red wine**, and cook for another hour. (This meal can be prepared a day in advance, if you like, and is probably even better that way. Just heat it up the next day and feed the whole damn neighborhood.)

CHICKEN-FRIED FILET MIGNON
This one really ticks off the purists. Slice **filet mignon** into half-inch-thick (1-cm thick) medallions and season generously with **salt** and freshly ground **pepper**. Set the meat aside until it's about room temperature. Dredge the medallions in a lot of **flour**, enough to really coat them, then fry in a pan with at least a quarter inch (½ cm) of hot **vegetable oil**. Your medallions should be well browned—figure about five minutes per side. Set aside. Keep the pan hot, but not quite as hot as before, and add a heaping spoonful (or two) of **flour** to the leftover oil. Stir in the flour and cook for a minute, then pour in about a half cup (120 ml) of **milk**. Cook and stir until you have a nice, thick, white gravy. Season with salt, pepper, and **nutmeg** and pour the gravy over your filets. Garnish with fried **onions** and serve with **mashed potatoes**. For Southern-fare junkies, this is a wet dream.

THE BEST LITTLE CHILI IN TEXAS
Sauté two chopped **onions**. Add a handful of minced **garlic** and cook for a few minutes. Add about two pounds of **ground beef**. Brown the meat well, then add a 16-ounce can of **tomato sauce**. Season with a pinch each of ground **cumin**, **cayenne**, and **cinnamon**, two heaping pinches of **chili powder**, and a good pinch each of **salt** and freshly ground **pepper**. Once you've got all your seasonings mixed in, go ahead and pour in a coffee cup or two of water just to keep things from getting sticky. Let the whole shebang simmer for two hours, adding water if it starts to look dry or if it seems like it might start to burn on the bottom. Throw in a dash or two of **Worcestershire sauce** in the last half hour of cooking, if you'd like. If you're partial to beans, follow the same recipe, but mix in a few heaping handfuls of cooked **red beans** in the last hour of cooking.

BEER-DROWNED SPARE RIBS
Rub **spare ribs** all over in **salt** and **pepper** and put them in a shallow baking pan. Cover the ribs with **dark beer** and throw in a big mess of peeled and quartered **onions** while you're at it. Cover the pan with aluminum foil and put it in a 400°F (205°C) oven to steam and soften. After about an hour, take it out and remove the ribs from the hot beer. Pre-steaming your ribs will ensure that they will be fall-off-the-bone soft and juicy, and you can do this part up to a day in advance. When you're closer to eating time, baste them in your favorite **barbecue sauce** and put them back in the oven at 300°F (150°C) for at least another hour to an hour and a half, or until they're soft and tender. (Ribs can vary in cooking time depending on the batch of ribs you've got, but you'll know they're done when the meat just pulls off the bone.)

veggie-licious

VEGETARIAN MAIN DISHES // Chef Rossi (unless otherwise noted)

Not feeling the meat? We've got you covered. These yummy dishes are filling, delicious, and flesh-free.

ISA CHANDRA MOSKOWITZ'S APPLE-PUMPKIN RISOTTO WITH CARAMELIZED ONIONS

Preheat the oven to 350°F (175°C). Hack a three-pound (1.4 kg) **sugar pumpkin** (or any winter squash) in half and remove the seeds and stringy bits with a spoon. (If you want, you can clean the seeds, drizzle them with **olive oil**, and bake at 350°F (175°C) for 15 minutes for a delectable snack.) Put the pumpkin halves cut side down on a lightly **oiled** baking sheet. Bake for about 35 minutes, or until the pumpkin can be easily pierced with a fork. Let cool, then peel off the skin and chop the flesh into bite-sized pieces.

While the pumpkin is baking, prepare the caramelized onions: Preheat a heavy skillet over low heat. Add one tablespoon of **olive oil** and two thinly sliced **sweet onions** and toss to coat. Cover, leaving the lid slightly askew, and cook for about 20 minutes, stirring occasionally, until the onions are a mellow amber color. Uncover and increase the heat to medium. Cook, stirring often, for 10 minutes, or until the onions are dark amber and some of the moisture has evaporated.

Start the risotto right after beginning the onions. Have five to six cups (1.2 to 1.4 L) of **vegetable broth** warming on the stove

Isa Chandra Moskowitz's Apple-Pumpkin Risotto With Caramelized Onions

top. Preheat a heavy-bottomed pot over medium heat. Sauté one small diced **yellow onion**, three minced cloves of **garlic**, one tablespoon of minced fresh **ginger**, and a half teaspoon of **red pepper flakes** in the oil for about seven minutes, stirring often. Add a cup and a half (340 g) of **arborio rice** and stir to coat. Add one-third cup (75 ml) of **dry white wine**, two peeled and diced **green apples**, and one cup (240 ml)of the broth. Stir until most of the liquid is absorbed. Repeat this step, adding one cup (240 ml) of the broth at a time, stirring occasionally, until you have one cup (240 ml) of broth left. This should take about 45 minutes. Add the pumpkin (it should be ready by this point) and the last cup of broth and stir. When most of the liquid has been absorbed, add a half teaspoon of **salt**, a half teaspoon of freshly grated **nutmeg**, and a quarter teaspoon of **cinnamon**. Cook for 10 minutes, stirring occasionally. Remove from the heat and let sit for 10 minutes, then spoon into serving bowls and top with the caramelized onions.

DELICIOUS DHAL

Get yourself a bag of dried **chickpeas** or **mung beans** and soak them in water overnight. Drain them, then put them in a pot and cover with water by about two inches (5 cm). Bring to a big rolling boil. Meanwhile, sauté a few handfuls of chopped **onions** and a plop of minced **garlic**. Add a pinch each of ground **turmeric**, ground **cumin**, **curry powder**, **salt**, and **pepper**, and then add a drizzle of water. Cook for a few minutes, then add to your boiling beans. Bring to a boil again and then lower the heat to medium and cook for about 30 minutes, or until everything is looking nice and mushy. Make sure to add water if things get sticky, and keep stirring. Garnish with **chili powder** and fresh **cilantro**. Serve with steamed **basmati** or **jasmine rice**.

VEGETARIAN JAMBALAYA

Melt a stick of **butter** in a pot. Throw in two chopped **onions** and sauté until they get soft, then add a handful of chopped **celery**, a plop of minced **garlic**, and one diced **bell pepper**. Sauté for a few more minutes, then add a 16-ounce can of **whole tomatoes**. Add a pinch each of fresh or dried **oregano**, **thyme**, and **parsley**, season with **salt**, **pepper**, and **cayenne**, and simmer for a few minutes. Stir in a nice handful of frozen **baby peas**, a coffee cup of cooked **red beans**, and a diced or sliced **zucchini** or any other squash you love. Broccoli is also nice. Simmer for a few minutes, and then stir in four coffee cups of **cooked white rice**. Pour into a baking dish and bake at 350°F (175°C) for thirty minutes. Serve with a few **biscuits**, if you want. You don't need much else, except a cold **beer**.

VEGAN CURRY

Sauté two diced **onions** in **olive oil** or **vegetable oil**. When the onions are soft, add four peeled and diced **carrots** and cook for a few minutes, then add one diced **bell pepper** and a head of **cauliflower** cut into small florets. Cook until the veggies all start to soften, then add two nice plops of minced **garlic**, a heaping pinch of **curry powder**, a heaping pinch of ground toasted **cumin**, a pinch of ground **turmeric**, and a pinch of **cinnamon**. Stir for a minute or two, until the spices smell up your apartment like Little India, then pour in a can of **unsweetened coconut milk**. Cover and simmer until all the vegetables are tender; you may need to add a little water if the sauce starts to get too thick. You want the curry to be nice and saucy, very wet. Season with **salt** and **pepper** and serve with steamed **jasmine rice** (or any rice you like).

VEGGIE-LICIOUS STEW

Sauté two heaping handfuls of chopped **white onion** in a drizzle of **olive oil**. Throw in a heaping handful each of chopped **celery**, **bell pepper**, and **carrots**. Sauté for a few minutes, then add some faster-cooking veggies, like a pound (455 g) or so of any of these: **fresh peas**, cut-up **broccoli** or **cauliflower**, or sliced **zucchini**. Sauté for a minute or two, then add a couple coffee cups of **vegetable stock**, and season well with **salt**, **pepper**, **paprika**, and **thyme**. Cover the pot, lower the heat to a simmer, and cook until the veggies are soft.

THREE-CHEESE PLEASE QUESADILLAS

Lay out **flour tortillas** on a baking sheet. Sprinkle with heaping handfuls of shredded **cheddar**, **Monterey Jack**, and **mozzarella**. Cover with another tortilla to make a sandwich and bake just until the cheese melts. These can be made a day in advance and stacked in the fridge. When ready to serve, get a heavy sauté pan or skillet super-hot, pour in a drizzle of **vegetable oil**, and fry those quesadillas until they start to brown on each side. Cut into wedges and serve with **salsa**.

ISA CHANDRA MOSKOWITZ'S ROOT VEGGIE CHOCOLATE CHILI

This recipe is a great way to eat what's in season in the middle of winter. Use two pounds (910 g) of **root veggies**—some great ones are rutabaga or turnip (they taste similar, so best to avoid using both), celery root, golden beets, parsnips, and even the humble carrot. Peel and dice them. Preheat a four-quart (3.8 L) soup pot over medium-high heat, and sauté a small diced **onion** and diced **red bell pepper** in a tablespoon of **olive oil** until the onion is translucent, about four minutes. Add three minced cloves of **garlic** and sauté for another minute. (For spicier chili, add a couple pinches of **red pepper flakes** when you add the garlic.)

Add a tablespoon of **mild chili powder**, two teaspoons each of ground **cumin**, ground **coriander**, and dried **oregano**, a half teaspoon of **cinnamon**, and three-quarters teaspoon of **salt**. Add a half cup of **vegetable broth** and two tablespoons of **cocoa powder**; cook for another minute, stirring. Add a cup (220 g) of washed **green lentils**, three and a half cups (840 ml) more broth, one 15-ounce can of **diced tomatoes**, and the root veggies. Cover the pot and bring to a boil, then lower the heat to a simmer and cook for about 45 minutes, until the lentils and root vegetables are tender. Stir in two teaspoons of **agave nectar** or **maple syrup**. Taste for salt and seasoning. Let your chili sit for 10 minutes or so for maximum flavor. Serve garnished with fresh **cilantro**, if you like.

SOBA NOODLES IN TOASTED SESAME DRESSING

Boil two packages of **soba noodles** until soft, drain, and put in a bowl of cold water while you make the dressing. Toast a handful of **white sesame seeds** and grind in a spice grinder. Puree two cloves of **garlic**, the ground sesame seeds, one good plop of **red miso paste**, two splashes of **soy sauce**, three good drizzles of **rice vinegar**, and a heaping pinch of **sugar**. Drain the noodles and toss with enough **olive oil** to coat (just a couple drizzles should do it), then drizzle with a nice amount of **sesame oil** and toss again. Put in a serving bowl and pour the dressing over the noodles. Top with sliced **scallions**, **bean sprouts**, and julienned **red bell pepper**. **Smoked tofu** or **grilled mushrooms** are num, too.

SPRING SAUTÉ

Start with fresh **fava beans** in the pods. You'll need to shell these so you have two coffee cups of beans, and then peel each bean, but, honey, they are worth it. Cut a

Isa Chandra Moskowitz's Root Veggie Chocolate Chili

pound or two (455 g to 910 g) of **asparagus** into bite-sized pieces. Blanch your fava beans by dropping them in boiling water for a minute, then drain and cool under cold water. Drop two heaping plops of **butter** in a frying pan. Melt it, then add the asparagus and fava beans. Sauté until soft, just a few minutes, then season with **salt** and **pepper** and remove from the heat. This spring vegetable dish becomes a full meal with the addition of a nice piece of seared tofu on top, or chicken or fish for non-vegetarians. Brush sliced **firm or extra-firm tofu**, **chicken breast**, or **fish fillets** with **olive oil**, then sprinkle with salt—sea salt, if you have it—and pepper. Grill, broil, or pan-sear until done, and serve with the vegetables.

COLD SESAME NOODLES WITH SNOW PEAS

Here's a fun recipe for the college-dorm kid in all of us who longs for noodles other than ramen. You can substitute a whole array of veggies—asparagus, sugar snap peas, broccoli rabe—for the snow peas, so experiment your heart out!

Cold Sesame Noodles with Snow Peas

Buy a package of **linguine**. Pick up a few handfuls of **snow peas**—about a pound (455 g)—and a bunch of **scallions**. Cook your noodles in boiling water until al dente (soft but firm to the bite) and in the last minute of cooking, throw in your snow peas (why wash two pots?). Drain the whole shebang and rinse under cold water. Slice up your scallions and toss them on top. Add **Ginger-Sesame Dressing** (recipe follows), toss, and you've got some tasty noodles ready to go. They can also be made a day in advance and kept in the refrigerator.

Ginger-Sesame Dressing

Mix together a plop of minced fresh **ginger**, a plop of minced **garlic**, a few splashes of **soy sauce**, a pinch of **red pepper flakes** (any kind), and a few drizzles of **sesame oil**. Whisk in a plop of **toasted sesame paste**, if you want.

MACKIN' CHEESE

Boil a box of **macaroni** until it is al dente (firm to the bite, not mushy), drain and cool under cold water, drain again, and set aside. In a large saucepan, make a roux by melting one stick of **butter** and whisking in about the same amount of **flour** (a half cup). Keep whisking while you pour in two cups (480 ml) of hot **milk**. Season with **garlic**, **paprika**, **cayenne**, **salt**, and **pepper**. Stir in two handfuls of shredded **white cheddar** and one handful of grated **Parmesan**. Stir and cook until the cheese is melted. Your sauce will be nice and gooey now, like an Alfredo. (Actually, minus the cheddar, this is how to make Alfredo sauce. So if you're hankering for Fred, just add some grated nutmeg.) Mix the cheese sauce with the pasta and pour into a **buttered** baking dish. Sprinkle extra cheese on top, then **bread crumbs**. Bake at 400°F (205°C) for 15 minutes, or until everything starts to look crusty.

on the side

VEGGIES AND STARCHES // Chef Rossi (unless otherwise noted)

Need a little something to go with that? These side dishes will be the perfect complement to any meal.

MOUNT COUSCOUS

Cook your favorite **couscous** according to the directions on the box. Let cool for a few minutes, then make like Richard Dreyfuss in *Close Encounters of the Third Kind* and pile it in a big mound. Top with just about any kind of **dried fruit** or **nuts**, such as pistachios, toasted cashews, slivers of sun-dried apricots, raisins, or dried cranberries. What makes this dish really sexy is the way you eat it: Grab a handful, mush into a tight ball, and plop into your mouth, just like in the old country. Then immediately proceed to insert jewels into your navel and belly dance until the sun comes up.

PARSNIP MASH

Peel about a dozen **parsnips**, then cut into bite-sized pieces. Drop the chunks in a pot of cold water, bring to a boil, and cook until soft (about 30 minutes). Drain and mash well while hot, mixing in a good plop of **butter**. Season well with **salt** and freshly ground **pepper**, and you're done! Serve alongside almost any kind of meat or grilled fish.

KIMCHEE MARINATED BOK CHOY

This dish plays on the spicy kimchee flavor that most spice-aholics love and also gives you a fabulous veggie side dish that you can make for yourself and have on hand to eat any time you want. Just wash and cut up **bok choy** or **napa cabbage** into bite-sized

pieces. You probably want about six bunches of bok choy because it shrinks down to nothing after it's marinated. Make a dressing by mixing up one heaping smidgen of **chili powder**, a good plop of finely chopped **onion**, a smidgen of minced **garlic**, a smidgen of minced **ginger**, a shot of **rice vinegar**, and **salt** and **sugar** to taste. It should be kinda spicy and kinda sweet—like you. Just toss up your bok choy in this and marinate overnight. The next day, you'll have a perfect zingy little snack to serve alongside an entrée, put in a sandwich, have as a salad, or pick at as is.

Parsnip Mash

MARTHA WAINWRIGHT'S SIMPLE GREENS

Greens are great all sorts of ways, but especially sautéed. Use whatever looks good from the grocery store—maybe some **Lacinato kale** and some **regular kale**. Cut off the thick stems. Rinse the greens but don't shake them out too much. Throw them into a heated pan (not too hot) with some water still clinging to them. Add a quarter cup of **olive oil** and about a quarter cup (60 ml) of water. Turn the heat down to medium-low, then mince or crush two **garlic** cloves and add them to the pan. Cover. After a few minutes, stir. The greens should be wilted and almost tender. Let some water boil off or, if the pan is dry, add a little more water and keep it covered. Season with **salt** and **pepper** and remove from the heat.

WASABI MASHED TATERS

Buy any good mashing tater like Yukon Gold—about three **potatoes** for every person you're gonna feed, as everyone loves mashed potatoes. This recipe's good for about 12 or so taters. Peel the spuds and cut up into equal-sized chunks, then put them in a big pot with enough water to cover the potatoes. Add a few pinches of **salt** and boil until soft. Drain your taters and mash them with a masher, electric mixer, or an egg beater—or just bang the hell out of them with a big whisk. Mix a coffee cup of **milk** with a heaping smidgen of **wasabi powder** and whisk it up good. Some folks prefer a little **cream** in there too. Then bring to a simmer in a saucepan and add it to the taters. Mix in a few generous plops of softened **butter**, then beat the taters again and season with salt and freshly ground **pepper**. This is great served with Asian-style grilled or roasted meats or fish, or even a teriyaki burger.

TSIMMES

Every Jewish mother has an opinion about how to make this traditional sweet-tasting dish: "It has to have prunes!" "Sweet potatoes, not carrots!" Well, bubelahs, this is my way, and oy vey if you don't like it!

Peel about two pounds (910 g) of **carrots**, then slice into half-inch-thick (1-cm-thick) ovals. Put them in a deep baking pan that you've rubbed with **butter**. In a pot, bring two coffee cups of **apple cider** to a boil. Add a drizzle of either **bourbon**, **Grand Marnier**, **triple sec, brandy, rum,** or **vanilla extract**. Add two heaping plops of **brown sugar**, a nice pinch of **cinnamon**, a few pinches of **salt**, and a heaping handful of **raisins** or **currants** and mix well. Pour the hot cider mixture over your carrots, making sure they're covered. Cover the pan with aluminum foil and cook at 350°F (175°C) for about an hour or until the carrots are super-soft.

ROASTED VEGETABLES WITH OVEN-DRIED TOMATOES

Oven-dried tomatoes are too fabulous for words. Buy a few pints of **cherry tomatoes**, cut them into halves, and toss with a shot of **olive oil**, **salt**, **pepper**, a plop of minced **garlic**, and some chopped fresh **rosemary**. Then spread them out on a baking sheet and bake at 350°F (175°C) until the tomatoes look dried but not burned. This can take an hour. Meanwhile, cut six **zucchini**, two heads of **cauliflower**, and two heads of **broccoli** into bite-sized pieces (carrots and most kinds of squash are delicious subs). Toss in olive oil, then put in a baking pan and roast until they're tender but still hold their shape. Toss with the tomatoes, season with salt and pepper, and that's it! This is great hot or at room temperature.

Mackin' Cheese, Wild Rice Salad & Roasted Vegetables with Oven-Dried Tomatoes

WILD RICE SALAD

Start with two pounds (910 g) of washed **wild rice**, 'cause this is too good not to make a lot of, and it keeps for several days. In a pot (large enough to hold five times the amount of the uncooked rice), add twice as much water as you have rice and bring to a boil, then cover and simmer for about an hour or until the rice is tender. Make a dressing with half a coffee cup of **olive oil**, a couple shots of **raspberry vinegar**, a couple drizzles of **honey**, and a nice dollop of **Dijon mustard**. Toss your rice in this and add a heaping handful each of sliced **shallots** and **dried cranberries**. Season with **salt** and **pepper**. This is great hot or cold, and even more delectable topped with toasted **almonds**.

FIVE-MINUTE BROCCOLI

On your mark, get set, go: Cut a head of **broccoli** into florets. Drop into boiling water for one minute. Meanwhile, sauté a plop of minced **garlic** in a generous amount of **olive oil** in a large sauté pan. Drain your broccoli and toss it in with the garlic. Sauté until just tender. Season with **salt** and **pepper** and serve. You can do this with cauliflower, zucchini, snow peas, spinach . . . just about anything that doesn't bite back— and even a few things that do.

the sweet hereafter

DESSERTS AND SWEETS // Chef Rossi (unless otherwise noted)

End your meal on a sweet note with one of these super simple treats.

JACK DANIEL'S ICE CREAM SAUCE

Melt about a coffee cup of **sugar** mixed with about half a coffee cup of water and cook until it looks syrupy and thick. Pour in two shots of **Jack Daniel's**. Then pour yourself a third one for being so hot. Cook the sauce for a minute or two, then ladle it over your favorite ice cream.

LINDSAY LARICKS' BLACKBERRY-LAVENDER POPSICLES

This frosty treat is based on one of the most popular snow-cone flavors offered by Fresher than Fresh, Laricks' dessert cart in Kansas City, Missouri, so you can get a taste of her genius at home.

Put two heaping cups (455 g) of **black-berries**, a cup (225 g) of **sugar**, a cup and a half (360 ml) of water, and two tablespoons fresh or dried **lavender buds** in a saucepan. Bring to a boil, then lower the heat and simmer for eight minutes. Mash the mixture with a potato masher to extract as much juice as possible from the berries. Put in the refrigerator to cool for about 30 minutes. Add six tablespoons (90 ml) of fresh **lemon juice**. Pour the mixture through a fine-mesh sieve into a large measuring cup with a pour spout (or something similar), then pour into ice-pop molds (or ice cube trays, disposable cups, or skinny highball glasses). Cover each mold with aluminum foil, then poke Popsicle sticks (or plastic spoons, swizzle sticks, or chopsticks) through the foil into the juice mixture. (The foil helps to keep the sticks in place.) Freeze for about four hours. Pop those suckers out of the molds and enjoy!

STRAWBERRY FANTASY

Take three pints (1.4 kg) of **strawberries** and thinly slice them lengthwise. Mix a coffee cup of **brandy**, **triple sec**, **Cointreau**, or **Grand Marnier** with a heaping spoonful or two of **sugar** and pour over the berries. Slice a store-bought **pound cake** (or muffins or biscuits) and use the slices to line the bottom of a deep glass baking dish. Cover with a layer of macerated strawberries, then a layer of **whipped cream** (whip it yourself or buy it), then another layer of pound cake, more strawberries, and whipped cream. Pop the whole shebang in the fridge for about two hours. Scoop and serve as is or with ice cream. It's sinfully fantastic.

Lindsay Laricks' Blackberry-Lavender Popsicles

Chocolate Pizza & Chili-Rum Chocolate with Pineapple Bites

CRAZY FRUIT COCKTAIL

Mix a 16-ounce can of **pineapple chunks and their juice** with three cored and diced **apples**, three **oranges** cut into segments, and a heaping handful each of seedless **grapes** and sliced **melon** (any kind). Or substitute your fave fruit—diced pear and sliced strawberries are fab—for any of these. Stir a spoonful of **sugar** into a coffee cup full of sweet **juice**, like pear or peach, and mix into your fruit combo. Serve in a martini glass if you're fancy.

CHILI-RUM CHOCOLATE WITH PINEAPPLE BITES

This recipe is great for entertaining. Peel a **pineapple** and cut it into bite-sized pieces (get rid of the heart; it's too tough to chew). Skewer your pineapple chunks with toothpicks or bamboo sticks. Bring a coffee cup of **cream** to a high simmer in a saucepan on the stove top. Whisk in a shot of **rum** and a plop of **butter**. When the butter is melted, stir in a coffee cup of **semisweet chocolate chips** and a good pinch of **chili powder**. Put the pineapple skewers on a tray or plate and drizzle the hot chocolate over them.

CHOCOLATE PIZZA

Buy any decent **frozen pizza dough** and follow the cooking instructions on the package. Once your dough is nice and toasty, brush it with **melted butter** and sprinkle generously with **semisweet chocolate chips**. Put it back in the oven until the chocolate is melted. Top with toasted nuts or marshmallows and cut into wedges. White chocolate is fabulous too.

CHOCOLATE MAMA MOUSSE

Drop a heaping coffee cup of **semisweet chocolate chips** into a bowl. Put a brimming coffee cup of **cream** in a saucepan and throw in a **cinnamon stick**. Bring to a boil, remove the cinnamon, and pour your boiling-hot cream into your chocolate. Stir until the chocolate is melted, then let it cool. In a large bowl, with a whisk, beat about two coffee cups of cream until a little thick, then beat in a heaping handful of **sugar** and keep whipping until thick. Fold the cream into your chocolate goop and chill. Spoon into glasses for individual helpings or serve family style in a big bowl. You can make it the day before, but a few hours ahead works too. Serve the mousse cold and top with **whipped cream** and **shaved chocolate**.

bottom's up

DRINKS AND COCKTAILS // Chef Rossi

Whether you're looking for an apertif, a digestif, or a party punch, these recipes will keep your glasses full. Cheers!

ELECTRIC LEMONADE

This is such an easy, tasty cocktail, you'll want to make it all the time. Just whip up a pitcher of your fave homemade or store-bought **lemonade**. Load a tall glass with **ice**, then fill it one-third full with **vodka** and two-thirds with lemonade, leaving an inch of room at the top. Top with **ginger ale**, then garnish with a **mint sprig** and a slice of **lime**.

PUNCH-DRUNK LOVE

This fabulous punch can be served in pitchers or a big retro bowl. Mix up one liter of **dark rum**, a half liter of **brandy**, four shots of **peach schnapps**, two liters each of **apple juice** and **pineapple juice**, four shots of **Rose's lime juice**, 16 ounces of **mango juice**, and two drizzles each of **vanilla extract** and **bitters**. Top with about two cups (480 ml) of **ginger ale**. Add **ice** and sliced **lemons**, **limes**, and **oranges**.

Punch-Drunk Love

APPLE BOMB

For a bubbly holiday drink, pour a shot of **vodka** and a half shot of **Grand Marnier** into a champagne glass. Fill with chilled **sparkling cider** and garnish with an **apple slice**.

PINEAPPLE-ITO

Everyone loves traditional mojitos, but they take a long time to make, which isn't practical if you're serving a crowd. Try this easy twist instead. Throw a handful each of fresh **mint** and **sugar** into a tall pitcher, then load with **ice**. Fill one-third with **white rum** or **vodka**, one-third full with **pineapple juice**, and one-third with **club soda**. Stir in the **juice of two limes**.

FIRE EXTINGUISHER RUM PUNCH

Fill a pitcher with **ice**. Fill it one-third full with **Jamaican rum**, add a few dashes of **bitters**, a drizzle each of **grenadine** and **lime juice**, then fill the rest of your pitcher with equal amounts of **pineapple juice**, **orange juice**, and **cranberry juice**. Serve with a **cherry** and a slice of **orange**.

TIPSY RUSSELL'S BUST BELLINI

For a fizzy, refreshing drink that is fruity enough to enjoy for breakfast, have your houseboy whip up this cocktail delight. Start with four parts of the chilled sparkling white wine **Prosecco** (or *frizzante*, as the Italians call it), then drizzle one part **peach nectar** over the top. Have houseboy garnish with **fresh fruit** and stir with his pinky. Cheers, darlings.

MINT JULEP

If you want to channel your inner Southern belle, a mint julep is where it's at. In a saucepan, combine equal parts **sugar** and water—figure a coffee cup of each—and bring to a boil, stirring until the sugar is totally dissolved. Drop in a heaping handful of fresh **mint**, remove from the heat, and let cool completely. Strain to remove the mint, then put the syrup in the refrigerator to chill. You can make this the day before you want to use it. When it's time to party, fill your glasses with **ice**, add a good drizzle of your syrup, and fill the rest of your glass with **bourbon**—two shots is good. Then garnish the glass with fresh mint. If you need those juleps right away, you can drop a spoonful of sugar into a glass and muddle with an equal amount of water and four or five mint leaves, then top with ice and bourbon, but it won't be as good as the syrup way.

MULLED WINE

Just pour one bottle of **dry red wine** into a pot, throw in a dash of **cinnamon**, a heaping spoonful of **sugar**, a tiny pinch of grated **nutmeg**, and a shot of **Cointreau**, **triple sec**, or **brandy**. Then bring to a light simmer and enjoy.

LETHAL HOT TODDY

Drink this one while sprawled across a bearskin rug. To make it, pour about six coffee cups of **apple cider** into a pot, then throw in about one shot of **rum** for every cup of cider if you want it lethal, about half that if you want it wussy. Add a pinch of **cinnamon**, a pinch of **brown sugar**, and a drizzle of fresh **lemon juice**. Bring to a simmer, and you're good to go. This is also great with brandy, tequila, or whiskey.

the green party

THROW A LOCAL-FOODS POTLUCK // Lisa Butterworth and Christina Amini

Hosting a local-foods potluck is an awesome way to hang out with your ladies while saving the world one bite at a time. Eating local (also known as a "locavorism") means relying on ingredients produced within a 150-mile radius from where you live, but there's lots of room for improvisation. You can be as specific as eating within your county or as loose as buying items grown in your state or region. The benefits of eating locally are plentiful: Not only is the produce fresher, tastier, and more nutritious than its industrially produced counterpart, but eating food farmed close to home also saves a ton of energy wasted in the mass production and transportation of our edibles. According to Steven L. Hopp, an environmental studies professor at Emory and Henry College, "If every U.S. citizen ate just one meal a week composed of locally and organically raised meats and produce, we would reduce our country's oil consumption by over 1.1 million barrels of oil every week." Talk about an easy change to make!

SET SOME GROUND RULES

To host your own local-foods potluck party, delegate apps, sides, desserts, and drinks to a dozen or so of your favorite friends. Make sure you have a couple of dishes for each course. (As the hostess, it's up to you to make the main dish.) Tell your guests the goal of the meal: To see how local you can go. Decide how strict you want to be. For example, should all ingredients (even staples like flour) be sourced from within 150 miles? If so, provide suggestions of farms, food co-ops, community-supported agriculture groups, farmers' markets and even friends with nearby gardens so people have a better chance of success. These days, even many supermarkets have an area of their produce section reserved for locally produced fruits and vegetables. And it's not only veggies that can be found in farmers' markets; some also feature bread, cheese, wine, and ciders.

If you just want to highlight in-season local foods—meaning the whole meal needn't be sourced locally—tell people that (and offer a list of veggies and fruits that will be in season if you think that'd help your besties). Have friends who are gardeners? Consider throwing a party focused on celebrating backyard bounties. And take the season into consideration: If you live in a colder climate, planning your party in late summer or early fall will give you far more options than holding it in February, when you might be forced to make a five-course meal entirely out of root vegetables (including dessert!).

LOOK BEYOND THE FARMERS' MARKET

Going local is a great way to discover indie businesses in your city, so explore your neighborhood for options beyond the farmers' market. On a quest for the perfect scoop you might stumble upon an eco-friendly ice cream shop owned by two cool gals. Perhaps you'll discover that your neighbor brews ales in his closet. Or, you can buy your beer from a local craft brewer, or take it to the next level and try brewing your own (see page 260). Since some of your guests may want to make food from scratch, make sure to give them plenty of advance notice; how else are they going to be able to bring along those homemade pickles from the local Kirby crop or have time to ferment their own kimchee?

SHOW AND TELL (AND EAT)

When people arrive with their dishes, have them also bring a list of the ingredients and sources. Half the fun of grubbing locally is finding out about the farm that produced the delicious Brussels sprout on your fork or the person responsible for that pint of ice cream you devoured. Fold paper into "table tents" and write what the dish is and where the ingredients came from. As you eat, think of the time you ate a similar plate using food sourced from far away; talk about any differences you notice. Take the time to appreciate the food grown so close to home.

By consuming only what grows naturally and in your region, you reconnect to where your food actually comes from, the people who produce it, and the passing of seasons. It's one thing to buy a bag of prewashed, impeccably packaged, who-knows-where-it-came-from spinach at the grocery store; it's an entirely different experience to grab a bunch at the farmers' market, dirt clods still clinging to the roots, passed from the hands of the farmer who dug it out of the ground herself. Sure, you might have to wash it more. But that soil has probably been feeding the region for years, and there's something so humbling (and tasty) about that. It might even inspire you to dig in the dirt a little yourself. To find out more about eating local, check out the Resources on page 356.

salon selective

HOW TO PARTY LIKE IT'S 1929 // Juliet Eastland

Descended from the Old English *sele*, or "hall," a "salon" came to mean a gathering designed to entertain and enlighten. It was a hit with French aristocrats in the seventeenth century, and with Gertrude Stein and her circle of famous friends in the 1920s. So why not invite your pals over and host a salon of your own? Some performances will be wince-worthy, some sublime, but all will be offered in the same spirit of bravery and openness. And that's the difference between hosting a party and hosting a "salon."

L'HISTOIRE DU SALON

The phenomenon of the salon reached its apogee in French aristocratic homes of the seventeenth and eighteenth centuries (although there's even proof that salons were hosted for the likes of Plato, Pericles, and Socrates as far back as fifth century BC). Guests gorged on decadent, multicourse meals, engaged in readings, music, and games, and oozed glamour. But salons purveyed more than folderol and foie gras. They were binges of bon mots, banter, and verbal and artistic prowess, and their intellectual influence extended far beyond the watered-silk walls. Conversations and creativity of the times were developed in the salons before they blossomed and exploded—often with revolutionary results.

Salon hostesses (*salonnières*) were almost always women, and they had the resources, connections, and stamina to preside over these intellectual bacchanals. Even more, they possessed discernment—the ability to recognize greatness of mind. They relished the sparks that flew from gathering a roomful of erudite characters and letting them have at it, whether it be philosophical discussion, musical performance, or revolutionary fomentation. However, barred from official participation in civic or political institutions, they recognized that men would do the public "work of change."

TODAY'S SALONS: HOW TO HOST ONE

The essence of salons—ongoing community, meaningful dialogue versus angry diatribe—may be particularly relevant in our cacophonous climate of newspapers, magazines, websites, television, and blogs. But it's up to you to carry on the tradition. Ready? Herewith, some considerations for the savvy salonnière:

Theme

What do you adore? What makes your heart beat faster? Maybe you're dying to discuss a specific subject, like horticulture, Caribbean drumming, or twentieth-century art. Or perhaps you're a political animal whose salon conversations will create momentum among like-minded souls ("Retaking the Presidency") or gather people of different political stripes ("Right and Left: A Discussion"). Teresa M. Dentino's years in finance spawned The Peninsula Women's Salon (www.thefinancial411.com), which empowers divorcing women through community building and financial education. New York singer/actor Joanna T. Parson parlayed her passion for performance into the twice-monthly Happy Hour Salon, which showcases 10-minute new works of music, literature, drama, and comedy (www.joannaparson.com). Kelly Close, founder of Close Concerns, Inc., favored an eclectic intellectual menu, so she established CPS Lectures in memory of her father, a polymath with omnivorous interests; lecture topics range from juvenile delinquency to "Sex and Work" (www.cpslectures.com). Whatever your theme, it will spring from you—your experience, your interests—and it is your ardor that will draw people in and get them as excited as you are.

Your Role

What's your style? If you schedule a roster of performances in advance, as Parson does, you may wind up an actual, on-stage emcee; if you facilitate a "lecture series," your role may be to contact interesting-sounding speakers and moderate the Q&A session. Journalist, editor, and Mediabistro.com founder Laurel Touby hosts an informal, ongoing cocktail-party salon for media folks at various local bars, where her role is simple: to facilitate mingling. "Tell everyone to show up at a certain time/date/bar/restaurant/home. Don't promise anything more than great company and stimulating conversation. Then, host—don't talk to one person for more than several minutes at a time, mix people up, force them to move around." Her efforts have spawned "marriages, friendships, feuds, and feisty discussions."

At the other extreme, speaker, futurist, and author John Renesch (www.renesch.com) avoids "hosting" altogether. Because he feels the hierarchy of "expert" speakers versus "nonexpert" listeners inhibits genuine discourse, his Presidio Dialogues—created to stimulate "holistic thinking and healthy lifestyles in the world of business"— resemble Quaker meetings rather than lectures: The group forms a circle, three or four people offer opening comments, then attendees speak when moved.

Don't be afraid to experiment. You might find that you prefer to sit back and let the evening unfold. Sure, you might e-mail the invitations, and you may impose minimal structure by calling out "Who's next?" but maybe you'd prefer to allow someone's song or reading to inspire conversation and debate. Do what works for the people you invite and they'll be back for more.

The Cast

When it comes to guests and, if your format calls for it, guest speakers, most salonnieres start, sensibly, with friends, family, and colleagues. (Ongoing word of mouth helps, too; almost all the people on Renesch's mailing list are original invitees, their friends, or their friends' friends.) Also consider inviting folks from different stages of your life, such as college friends, coworkers, artists, and business acquaintances. Just remember, you control the numbers. You can pare your list or "close" your event after a certain point. Touby preserves the intimacy of her salons by choosing small barroom settings; space fills quickly, and if guests RSVP late, they have to wait until next time. Start by inviting the folks you like, those you think will contribute to the evening.

Location, Location, Location

Where will you put people—and how will you afford it? Oregon writer Colin Lingle wanted to address environmental concerns, but with minimal space and resources, he had his own environmental issues. So he hosted his Green Salon in his living room for a few friends. His only cost: snacks. ("Never underestimate the power of a superb cheese plate to change the world.") Once your salon is established, you might accept offerings, either financial (no shame in a tip jar) or culinary. Because her salon members are at a particularly vulnerable time in their lives, Dentino rents rooms that have serenity and a "sense of grace;" a members' fee helps offset this cost. Parson charges audience members five dollars to offset the rental of her small theater space. Ask your local church/community center/bookstore about obtaining space, perhaps in exchange for community service. Visit local venues; your salon might be just what they need to boost their PR. Alternate locations or split costs with a cohost. Hold a fundraiser. Be creative!

Frequency

When it comes to salon meeting times, it's important to be flexible. Regularity is not always feasible, so Close's salon convenes "every so often." Dentino's meets several hours a week for four weeks. Lingle's salon met for only three sessions (although to great effect; one attendee was inspired to start "greening" his workplace). Bottom line is, go with the flow. Host a few events. See how they go; tinker with their format and theme, if need be, and evaluate your financial resources and time constraints. Then consider a long-term commitment.

E-Communication

You'll need to keep your peeps posted, and the Internet makes it easy. Renesch uses an e-newsletter service to publicize time, place, and topic. Parson e-mails a "wrap-up" to her entire list summarizing each performance. "The people who came to that salon are interested because everyone wants to read a review of something they've seen," she explains. "[Those] who usually come but missed that night want to know what they've missed; those yet to come are constantly hearing about the event and feeling like they're part of the community." She also holds an annual "Audience Appreciation Awards" ceremony, whereby people nominate favorite acts on her website. Start a Facebook page for your group and consolidate RSVPs and discussion forums in one place.

Not Up to Hosting a Salon? Join One!

When you get together with a group of people, you may have a chance to hear live opera, learn about haiku, or meet a Broadway cast member. Or you might rethink a cherished belief, beat addiction, propose a workplace innovation, influence government, banish loneliness, or fall in love. As Renesch says, "Miracles occur." There's no limit to how much you can learn and grow—all within the comfort of your own living room.

party girl

THE EASY WAY TO HOST A COCKTAIL SOIREE // Chef Rossi (unless otherwise noted)

It's always the right time for a cocktail party for you and all your besties. Staying in means you can dress up or down (or come in costume like the true nerd you are), plus you get to choose the music. And, by making the drinks and food yourself (or going potluck style and inviting friends to bring things too), you'll save cash. To make sure attendees know to expect small bites, start your party later—say, 9 p.m.—and use the words "You are invited to a cocktail party." That's English for "booze and light munchies," not "all-you-can-eat buffet." Here are a few recipes to get you rocking.

drinks

Any successful cocktail party needs some cocktails. A great way to set up your bar is to provide wine, beer, soda, and maybe one signature drink or vodka and some mixers. Here are a couple fancy-drink options.

POMEGRANATE PASSION

Mix four parts **champagne** and one part **pomegranate juice**. Don't get cute and try to float pomegranate seeds in it. A guest will wind up chugging the drink and will sound like a cat with a furball when those seeds hit the back of her throat.

WHITE SANGRIA

If you want to avoid serving anything red to save your white leather furniture (or outfit), try this. Dump three bottles of hearty **white wine** into a punch bowl, add two shots of **peach schnapps**, two cups (480 ml) each of **peach juice**, **orange juice**, and **apple juice**, and then fill with sliced **apples**, **oranges**, and **limes**. A shot of **brandy** is nice too.

food

If you're working until five that night, try to get as much prepared in advance as you can. Then just put out your grub buffet style and let guests help themselves. Table optional.

BUFFALO SHRIMP

Peel and devein as many **shrimp** as you want to serve, or buy them already cleaned. Then make a spice mix by combining a good pinch each of **salt**, freshly ground **pepper**, **paprika**, and **garlic powder**. Toss up your shrimp in this mix and then grill them. When your shrimpies start to curl and turn orange, they're done.

Then toss shrimp in Mama Rossi's Buffalo Toss: Melt one stick of **butter** and mix with two good dashes of **Tabasco sauce** and a nice drizzle of **Worcestershire sauce**. Garnish with a heaping handful of sliced **scallions** or **chives**.

FETA AND TOMATO CONCASSÉ ON CROSTINI

Slice a couple of **baguettes** into quarter-inch-thick rounds. Brush them with **olive oil** and sprinkle with a pinch of **salt**. Bake at 300°F (150°C) until crisp. Meanwhile, cut one pound (455 g) of **feta** into the tiniest little squares you can and about six **plum tomatoes** into a super-small dice. Toss them together with a few dashes of olive oil and a heaping handful of chopped fresh **basil**, then salt and **pepper** to taste. To serve, spoon your concassé onto the crostini.

SMOKED TURKEY FINGER SANDWICHES

Get a pound (455 g) of sliced **smoked turkey**. Then spread **cranberry relish** or **apricot mustard** (recipes follow) on a slice of **whole-grain** or **raisin-walnut bread**, top with a nice amount of turkey and another slice of bread, and cut up into little fingers or triangles, or get cute and punch out with a cookie cutter. The same idea works great for smoked ham, too.

Cranberry Relish

Throw the following into a food processor or blender: a heaping handful of fresh **cranberries**, a minced **jalapeño**, a heaping handful of **sugar**, one **orange segment**, and a spoonful of minced fresh **ginger**. Puree until you get a nice chunky paste.

Apricot Mustard

This is so easy you'll think you're doing something wrong. Mix up equal parts **apricot preserves** and **grainy mustard**, then use as a fixing for ham, turkey, or chicken. It's yum-a-licious.

CHICKEN 'N' WAFFLES

If you have the time (and a waffle iron), make waffles from scratch, or get a box of your favorite **plain frozen waffles**. Thaw them, then use a cookie cutter to stamp out shapes, or just cut a regular-size square waffle into four square minis. Marinate four or five boneless, skinless **chicken breasts** overnight in a few glugs of **barbecue sauce**, a glug each of **Worcestershire sauce**, **apple cider vinegar**, and **olive oil**, freshly ground **pepper**, a few pinches of **garlic powder**, and a pinch of **cayenne**. Put in a baking dish and bake at 300°F (150°C) until cooked through (40 minutes to an hour). Shred using two forks or your fingers. Save all the drippings from the baking dish and pour it over your pulled chicken. Toast your waffles until crisp, then dollop the chicken on top.

EASY-BREEZY RAVIOLI

Putting out hot pasta for a party is a real drag, so here's a fabulous munchie that you can put out hours in advance. It won't get stale or funky. Boil your fave small **ravioli**, or do a combo—maybe a green spinach, an orange pumpkin, and a white cheese. Boil just until the ravioli float, then drain and cool under cold running water, drain again, and toss in **olive oil**. Skewer the ravioli with bamboo skewers or long picks and arrange on a platter with one or several of the following **dips**.

Sun-Dried Tomato Tapenade

Just puree a heaping handful of **sun-dried tomatoes** with a shot of **olive oil** and a plop of minced **garlic**. That's it!

Black-Olive Pesto

Buy pitted **kalamata olives** and puree a heaping handful with a shot of **olive oil** and a good pinch of fresh **rosemary** or **thyme**.

Traditional Basil Pesto

Puree a bunch of fresh **basil** with a generous pinch of **pine nuts**, a generous pinch of grated **Parmesan**, a **garlic** clove, and a shot of **olive oil**.

AMY SEDARIS'S CHEESE BALL

Amy makes this all the time and you should too. Let two eight-ounce packages of **cream cheese**, two cups (455 g) of shredded **smoked Gouda**, and one stick of **unsalted butter** come to room temperature. Beat them all together in a mixing bowl with two tablespoons of **milk**, **cream**, or **half-and-half**, and two teaspoons **A-1 steak sauce**. Form into a ball (or several small balls) to suit your function/needs. Roll in two cups (400 g) of crushed **nuts** (Amy likes walnuts) and refrigerate. Remove from the refrigerator and let soften at room temperature for about 20 minutes before serving. Serve with crackers of your choice.

take it outside

MAKE YOUR NEXT BARBECUE A WALK IN THE PARK // Chef Rossi and Lisa Butterworth

When the weather turns warm, there's no better place to be than in the park with your pals. Add a delicious spread of food, a tasty cocktail, and a bumping boom box, and you've got the makings of the best day ever. We've done all the planning for an epic outdoor shindig, so simply read on for a bunch of finger-lickin' recipes, and even tips for lighting a grill. You can also lend your outing an eco-friendly slant, not to mention a little class, by bringing real dishes instead of disposable ones. So hit up the grocery store or your farmers' market, grab your girls, a few blankets, that croquet set gathering dust in your closet, and a cooler, and get ready for some fun in the sun.

BREAD AND BUTTER PICKLES

Slice two **English cucumbers** into quarter-inch-thick (5-mm-thick) rounds, and thinly slice two small **red onions**. In a large bowl, toss cucumbers and onions with two tablespoons **kosher salt** and refrigerate for one hour. Rinse and drain. Pat them dry with paper towels or a dishcloth and place them in a glass bowl.

In a small saucepan, combine another two tablespoons **kosher salt**, two cups (480 ml) **cider vinegar**, one cup (225 g) **sugar**, a tablespoon of **whole black peppercorns**, a teaspoon of **mustard seeds**, a half teaspoon of **celery seeds**, a quarter teaspoon fresh **ground pepper**, and a half teaspoon **red pepper flakes**, and stir well. Bring to a simmer over medium heat and let simmer for five minutes. Pour the mixture over the cucumbers and onions (they should be covered with liquid) and let cool. Cover and refrigerate overnight.

Once they're done, you have the perfect pickled topping for burgers, dogs, and sammies alike.

GRILLED GREEN TOMATOES

Forget all that fried green tomatoes stuff. These are easier and just as tasty. Slice **green tomatoes** into half-inch-thick (1-cm-thick) circles and toss in **olive oil**, **garlic salt**, and **pepper**. Grill on both sides until well marked but still firm, then drizzle with **balsamic vinegar**.

GRILLED CORN ON THE COB

Shuck the **corn** halfway and remove the silk, then fold the husk back up and soak the corn in ice water for a minute or two. Take it out of the water and, with the husk still on, let it steam over medium heat on the grill until tender. Serve with a tub of **butter**. Mmm, calories.

VEGGIE BUNDLES

This works for **broccoli**, **asparagus**, **zucchini**, **yellow squash**, and a whole bunch of other veggie delights, so pick your fave or mix and match. Depending on what you choose, cut broccoli into florets, trim the ends off asparagus, and slice zucchini or yellow squash into half-inch-thick (1-cm-thick) pieces. Toss your veggies in **olive oil**, **salt**, and **pepper**. Place a heaping handful on a sheet of aluminum foil, slide in a plop of **butter**, then fold into a packet. Grill for about 10 minutes.

WARM POTATO SALAD

Wash and quarter some medium-sized **potatoes** (cut them into eighths if they're huge). Any kind of potato will do, but Red Bliss or Yukon Gold are especially tasty. Dip yer taters in **olive oil**, then season with **salt** and freshly ground **pepper**. Wrap in aluminum foil and grill over medium heat until tender. Toss the potatoes in a little more olive oil and a drizzle of **champagne vinegar** or **cider vinegar**. Season to taste and garnish with chopped **scallions**. Serve warm

SIMPLE AND DAMN GOOD STEAK

Take your favorite cut of **steak** and season generously with salt and freshly ground **pepper**. Brush with a little **vegetable oil** to keep things from getting sticky. Throw your meat down on the super-hot zone (toward the middle of your grill) just long enough to sear it on both sides, then plop it in the medium-hot zone (toward the edges) and baste generously with **Berry Barbecue Sauce** (recipe follows) or your favorite barbecue glaze. Cook to desired doneness. A nice steak should take anywhere from 10 to 15 minutes, depending on the size and how you like it.

Berry Barbecue Sauce

Preheat a saucepan over medium heat. Sauté one small, finely chopped **onion** in one tablespoon of **peanut oil** for about 10 minutes, until lightly browned. Add three cloves of minced **garlic** and a one-inch (2½ cm) chunk of minced **ginger**, sauté for a minute more. Add two cups (455 g) of **berries** (blackberries, raspberries or blueberries work great), a half cup (120 ml)

how to light a charcoal grill

Forgo chemical-laden lighter fluid by using a DIY chimney starter.

With a punch-type can opener, make a few holes around the edge of a coffee can, then use the can opener to remove the bottom (figure 1). Take the grill grate off your barbecue and place your chimney in it with the holes at the bottom. Scrunch up a piece of newspaper so it forms a ring and place it in the bottom of your chimney (figure 2). Fill your chimney to the brim with charcoal and use a match to light the newspaper in several places through the holes (figure 3). Allow the briquettes to turn ashy (about 20 to 30 minutes), then use tongs to carefully remove your chimney. Spread the coals evenly, replace your grill grate, and start cookin' (figure 4).

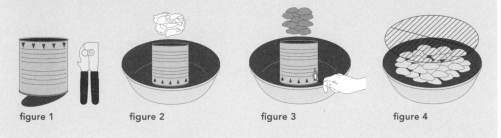

figure 1   figure 2   figure 3   figure 4

of **veggie broth**, and two tablespoons of **soy sauce**, and bring to a boil. Once boiling, add two tablespoons **ketchup**, two to three teaspoons **chipotle powder** or **smoked paprika**, half a cup (120 ml) **molasses**, and a couple tablespoons of **sugar** (to taste). Lower heat and let simmer for about 45 minutes, until it's reduced by half. It should be nice and thick. Adjust seasoning if necessary. Turn the heat off and let sit for about 15 minutes before using, stirring occasionally. When it's done, slather it on steaks, veggie dogs, burgers, or just about anything.

SHRIMP AND NECTARINE KABOBS
To make a garlic-herb oil, combine a quarter cup (60 ml) **olive oil** and a couple cloves of minced **garlic** in a small saucepan. Stir over medium heat just until the garlic is aromatic (probably under a minute); you don't want it to brown. Remove from the heat and immediately stir in a couple tablespoons of **herbs**, like basil, rosemary, and thyme—whatever you have handy; set aside. Cut three **nectarines** (plums and peaches work, too) into half-inch-thick (1-cm-thick) slices. Grab a pound of large peeled and deveined

shrimp and slice one **lemon** thinly. Thread the shrimp, lemon, and nectarines onto skewers alternately. Brush lightly with garlic-herb oil. (For a little kick, sprinkle kabobs with **cayenne**.) Throw them on the grill for a few minutes per side or until the shrimp is pink and cooked through. Drizzle with extra oil for added flavor.

LEMON-BUTTER FILLET

Buy **salmon**, **snapper**, **cod**, **halibut**, **trout**, or almost any kind of fillet you like. Brush your fish with melted **butter**, season with **salt** and **pepper**, and sprinkle with fresh **lemon juice**. Top with sliced **plum tomatoes** and fresh **rosemary**. A few

capers won't hurt, either. Wrap in aluminum foil (one fillet per packet makes for easy serving) and grill for 10 minutes.

PIZZA

Start by brushing a precooked **pizza crust** with **olive oil**. Cover with **tomato sauce**, shredded **mozzarella**, and your fave toppings—**pepperoni**, **broccoli**, **mushrooms**, or whatever you like. Season your pizza well with **salt**, **pepper**, and **oregano** and add a pinch of **red pepper flakes**, too, for a bit of heat. Seal inside a foil packet, leaving room on top so the cheese doesn't get stuck. Grill for about 10 minutes.

family supper picker-upper

MAKE A CLASSIC SUNDAY DINNER // Chef Rossi

Maybe you grew up eating mostly things that came out of cans. Maybe your mom wasn't big into the homemade, instead relying on precooked grocery-store chickens and iceberg lettuce. That's okay. There's still hope for you. Here's an old-school chicken 'n' potatoes menu (including a kicked-up iceberg salad!) to help bring back the kind of family memories you wish you had.

MASHED-UP TATERS

Go for at least twelve **potatoes** (or figure on about three potatoes for every person coming to dinner). Get whatever kind floats your boat; Yukon Gold potatoes are great. Peel the taters, cut them into chunks, and put them in a pot with enough water to cover. Add a few pinches of **salt**, and boil until they're soft. Drain your taters, then mash them up.

Look at your taters and put about one-third of that amount of **heavy cream** in a pot (you can also go half milk, half heavy cream). Throw in a handful of peeled **garlic cloves**. Heat until it's simmering, then whisk in the mashed taters. Mix in a few generous plops of softened **butter** and beat it all to hell. For folks who like to take it easier on themselves, an electric mixer or an egg beater is fabulous for this. Finally, season your taters to your liking with **salt** and freshly ground **pepper**.

CHICKEN NOT LITTLE

Buy a whole **chicken** cut into eight pieces and marinate it in a little **olive oil** with a nice pinch each of **oregano**, **rosemary**, **thyme**, **salt**, and **pepper**. You can do this overnight or for a couple of hours. Then throw your chicken in a baking pan and roast it at 350°F (175°C) until well done, which may take an hour. For a quickie sauce, just pour the drippings from the pan into a skillet and add a cup of **white wine**. Cook to reduce it by about half, then pour it over the chicken with a touch more salt and pepper. If you're a thick-gravy fan, you can add a pinch of **flour** mixed with **butter** or **vegetable oil** to thicken things up.

ACTUALLY DECENT ICEBERG SALAD

Maybe you think icebergs did to salad what they did to the *Titanic*, but folks love this stuff, so here's a good way to use it. Wash a head of **iceberg lettuce** and discard the crappy outer leaves and the core. Cut it into about eight big wedges, and put one wedge on each salad plate. Make a dressing out of one heaping plop of crumbled **bleu cheese**, one plop of **mayo**, one drizzle of **balsamic vinegar**, a shot of **olive oil**, and **salt** and **pepper** to your liking. Pour over your wedges. Shaved **Parmesan** on top of it is sexy too.

A traditional family supper doesn't have to be a parade of bland basics.

a little dip'll do ya

THROW A FONDUE PARTY // **Chef Rossi**

Sure, fondue is retro, kitschy, and deliciously, deliciously cheesy. But there's no rule that says fondue has to be a chafing dish filled with hot cheese goop into which you dip annoying little croutons. Like Italian? Have a ravioli fondue party. Everyone brings a favorite kind of ravioli; boil them and serve with pick-your-own fondue forks around a pot filled with hot, cheesy alfredo sauce. Crazy for chocolate? Serve skewered fruits around a simmering pot of chocolate fondue. Here are a few ideas to get you started. They can all be done with an authentic fondue set or with any hot plate, a small pot, and some skewers.

TWO CHEESEY FONDUE

Mix up about a coffee cup and a half of **milk** with a pinch of **cayenne**, a pinch of **dry mustard**, a plop of minced **garlic**, a splash of **Worcestershire** and a heaping spoonful of **flour**. Whisk well and heat over super-low heat in a pot until it just starts to bubble, then stir in two heaping handfuls of grated **cheddar** (any kind) and **smoked gouda**. Once the cheese melts, it's ready to serve. Some folks may add salt but I think the cheese is salty enough. Added bonus: Believe it or not, you can substitute **beer** for the milk in this recipe and it works great . . . maybe even better.

VEGAN RAGOUT FONDUE

Sauté one diced **onion** and a smidgen of minced **garlic** with a nice plop of **tomato paste**. Stir in a few chopped **green bell peppers**, a few chopped **tomatoes**, and a few shots of **tomato juice**. Season with **paprika**, **salt**, and **pepper** to taste. Simmer for about 15 minutes. Puree the ragout until it has the texture of chunky tomato sauce, sprinkle with **oregano**, and serve in a fondue pot surrounded by thinly sliced **garlic bread**, **toast**, or **bread sticks** for dipping. For something really filling, you can serve this with skewered vegan **ravioli** or **tortellini**.

BUTCH FONDUE

Start with boneless **chicken**, **beef**, or **lamb**, or **tofu**. Or go mad and serve them all. Cut into bite-sized cubes. Make a little seasoning mixture by mixing a pinch of **garlic powder**, a pinch of freshly ground **pepper**, a pinch of **salt**, and a little itty-bitty smidgen of **cayenne** and set aside. Arrange the skewers around a fondue pot filled with **vegetable oil** over medium-high heat. Put the oil to the sizzle test: If you flick a drop of liquid in it and it sizzles immediately, it's hot enough. (Lesser cooks also call this the spit test, but that's just plain disgusting.) Have your guests spear the meat with fondue forks or skewers. Dip the meat into the oil and leave it there until it is cooked. This won't take long, probably just a few minutes, unless you've got a taste for well-done. Put the seasoning mix out in a bowl and let guests sprinkle to their liking. Serve with Vegan Ragout Fondue (recipe above) or your favorite barbecue sauce.

CHOCOLATE FONDUE

In the top of a double boiler over simmering water, melt down a few handfuls of **semisweet chocolate chips** with a couple plops of **butter**. After the chocolate has melted, stir in a shot of **heavy cream** and a shot of **amaretto**, **Grand Marnier**, **rum**, or **cognac**—whatever floats yer boat. Serve the chocolate warm in a small pan or fondue pot surrounded by **strawberries**, sliced **pineapple**, **bananas**, and **finger cookies** for dipping.

party time

DIY PIÑATA AND BANNER // Meghan Keys, Lisa Butterworth, Jenna Warner

If you're looking for inexpensive ways to spice up your soirées, we've got the crafts for you. Cheap, fun, and easy to make, a piñata guarantees a smashing good time. For bonus flair, whip up a DIY banner with fabric scraps.

materials

Newspaper

Scissors

Sheet of plastic

1 cup flour

2 cups cold water

Bowl

Large balloon

Additional balloons of various sizes, for creating a different shape (optional)

Masking tape (optional)

Card stock (optional)

X-ACTO knife

Colorful tissue paper

Liquid glue

Spray glue (optional)

Long needle and thick thread

Candy (or condoms and plastic mini liquor bottles), for stuffing the piñata

Cut the newspaper into strips 3" to 4" wide and 12" to 14" long, which are long enough to cover a large blown-up balloon (the body of your piñata). If you plan on combining balloons to make your piñata a different shape (we used masking tape to hold a smaller balloon on top of a larger one to create the head and body of the bird), cut several newspaper strips long enough to connect the balloons.

Cover your work surface with the sheet of plastic. Using your hands, mix the flour and water together in a bowl until you have a smooth, clump-free liquid. The consistency should be slightly runny; add a touch of water if necessary.

Blow up your balloon. You may want to place it in a bowl while you apply the strips.

Soak a strip of newspaper in the flour mixture for a few seconds. Use your fingers or the side of the bowl to remove the excess liquid from the strip (the more flour mixture on the paper, the harder your piñata will be), then place it on the balloon and smooth it out. Repeat until the balloon is covered, slightly overlapping strips to avoid any holes. Let dry overnight or at least a few hours.

Once your piñata is dry, reinforce the top area where it will hang by adding several more layers of papier-mâché. For an extra-solid hold, add pieces of masking tape to the spot, then cover with papier-mâché strips and let dry.

Feel free to add non-papier-mâché details to enhance your piñata's design (we added wings, tail feathers, and a beak). To do so, cut cardstock into your desired shapes. Attach them by using your X-ACTO knife to cut slots in your piñata (it's OK if the balloon inside pops) just long enough for each piece of cardstock to snugly fit into.

Decorate your piñata by cutting tissue paper into 2"-by-4" strips. Along one 4" edge of each strip, make several snips about 1¾" long, about ¼" apart, leaving ¼" at the top of each strip intact. Run a thin line of liquid glue along the uncut edge, then place the strip on the piñata with the snipped edge hanging down; start at the bottom and work your way up until the piñata is entirely covered. Stagger the placement to create the classic, fluttery look of a traditional piñata. If you want, you can use spray glue and full sheets of tissue paper for a sleeker look.

If the balloon inside is still intact, poke your needle through the piñata to pop it. Then use the needle and thread to sew a loop about 2" long at the reinforced top of the piñata.

Using an X-ACTO knife, cut a small, three-sided opening (hinging at the top) toward the upper backside of your piñata. Fill it with goodies, then close the flap. To hang, tie a rope or cord to the loop, and drop it over a tree branch (or through a secure hook fixture) so that it can be pulled up and down. Swing, batter, swing!

diy banner

Let the world know you're having a party by hanging this cute banner.

First, gather a variety of fabric in complementary patterns. Then cut one triangle with a 6" base that is 10" from base to tip. Use this triangle as a model and cut others, making sure to use all your fabrics. The desired length of your banner will determine how many triangles you need (for ours, which was 36' not including tails, we cut 45 flags). Now it's time to attach the triangles to twine. Lay a fabric triangle right side down on your ironing board. Grab a ball of twine and, leaving a 2' to 3' tail, rest it on top of the fabric, parallel to the 6" side about ¼" from the edge. Cut a piece of iron-on adhesive (we used Steam-A-Seam) that is slightly shorter than the width of the triangle where the twine rests, and place it on the fabric just below the twine. Fold the edge of the triangle over the twine so that it completely

covers the adhesive. Activate the adhesive by resting your heated iron on it for 5 to 10 seconds (or however long is recommended on the adhesive's package). Repeat this step, securing the triangles about 2½" apart in alternating fabric patterns, until you've reached the desired length of your banner. Leave a 2' to 3' tail of twine on the other end as well.

step up to ginger brew

MAKE YOUR OWN GINGER BEER // Kathryn O'Shea Evans

Drinking your first ginger beer is like reliving your first great kiss: It'll leave you hot, woozy, and thirsting for more. Because it's nonalcoholic, ginger brew can be enjoyed by anyone, anywhere, from the playground to the Greyhound.

Keep in mind that the more ginger you add, the hotter your brew (and as we all learned with our first great kiss, the hotter the better). Getting the carbonation right can be tricky if there's any ginger sediment left in the juice after it's strained. If there's no carbonation after you've refrigerated the bottles, all you have to do is pull the brews out of the fridge for a while; the bubbles happen when the yeast eats the sugar, and the yeast can't work its magic in a cold fridge. If the bottles are not refrigerated soon after the 48 hours suggested here, the carbonation may burst off the lids. Those yeasty beasties are tricky, but if this recipe is followed pretty closely, you shouldn't have a problem.

materials

3 cups (720 ml) honey

3 egg whites, beaten

6 tablespoons (85 g) chopped fresh ginger

Juice of 4 lemons

Juice of 1 lime

6 tablespoons (45 ml) pineapple juice

¼ teaspoon active dry yeast

Sieve and cheesecloth

About twenty-two 12-ounce bottles with caps (available at brew shops)

Makes about 2 gallons (7.5 L)

In a large pot, dissolve the honey in 2 gallons (7.5 L) water. Add the egg whites and ginger. Bring to a boil, simmer for several minutes, skim the scum off the top, and set aside to cool to lukewarm. Add the lemon juice, lime juice, pineapple juice, and yeast and give it a stir. Let stand for one minute, then pour through a sieve lined with rinsed and squeezed cheesecloth into a clean container. Bottle the ginger beer (ask the folks at your local brew shop for details if you're a newbie). Let sit at room temperature for 48 hours, then pop the bottles in the fridge and enjoy. The ginger beer will keep for at least a few weeks in the fridge.

krazy for kombucha

FERMENT YOUR WAY TO THIS HEALTHFUL DRINK // Molly Kincaid

The first time you tried kombucha, you probably thought it tasted like fruity beer. This fizzy, fermented tea originated in ancient China and is touted for its digestive and immune-boosting qualities, but at four bucks a bottle, it comes at a price. Fortunately, it's super-easy to make at home. Just get yourself a culture—a symbiotic colony of bacteria and yeast (a.k.a. a "scoby")—and you're on your way.

materials

2-gallon (7.5 L) glass jar

Distilled white vinegar (for cleaning)

1½ gallons (5.7 L) freshly brewed green or black tea

1½ cups (340 g) sugar

Scoby (see tip below)

Clean plastic soda bottles with caps

Makes about 1½ gallons (5.7 L)

Rinse the large pot, the glass jar, and a large spoon with vinegar so you don't contaminate the scoby. Put the tea in the large pot and stir in the sugar. Let sit at room temperature overnight. In the morning, pour the tea into the glass jar, carefully place the jiggly scoby blob on top, cover the jar with a clean dish towel, and secure it with a rubber band or string. Store in a warm spot, out of direct sunlight, for one week. The mutating culture will look like a cross between a Man o' War and brains; don't worry, it's normal. At the end of the week, carefully remove the scoby and place it in a sanitized bowl. The acidity in the kombucha should have killed any contamination, but if you see mold on your culture throw the batch out and start anew. To add carbonation, funnel the kombucha into a few clean plastic soda bottles. Screw the lids on tightly; the pressure created by the fermenting tea will add the necessary fizz. Store at room temperature for another five to seven days, then unscrew those babies and drink up.

You can easily purchase a scoby online (check out www.getkombucha.com), but since the culture reproduces with every batch, kombucha brewers always have extras—ask around or try Craigslist.

this ale's for you

BREW YOUR OWN BEER // Aimée Dowl

This starter recipe is for basic malt ale and involves no grain or flavor additions, which you can play with after mastering the basics. Be patient: Every homebrewer produces the occasional dud batch, but that's a small price to pay for your own delicious, homemade potations.

The brewer's number-one enemies are common microbes that can transform a beer's flavor into the taste of dirty cardboard. Anything that will come into contact with the beer should first be washed in a bleach solution (1 tablespoon per gallon of water) and then rinsed in plain water. Your local homebrew supplier will have all of the supplies you need, or check out the Resources on page 356 for more options.

Brewing your own beer can cost as little as 50 cents per serving and won't clutter landfills with bottles and packaging.

materials

Two 3 ½-pound (1.6 kg) cans malt-extract syrup in light, amber, or dark

2 ounces (55 g) fresh hops in pellet or leaf form with an alpha-acid level of about 6 percent

Hydrometer or thermometer

5-gallon (18.8 L) or larger stainless steel pot

Glass or food-grade plastic carboy (like an office water-cooler bottle) or a 5-gallon (18.8 L) plastic pail with a hole drilled in the lid for an airlock (see instructions) to use as a fermenter

Funnel (if needed)

Sieve

Airlock (rubber stopper with a tube running through it)

One 2-ounce (55 g) package ale yeast

Another carboy or pail without a lid

Plastic racking cane (a rigid, hooked tube) and about 5 feet (1⅔ m) of siphon hose that fits onto the end of it

1 cup (225 g) dextrose (also called priming sugar)

Twelve 16-ounce (455 g) clear glass bottles, 12 bottle caps, and a capping machine

Makes 12 bottles

Bring 5 gallons (18.8 L) tap water to a rolling boil and add the malt-extract syrup. This steaming stew is called the wort. After the extract dissolves completely, add 1 ounce (30 g) of the hops and boil for 1 hour. Add another ounce of hops just before turning off the heat. Plunge the pot of wort into an ice bath until a hydrometer or thermometer reads 70°F (20°C).

Pour the cooled wort into the fermenter (through a funnel if using a carboy), straining out the hops with a sieve. Cap with the airlock and shake the fermenter like mad to oxygenate the wort. (Get a friend to help.) Remove the airlock and slowly add the ale yeast. Put the airlock back on and fill it halfway with water. Store the fermenter at room temperature, away from bright light. Within a few hours, the yeast will start rapidly firing carbon-dioxide bubbles through the water in the airlock. The beer may appear cloudy for up to several days. Kreusen, a fermentation by-product that accumulates as a thick layer of dirty foam, will quickly develop on top of the beer. When the bubbles rising through the airlock slow to about one per minute and there is no more cloudiness in the beer, it's time to bottle.

Transfer the beer into the other carboy or bucket. To do this, place the fermenter on a table and the empty carboy or bucket on the floor. Fill the connected racking cane and siphon hose with water, stopping the ends with your thumbs. Hold the ends so that the middle of the hose falls toward the ground in a U-shape. First loosen your thumb on the racking cane and insert it into the fermenter, then point the other end of the hose into the lower container and release your thumb—the siphoning will start. You will be transferring the beer between the sediment layer, called trub, on the bottom of the fermenter and the kreusen layer on top—do your best not to transfer any trub or kreusen.

Dilute the dextrose in 1 cup (240 ml) boiling water, then let cool to room temperature. Pour this liquid into the beer and mix well. Siphon your beer again, this time into the bottles, and seal them off using the capping machine. Store the bottles for about 10 days in a cool, dark place. As the yeast works on the dextrose, the beer may become cloudy again. Wait until the cloudiness completely clears and sediment forms at the bottom of the bottle (about one week); then you can put the stored bottles in the fridge until you are ready to drink them. When you pour out the chilled nectar, leave the sediment behind in the bottle.

mean beans

ROAST YOUR OWN COFFEE // Monique I. Cuvelier

materials

⅓ cup (70 g) green coffee beans (see Resources on page 356)

Hot-air popcorn popper with the top removed (the Toastmaster air-popping popper works great, but whatever brand you choose, make sure it has air vents on the side that blow in the air; roasting is hot business, and using the wrong type of machine could be a fire hazard)

Cardboard box large enough to comfortably fit the popper (with a hole poked in the side for a thermometer)

Empty can with both ends and label removed (wide enough that it doesn't drop inside the popper

2 oven thermometers (optional)

Metal colander

Glass jar with lid

There's nothing better than a really fresh cuppa, but did you know that a jerry-rigged popcorn popper makes better coffee than most coffee shops? Here's how to roast fab coffee fast and cheap.

If possible, take your roasting production outside. Roasted coffee smells delicious, but roasting coffee stinks like milky breath and smokes more than a '72 Pinto tailpipe.

Put the popper in the cardboard box, which will help keep the temperature around 90°F (30°C) while roasting. Stick a thermometer through the hole in the box. Turn on the popper. If it's too cool, fold down one of the box's top flaps; if it's too hot, open it up again. On a really hot day, ditch the box altogether. Pour in the beans, agitating with the wooden spoon until they start to hop around by themselves, about 1 minute. Place the can on the top of the popper to act as a corral for the beans and prevent them from leaping out as they expand.

Now listen to the beans, because they'll go through two sets of popping. The first, called the "first crack," sounds like small twigs breaking and happens after about four minutes. Stop roasting now for a super-light city roast. For a full-flavored French roast, sit tight and listen for the "second crack," after about six minutes, which sounds more like a mouthful of Pop Rocks. Use tongs to dangle a thermometer inside the popper; when it reads 450°F (230°C) (after about seven minutes), the beans are done.

Immediately pour the beans into the colander and toss to cool and stop the cooking process. When they're warmish, put them in a jar and leave the lid off for the first 12 hours—freshly roasted beans vent carbon dioxide and can turn a sealed jar into a coffee bomb. The coffee is ready to grind and use right away, but becomes mouth-meltingly delicious between 4 and 24 hours after roasting. You've got three days to drink up while the freshness lasts.

mighty fly hot chai

MAKE A CHAI MIX // Hannah Simpson

A warm mug of hot chai is the spicy-sweet icing on the cake of a cold night, and having this mix on hand means you'll never be more than a few minutes from bliss.

materials

2 cups (455 g) superfine sugar

1 cup (225 g) instant white tea powder

1 cup (225 g) nondairy creamer

1 cup (225 g) instant nonfat dry milk

1 cup (225 g) Coffee-Mate Latte Creations (original or vanilla)

4 teaspoons ground ginger

4 teaspoons cinnamon

2 teaspoons ground cloves

2 teaspoons ground cardamom

2 teaspoons ground allspice

1 teaspoon white pepper

Three 1-pint (480 ml) jars with lids

Mix all the ingredients in a large bowl. To give your mixture a uniform appearance (some of the ingredients are more granular than others), process it in a blender or food processor 1 cup at a time. Divide among the jars and put the lids on tightly.

To serve, put 2 tablespoons in a mug and fill with boiling water. Wait a few minutes before sipping, to allow the spices to settle at the bottom. Now drink up!

nothin' but 'nilla

HOMEMADE VANILLA EXTRACT // Clotilde Dusoulier

Vanilla extract is a necessary staple in every baker's kitchen and a pricey one to boot. Turns out making your own could not be simpler and once you taste the heavenly flavor of your DIY version, you'll happily kiss the dullness of store-bought brands good-bye. Plus, homemade vanilla extract makes a great gift for foodies.

materials

1-cup (240-ml) glass jar or bottle with tight-fitting lid

3 medium or 1½ large vanilla beans

Light rum (or any liquor that's 40 percent alcohol)

Sterilize the glass jar or bottle by filling it with boiling water. Let it rest for 10 minutes, and pour out. Using a sharp knife, slice the vanilla beans lengthwise to expose the seeds. Tuck the beans in the jar and fill with light rum. Close the jar, shake it a few times, and place it in a cool, dark cabinet, keeping it there for eight weeks. Shake the jar once or twice a week; the mixture will get darker over time. You can start using your extract at the end of the eighth week.

The best part is, as long as you have both ingredients on hand, you'll never have to wait for your vanilla extract again. When you've used about 20 percent of the jar's contents, simply top it off with more rum and shake again. Add a fresh vanilla bean once or twice a year. If you continue to "feed" it this way, the extract will keep forever; just remove some of the older beans if the jar becomes too crowded.

Though this recipe suggests using light rum, you can use whatever liquor you prefer, provided it's about 40 percent alcohol.

infuse your booze

FLAVORED VODKA // Kelly Carámbula

When it comes to infusing, the flavor possibilities are endless—you can use anything from fruits to herbs to nuts, as long as they're fresh and of the best quality. The result is a full-flavored vodka you can use to make cocktails or enjoy on the rocks. It's a super-simple way to create your very own fancy concoctions without going broke. Cheers to that!

materials

Flavor base, such as fresh lemons, limes, oranges, melons, berries, cucumbers, ginger, mint, basil, lemongrass, vanilla beans, or chiles

1 (750 ml) bottle good-quality vodka

1 large glass jar with a lid (a container with a spigot at the bottom or a regular canning jar)

Sieve and cheesecloth

Thoroughly wash your fruit, vegetables, or herbs. Citrus fruit, melons, cucumbers, and strawberries should be sliced to expose the flesh, while other berries (such as blueberries or raspberries) and herbs can be left whole. Place enough infusion ingredients in the jar to fill it about halfway, and cover with vodka to the top of the jar. Tighten the lid and put the jar in a cool, dark place, like a pantry or cupboard. Strong flavors like citrus can infuse in as little as three days, while subtler flavors, like cucumber, can take up to two weeks. It doesn't hurt to do taste tests every now and then to see how the flavor is developing. Once you've arrived at your desired flavor (whether that's just a light hint of your infusion base or the deeper taste of a longer steeping period), it's time to strain the vodka. Line a fine-mesh sieve with cheesecloth, place it over a large bowl, and pour your infusion through. Discard the solids (or eat them up) and pour the vodka back into the glass jar. Store your infused vodka in the freezer or whip up a tasty cocktail like the one below.

OH, HONEY!

Make up a batch of mandarin-orange-infused vodka. In a cocktail shaker, combine 1½ ounces (45 ml) infused vodka, ½ ounce fresh-squeezed juice from a mandarin orange (about ½ an orange), and ½ ounce honey syrup. (To make syrup, heat water over low heat for about 1 minute, remove from the heat, and add an equal amount of honey and stir until smooth.) Add a handful of ice to the shaker and swirl for about 15 seconds. Pour into an old-fashioned glass and top off with 1½ ounces (45 ml) club soda. Stir to combine and garnish with a slice of orange.

need for mead

A SPICY BREW THAT PACKS A PUNCH // Tracie Egan Morrissey

Mead has been intoxicating the masses since 500 BC. But unless you enjoy being hit on by long-haired flautists at the Ren Fair, you'll have to make this sweet libation yourself. Most mead making requires a three-month fermentation period and some brewery equipment. But if you like your booze like you like your men—cheap, fast, and easy—follow this recipe, which uses common household items and is ready after just 10 days.

materials

8-quart (7.5-L) stainless steel or enamel pot

3 quarts (2.8 L) purified water, plus more for topping off

½ cup lemon peels

1 tablespoon strong brewed tea

1 teaspoon cinnamon

2 pounds honey

Mesh tea strainer

1 packet wine or champagne yeast (not baking yeast)

3 feet (1 m) aquarium tubing no larger than 1 inch (2½ cm) in diameter

2 sterilized 1-gallon (7.5 L) glass jug

Sterilized wine bottles or 2-liter plastic soda bottles

Makes 1 gallon (7.5 L)

Bring the water to a boil in the large pot. Lower the heat to a simmer and add the lemon peels, tea, and cinnamon. Stir in the honey and continue to simmer. A scummy froth will rise; skim it off with a mesh tea strainer. Repeat for about 20 minutes until no more froth rises. (Warning: If you're half-assed about the skimming process, your result will taste like turpentine.) Remove from the heat, cover, and set aside at room temperature overnight.

Stir in the wine yeast, cover and set aside at room temperature. Wait 24 hours and your concoction should be foaming like a mofo. Siphon the mixture using the aquarium tubing. To do this, put one end of the tube in the mixture and suck gently on the other end. Quickly move the tube from your mouth before the mixture hits your lips, and put it in a sterilized gallon jug. When it's full, cover the top with 4 folded paper towels and a rubber band. (This allows gasses to escape.) Let that ferment for at least 48 hours. A layer of yeast will settle at the bottom. Siphon the mixture into another sterilized jug, leaving the yeast layer behind. Clean the jug well, fill it back up with the mixture, top off with purified water, reseal, and store in the refrigerator overnight. The next day, siphon the liquid into sterilized wine bottles or soda bottles. Cork or cap tightly. Store in the fridge and after three to five days you can drink and be merry! Huzzah!

confection perfection

DIY CANDY CORN // Melisser Elliott

materials

1 cup (225 g) granulated sugar

⅔ cup (165 ml) corn syrup

5 tablespoons vegan margarine

1 teaspoon vanilla extract

2 ½ cups (250 g) confectioners' sugar

⅓ cup (45 g) powdered soy milk

Pinch of salt

Yellow and red food coloring

Makes at least 100 pieces

Candy corn is the quintessential Halloween treat, and who knew you could actually make it at home? This DIY version is a bit time consuming, but the end result is well worth it. Best of all, it's vegan, so all your pals can enjoy it.

In a large saucepan, bring the granulated sugar, corn syrup, margarine, and vanilla to a boil. Lower the heat to medium and boil for 5 minutes, stirring occasionally. Remove from the heat.

In a bowl, sift together the confectioners' sugar, powdered soy milk, and salt, then add this to the syrup in the saucepan and stir until combined. Let the doughlike mixture stand until slightly warm to the touch, about 15 minutes, then divide into three equal pieces. Add several drops of yellow food coloring to one piece of dough; knead until smooth and the color is even. Make another piece of dough orange by adding a couple of drops each of yellow and red food coloring and knead until the color is even. Knead the remaining piece of dough until smooth.

Roll each piece into ropes of equal length (no thinner than ¼ inch thick or they will break). Lay the ropes next to each other and push them together to form one tricolor slab. Using a sharp knife, make diagonal cuts across the slab, alternating their angle to make triangles from top and bottom. Round the corners of the triangles to make candy-corn shapes; they'll be a bit larger than the store-bought kind. Homemade candy corn can be stored on parchment paper in an airtight container—enjoy them whenever your sweet tooth strikes! They will keep for quite some time.

churn it up

WHIP UP SOME BUTTAH // Jenny Rose Ryan

A little whipping goes a long way—not only is DIY butter fresher and tastier than its store-bought sister, but you can also experiment with different creams from your farmers' market or add tasty herbs to kick it up a notch. Now when you serve bread and butter at your next dinner party, you'll be able to say, "I made that!"

materials

1 cup (240 ml) heavy or whipping cream

1 or 2 pinches of salt (optional)

Mixer with whisk attachment

Dried rosemary or basil (optional)

Butter molds (optional)

Makes about ⅔ cup (80 g)

Put the cream in a stainless steel or stand-mixer bowl. If you like, add the salt. Beat the cream on medium-high with your mixer's whipping attachment, periodically scraping the sides of the bowl with a spatula. Continue to beat the cream beyond "soft peaks"—it will begin to resemble mashed potatoes and take on a light yellow hue. After another minute, the cream will get yellow and grainy and liquid will start to pool in the bowl; slow down the mixing speed to prevent sloshing. As the butter lumps together, buttermilk will continue to pool. Pour out the buttermilk and reserve it for baking. Put the lump of butter in a clean bowl. Run cold water over it and knead it for a few minutes, changing out the water until it runs clear. Want to get fancy? Stir in dried rosemary or basil. Roll the butter in waxed paper and refrigerate, or chill it in molds to make cute shapes. It will keep in the refrigerator for at least one week. You can also whip it a little more to create a fluffier texture that's great for spreading on muffins or bread.

culture club

MAKE YOUR OWN YOGURT // Erin Hanusa

You know that yogurt can feed your belly, moisturize your skin, and tame the yeasty beast, but you may not know that it is ridiculously easy to make. Of course you can make yogurt with store-bought milk, but milk that comes straight from the cow is even better. Full of vitamins A and D, raw milk possesses all its natural enzymes, so more of its calcium gets to your bones, and it's sweeter and easier on your stomach. In this recipe, you'll heat the milk enough to kill off at least some germies, so it's technically not a raw milk yogurt (but you'll still get lots of health benefits). To find fresh, unpasteurized, cream-topped milk, check out co-ops, local farms, or www.realmilk.com. With milk in hand, you're halfway to a batch of the freshest, tastiest yogurt you're ever gonna eat.

materials

1-quart glass jar with lid

Large spoon

Large pot

1 quart (960 ml) fresh raw milk (or pasteurized organic milk)

Candy thermometer with clip

¼ cup (60 ml) plain yogurt (Brown Cow or Stonyfield Farm are good), at room temperature

Makes 1 quart (960 ml)

Sterilize the jar and spoon by boiling them in the pot for 10 minutes. Remove from the pot and pour out the water. Pour the milk into the hot jar and set the jar inside the empty pot. Clip the thermometer inside the jar. Pour water into the pot until it comes halfway up the side of the jar and put over medium-high heat. When the thermometer reads 185°F (80°C), remove the jar from the pot, and put on the lid. When the temperature hits 110°F (45°C), open the jar, stir in the room-temp yogurt, put the lid back on, and wrap the jar in a towel. Stick the whole thing into your oven. (Don't turn the oven on; being in the oven just keeps the yogurt a little warmer.)

After about five hours, check the yogurt. If it's too runny, let it sit (up to 12 hours) until it firms up. Make sure to keep it warm enough; open the lid every once in a while to check that the temp remains around 110°F (45°C). The longer yogurt sits, the tarter it gets, so play around to find the balance of firmness and tartness you prefer. Refrigerate the yogurt until you're ready to eat it. Then stir in fruit or sweeteners, or eat it plain.

around the whey, girl

HOMEMADE MOZZARELLA // Jenny Rose Ryan

Whether you're an experienced chef or a mere ramen cooker, making your own cheese is surprisingly simple. All you need are a few ingredients, a couple of inexpensive curd-inspiring substances, and basic kitchen implements, and you'll be eating your own homemade mozzarella in no time. By making cheese yourself, you control the ingredients' quality and, if you source your milk from a local organic dairy, you can even vouch for the cows that made it. Just follow these easy steps for a delicious DIY endeavor.

materials

¼ tablet vegetable rennet (available at www.cheesemaking.com)

¼ cup (60 ml) unchlorinated water (Brita-filtered or bottled water works well)

1 gallon (3.8 L) whole milk (not ultrapasteurized)

6- to 8-quart (5.7 to 7.5-L) stainless-steel pot

1½ to 2 teaspoons citric acid (also at www.cheesemaking.com)

Thermometer

Large microwave-safe bowl

Salt

> Makes 1 large chunk of cheese—about the size of 2 fists

Dissolve the vegetable rennet in ¼ cup (60 ml) cool (but not cold) unchlorinated water and set aside. Next, pour the milk into the pot and add the citric acid as you heat the mixture to 90°F (30°C), stirring all the while. As you near the 90°F (30°C) mark, your milk may start to curdle (the solids separate from the liquid), which is exactly what you want.

When the mixture reaches 90°F (30°C), add the dissolved vegetable rennet and stir from top to bottom (similar to the way you "fold in" eggs while baking) for 30 to 60 seconds. Stop stirring after it's mixed, and turn off the heat. Let sit for three to five minutes as the curd continues to form. The longer the set time, the firmer the curd, and as you become a mozzarella-making master, you'll be able to tweak the cheese to your preference, determining exactly how firm a curd you like.

After the curd sets, use a sharp knife to cut it into 1-inch pieces, like a checkerboard, and fish them out with a slotted spoon. Drop the curds into a microwave-safe bowl, then knead them a little with your knuckles (like bread dough) to release some of the whey. Drain off the whey by holding the curds and tipping the bowl. Heat the lump in the microwave, uncovered, on high power for one minute. Drain again and knead the cheese with a spoon or your hands until it's cool to the touch. Microwave two more times for 30 seconds each, kneading and draining between heating. Continue to knead until the curd becomes smooth and shiny. Depending on the strength of your microwave, you may need to heat it

for another 30 seconds to reach this consistency. Add salt to taste. The curd becomes a real lump of cheese once it has a stretchy, rubbery texture. Form your cheese lump into a ball, then drop it into ice water to cool or refrigerate.

That's it. You made cheese! Now eat it sliced in a caprese salad with tomatoes, basil, olive oil, and balsamic vinegar; shredded on pizza; or in huge handfuls before your roommate or partner discovers it's there. Best to eat it within a couple of days, but it will keep longer in an airtight container.

home-tapped sap

FORAGE FOR MAPLE SYRUP // Ava Chin

If you have sugar-maple trees in your region, you can skip the middleman and forage for your own syrup. Don't have access to a tree of your own? Ask your neighbors if you can tap theirs. Then invite them over for brunch so they can sample the taste of sweet syrup-making success.

tree-tapping

materials

Power drill with ⅜" drill bit

Hammer

Two 3- to 5-gallon (11½- to 19-L) galvanized steel buckets (with tops or aluminum foil to cover)

3"-long, ⅜"-diameter (7 ½-cm-long, 1-cm-diameter) pipe (aluminum or steel only; copper will harm the tree) or a traditional tree tap

About 5' (1½ m) of ¾"-diameter (2-cm-diameter) PVC tubing— long enough to extend from the tap to a grounded bucket (unnecessary if using a traditional tree tap that your bucket hangs from)

Identify a mature sugar-maple tree at least 10" (25 cm) in diameter or with a 31" (78 ½ cm) circumference (anything smaller is too young to tap and could damage the tree). You'll want a healthy tree with lots of branches and leaf coverage. If you're unfamiliar with the tree's look, Google "sugar maple" or *Acer saccharum* for images. Sugar maples are most easily identifiable by their leaves, which the Canadian flag's symbol was modeled after. The tree will be bursting with sap when temperatures hit over 40°F (4°C) during the day, then dip to freezing at night.

Determine the tapping point on the tree: Southern-facing points are better in colder temperatures (early in the season) when the added warmth of southern exposure stimulates sap flow; cooler northern-facing points are useful later in the season, when temperatures above 50°F (10°C) signal the tree to quell production. At about shoulder height, drill slightly upward about 1" to 1½" (2 ½ to 4 cm) in so that gravity can do its work, allowing the sap to flow without harming the tree. Gently hammer in a ⅜" (1 cm) diameter pipe or tap; sap should immediately flow in quiet drips. Slip PVC tubing onto the pipe, and run the opposite end into the bucket, or simply hook the bucket if using a traditional tree tap.

The length of time it takes to fill a bucket with sap depends upon the tree and the temperature. There's more sap production early in the season and less as the weather warms up. When the bucket is full, replace it with a reserve bucket. Three gallons (11 ½ L) of sap makes just over a cup of syrup.

syrup-making

materials

Wide, shallow pan or pot for boiling

Candy thermometer

Mason jars

Funnel

Cheesecloth (optional)

Fill a wide, shallow pan or pot half-full with sap, leaving room so that the eventual boil will not overflow. Cook over high heat until liquid is at a rolling boil. An outdoor cooking space over burning wood is ideal for sugaring—boiling sap down to syrup—but you can do it on your kitchen stove as well; just be sure to use fans and vents if you are indoors, to prevent excessive moisture. Closely monitor cooking temperature with your candy thermometer, especially when it gets close to 219°F (104°C)—it will have started boiling around 160°F (71°C). Syrup is done when it hits that temperature—or when the sap is a deep, golden color, the thickness of good balsamic vinegar, and about a quarter-inch of liquid remains in your pot. (Note: This can take several hours depending upon the consistency and sugar quantity of the sap.)

Funnel syrup into a mason jar. Filter through cheesecloth to remove any sediment or leave unadulterated for super-authentic goodness. Your syrup will keep for about six months in the refrigerator.

pluck and shuck

GATHER YOUR OWN CLAMS // Katherine Goldstein

Clamming can appease your desires to be a hunter, gatherer, mermaid, and gourmet chef all at once. Everyday life is filled with food on the go, and there's something satisfying about slowing down and creating a meal from the fruits of your labors. So, before the water gets too cold in late summer, find some time to find your food. You'll swell with pride once you've shepherded your super-fresh (and free!) seafood from muddy waters to rave culinary reviews.

FIND IT!

Quahogs are a good choice for a first-time clammer because they sit on the bottom of ponds near the ocean throughout Long Island and New England and can't run away from you. Californians can get in on the clamming action in Pismo Beach and San Luis Obispo State Park. Places in the Pacific Northwest, like Tillamook, Oregon, have marinas that will give you the scoop. Wherever you decide to try your luck, ask around to locate a prime spot, and be sure to find out if you need a shellfish permit—you don't want to get hauled off by the Coast Guard!

PLUCK IT!

To become a clam goddess, all you need is a bucket, your bikini, and your bare feet. Quahogs like the reedy muck of brackish ponds, which are usually much warmer than the ocean, so strip down and wade in. Get quiet, focus, and feel for their distinctive, hard shape just below the surface of the pond bottom; in other words, become one with the clams. Then, since you'll often be more than waist deep, cup your feet around the clam and do a plié so you can grab it with your hands. Examine to make sure it's not a rock, throw in bucket, and repeat! Depending on your luck, a half hour to two hours should get you a bucket or two (buy more at a local fish market if you come up short). Keep the clams chillin' in pond water until you're ready to head home. In the kitchen, fill up large bowls of cold water with a few heaping spoonfuls of salt, and let the clams soak for at least 20 minutes to filter out some of the dirt, then scrub them vigorously under running water with a stiff brush before shucking or cooking.

SHUCK IT!

For easier shucking, put clean clams in the freezer for 45 minutes or in ice water for 1 hour. Wear a glove or cover your palm with a thick towel and cup the clam in that hand. Take a clam knife (OXO makes a good one) and press it between where the shells meet. Once the knife is inside the clam, twist it until the shell pops, moving the knife toward the top of the shell to cut the muscles so it will open. Run the knife under the clam meat to loosen it for easy eating. Serve with lemon, cocktail sauce, or horseradish. And as a rule of thumb, any that open with no effort or refuse to budge are bad, so throw them out.

STEAM IT!

Shucking's not the only way to get the little devils open. Fill a large pot with two inches (5 cm) of water and bring to a simmer. Pile in the clams and steam for 5 to 10 minutes, removing them as the shells begin to open. Pry the shells open with your fingers or a blunt knife. Eat the steamed clams with butter and condiments.

FRY IT!

Here's a recipe for Seat-of-Your-Pants Fried Clams: Combine one cup (255 g) flour, one cup (255 g) cornmeal, three-quarter tablespoon salt, and one teaspoon pepper in a large Ziploc bag. Add raw shucked or steamed and shelled clams and shake until well coated. In a skillet, heat up three-quarter inch (2 cm) of vegetable oil over medium heat until crackling hot. Turn up slightly when you put the clams in, fitting as many into your pan as possible without them touching. Fry for about one minute, or until brown. Drain on paper towels and squeeze lemon juice on top. Serve with tartar sauce.

MOVING & SHAKING

buy curious

BUYING AN OLD HOUSE // Shelley Cadamy

Whether you think that haunted-looking Victorian down the street is in need of your TLC or you grew up in a cookie-cutter house in the burbs and crave a historic home, buying an old house is possible, even on a tight budget. Follow these tips and you'll be rocking on your porch in no time.

FIND A FIXER-UPPER

It might be a no-brainer, but fixer-uppers are cheaper than a fully restored home. They also have probably retained more of their original fixtures, because they've escaped the "improvement" of having the claw-footed tub replaced with a newfangled plastic stand-up shower or faux-rock vinyl floor hastily pasted over timeworn parquet. Since you'll be doing the work yourself, you can make sure it's done right. Plus, there is something wonderful about sitting at your day job all day and then whacking away at a plaster wall in the evening.

The city planning department should be able to give you information on historic and current property values in neighborhoods that interest you (and they often have this info on their website). Once you find a place you like, it's imperative that a trusted home inspector examine the house before you buy it. Ask your friends or your real estate agent if they can recommend someone. Take the inspector's advice and hire any additional experts (engineers, etc.) to look at the house before you sign on the dotted line. Together with your realtor, determine what the potential market value of the house could be and make sure the cost of any necessary repairs will not exceed that amount.

CONSIDER A 203K LOAN

A good way to finance your restoration is a 203K loan from Housing and Urban Development (HUD)—yes, it's available everywhere in the U.S. This loan program allows a home buyer of limited means to finance both the purchase of a house and the cost of its rehabilitation through a single mortgage. Basically, any single-family dwelling is eligible. Most improvements are eligible as well, except for luxury items, like swimming pools and saunas. In addition to this HUD program, some cities and states offer grants for historic home renovations. Talk with a trusted mortgage professional (again, referrals are your friend) to find the options that will work best for you.

THE HOUSE IS YOURS

Once you close, decide what repairs you can do yourself. Consider the amount of time a job will take, in addition to the cost, when you're budgeting. If you're going it alone, the time you spend working is cash that stays in your pocket . . . which you might just need to cover those extra costs you can't see until you tear down a wall. You can learn an amazing amount from do-it-yourself books and from sites like www.oldhouseweb.com and www.oldhousejournal.com.

To kick off the work on your house, host an All-Girl Demolition Day, where your ladyfriends rip down paneling, pull up carpet, and haul off trash and debris. In return, feed them pizza and beer.

If you need to make substantial improvements that must be completed by professionals—such as the installation of air conditioning, heating systems, or electrical work—consider hiring a general contractor. For example, replacing a basement wall might require a plumber, electrician, and concrete team to all show up at the same time for several days. By hiring a general contractor to coordinate the various teams, you save money and days off from work. If you want to serve as your own general contractor and hire these teams yourself, approach it as you would any other hiring process. Do interviews, get references, and ask for photos of past work. Don't be afraid to interview 14 electricians; it may take that long to find one who comes across as reliable and has those other reference items to match. Beware of anyone who will not provide references, is not properly licensed in your state, or who suggests, "All that needs to be ripped out, 'cause it's old." And, if at any time in the process you don't like how things are going or the budget is being ignored, don't be afraid to fire them.

When your house is finally done, you'll have the satisfaction of knowing you brought a gem out of the rough, and you'll also be glad to watch your sweat turn into real equity as the housing market recognizes your newfound expertise.

When choosing an old house, look for the worst house on the best block you can afford.

home, a loan

FINANCING A HOUSE // Jenny Ramo

So, you have decided you want to own your place. Congratulations! Now it's time to talk money. The home-financing process isn't that complicated when you get right down to it. You just have to know what you're agreeing to do before you sign away your paycheck. Don't like it? Don't sign.

THE DOWN PAYMENT

The down payment is the money you pay the seller yourself. In an ideal world, you will sock away enough for a 20 percent down payment on the house you want to buy, but even if you only manage to save 10 percent, most lenders will allow it. Some lenders will even go as low as 3 percent, but remember: The larger the down payment, the lower your mortgage loan—and your monthly payments—will be. Even if the economy is down, a mortgage can be a good thing: in recessions, interest rates are generally reasonable, and if boarded-up houses are cropping up everywhere, you can help heal a community you love.

There are many ways to creatively piece together enough money for a down payment. Here are some sources to get that money.

High-Interest Savings

Set up a savings account with an online bank that pays high interest (just make sure your online account is FDIC-insured and checks out with the Better Business Bureau). Don't get an ATM card for this account; without one, transferring money to your regular checking account will take several days, at which point any urge to blow a bunch of money will usually subside.

Parental Savings and Loan

Since the dawn of time, parents have helped their children settle comfortably into their grown-up lives. If they will lend you the money or can borrow it for you, suck up your pride and just be grateful.

Get a Loan for the Down Payment

You can get two loans to cover the entire price of the house: a loan for the down payment and another loan for the rest of the house price. The good side to this is that you can buy a house without having the money for a down payment. The bad side is that if you sell your house for less than you paid for it, your debt to the bank is still based on the original price.

Take Money Out of Your IRA

Usually if you take money out of this fund before you are 812 years old (actually, it's 60, but that seems like 812), you pay a penalty. But, if you are a first-time home buyer, you may be able to withdraw without the fee. Obviously, you miss out on the tax-free development of that money, but it may be worth it to get some equity in a home.

THE MORTGAGE

The mortgage is the amount you borrow from the bank to pay the seller the rest of their money. Before you choose what kind of mortgage you want, consider these factors.

How Are the Rates?

Mortgages come in many shapes and sizes. You can pay it off at an interest rate that stays the same for the whole term, or with an interest rate that starts low and changes in five years.

Adjustable-rate loans can be tantalizing with their low initial rates, but you also can't predict where the rates will go when they readjust. Choosing a fixed-rate mortgage means you will have the same payment for the life of the loan. If interest rates are high when you're shopping for a loan, you might decide to choose one with an adjustable rate, because the rate was already high when you started. If interest rates are low, you will want to lock them in for the whole 30 years of your mortgage, so your payment doesn't skyrocket when interest rates do.

How Long Will You Live in the House?

If you think you'll be moving out in a few years, it might be worth it to take a mortgage that starts with a low interest rate and changes in five years. But if you've found the house you want to grow old in, you'd be better off getting the 30-year mortgage at a slightly higher rate, as it will be stable even if interest rates double.

What Monthly Payment Can You Afford?

You can find mortgage calculators online which allow you to calculate how much your monthly payment will be. If you put down less than 20 percent, you may have to pay something called PMI or mortgage insurance—so factor that in.

THE NEGOTIATION

One thing most people fail to do when getting a mortgage is negotiate with the mortgage broker. Not only is the rate negotiable, but so is how much you have to pay for the transaction. Generally, the following fees (that can add up to several thousand dollars) can be potentially negotiated away: origination, appraisal, administrative, and your credit report.

The origination fee can be anywhere from 0 to 2 percent of the transaction. This pays the broker for her work. To figure out how much of a risk the bank is taking by giving you a loan on the house you have chosen, they appraise it and charge an appraisal fee. The bank often asks for an administrative fee to cover the processing of the loan. Almost anyone who has rented an apartment has had their credit checked with a credit report. It does not cost much, and if the broker really wants your business, she should simply swallow the fee.

Call up five or six mortgage brokers; they'll ask you for your financial stats (income, savings, expenses, how much you plan to spend on a house) and run your credit report. If you have good credit, low debt, reasonable income, and some cash on hand, you should be able to get preapproved for a loan. Get information from each broker on the loans they're offering, including rates (fixed or adjustable), length of term (15 or 30 years), and the size of the loan they're willing to preapprove. Think about what you want and can realistically afford, not what the mortgage broker wants to sell you.

Then call each back, let them know you've spoken with other brokers, and ask if they can do any better on some of the fees and on the interest rate. When one offers you a good price, call the others and let them know the best deal you have been given, and see if they can beat it. It is a great way to negotiate, as you also get a sense of the broker you are working with and how they answer the tough questions.

whose house? my house!

BEING A LANDLADY // Vikki Warner

If you can't afford that cozy, immaculate, single-family dream house, buying a multifamily crash pad might be your key to home ownership. By channeling your inner Mrs. Roper, you'll have built-in contributions to the mortgage. So, stop fantasizing about being a homeowner and start putting your plan into action.

GET IN THE MOOD

Buying a multifamily house is not the first option prospective buyers think of, and for that reason, it's a quiet but powerful way to start your empire. All you need is the willingness to save up some money; wield a drill, paintbrush, or sander; and keep a calm head and a bit of cash in the coffers. You'll have the security of knowing you'll never be kicked out of your apartment because the landlord found someone who would pay more in rent. It will also give you the freedom to do what you want with your place and to be the landlady you wished you'd had.

CALCULATE THE CASH

Once you've socked away enough money for a down payment and have figured out the size of the loan you're looking to take on (see page 280), you can figure out how much income from rentals you need to offset the monthly mortgage bill. As you house shop, familiarize yourself with the rental market in each neighborhood so you can estimate the value of the units in the house based on their features. In the planning stages, it's best to lowball on your rent estimates so you know your bills will be paid even if you get a little less than you'd like. So, if you receive $1,500 in rent monthly, which is then applied to a $1,900 mortgage bill, and your tenants pay their own utilities (outside of the wayward water bill or repair), then the mortgage will be the only house-related expense. It's a good idea to have at least one month's mortgage just hanging out in your savings account, in case of a tenant's quick departure or inability to pay, or a sudden problem with your own finances.

DON'T AVOID THE ICKY TAX STUFF

Be sure to investigate any tax incentives available in your future neighborhood. Owning a multifamily home is a good tax proposition—you can take advantage of both income-tax deductions (which lower your taxable income) and property-tax credits (which are taken off the top of your city tax bill). City property-tax credits include incentives like "homestead" credits for owner-occupied multifamily homes, and some cities also offer tax credits to buyers of foreclosed houses. A visit to City Hall can help you sniff out property-tax credits that apply to your situation—they can change yearly, so stay on top of the new rules.

If you're looking at a fixer-upper, consult with an accountant who knows about what income-tax deductions you can get. Stuff like mortgage interest, repair costs, and buying energy-efficient appliances is often tax deductible, and in some areas, every dollar spent to renovate a multifamily house is tax deductible. It's important to get an independent inspector to nitpick the house from attic to basement. You'll get a thorough picture of what needs attention, both now and later, and what's in good shape already.

REPAIRING YOUR HOUSE, LOSING YOUR MIND

Fixing the problems identified by the inspector eats up tons of cash, so keep this in mind as you consider your potential purchase: Everything costs more than you expect it to, no matter how well you plan. One major way to avoid spending more than you have to is to learn how to make repairs or improvements yourself. Try to make improvements constantly; even little ones can keep you motivated. For what you can't do alone, call on friends to help; you can thank them by throwing a big party when the work is done.

DUDE, I HAVE TENANTS. WEIRD.

Before you make an offer, visit the neighborhood you're considering at all hours to make sure it's not crazy loud or filled with unsavory characters. Buying in a city where you have friends is key if you want to be a landlady— this way you have a prescreened network of potential non-creepy tenants.

If you start by renting only to people you know, you can take a lot of guesswork out of being a landlady. But if you can't rent to people you know, look for referrals from friends or coworkers, and get a sense of prospective tenants' interests, habits, and personalities to make sure you want to have them around. It can be tempting to rent to any old person just to get the bills paid, but it's always better to wait, get the word out to everyone you can, and calmly sort through your options.

Building good relationships with tenants is the easiest part of being a landlady—if you choose them wisely and maintain a cool head. Be accessible when they have requests, even if you can't fulfill them right away; at least offer some plan of action for the near future. It sounds odd, too, but don't expect rent checks on time; if you're prepared to shell out a bit extra in the event a tenant can't pay on the first of the month, you can avoid stressing about the mortgage—and you'll get the cash back in a day or two. Finally, check with your city's housing authority for landlord/tenant laws and find a good boilerplate lease agreement to have on hand—many are available online.

ira, 401(k), wtf?

A GUIDE TO SAVING AND INVESTING // Amy Keyishian

There are still plenty of us out there who don't know a 401(k) from a 40 DD, a money market from a flea market, or a mutual fund from a mutual orgasm. And you may feel that, unless you're on the fast track to a corporate career, financial planning is as irrelevant to your life as nude pantyhose or a Brooks Brothers blazer. While it may seem impossible to wrap your mind around saving, investing, and generally being responsible with the few dollars you make, there's nothing to say you can't learn to organize your money so it'll work for you. It's really just a matter of mind-set.

Women tend to be good savers, smart spenders, and sensible shoppers. We do make less than men, so we have to invest smarter just to break even, but research shows that women control something like 80 percent of all consumer purchases, so we must be doing something right. So get your slice of the financial pie. You're going to need it in the long run.

WHO, ME? YES, YOU

At the moment, you make so little, you can't imagine you could actually set anything aside. "I know, I know—I know that check-to-check feeling so well," commiserates Dayana Yochim, senior writer for Motley Fool (www.fool.com). "But there's really no such thing as 'too little to save.' Even if it's just five bucks a week, it'll get you into the habit of putting something aside." Once you see your nest egg grow, she promises, you'll get addicted to the heady thrill of having something to fall back on.

The reasons for saving are more than just a finger-waggy "should," according to Galia Gichon, a financial educator and founder of www.downtoearthfinance.com, which provides independent financial education to women. "We make less than men, so we save less than men," she points out. "We also live longer, and women tend to take off about 11 years from their working career to care for children and parents—those are times when you're not working, and therefore not saving." Even if you don't have kids—or if you don't want to burden the kids you do have with a looming need for help later—you've still got to come up with a plan for your later years. The vague sense that some husband/book-sold-for-film-rights/lotto jackpot will come to your rescue is not actually going to pay the bills.

If you can't get excited about saving for your gray days, there's also the here and now to consider. If you want a piece of that real-estate pie, you'll need money for a down payment, which means a couple years of serious saving. Why own instead of rent? "If you own a home, you have equity," says Gichon. If you spend $12,000 a year on rent, it's gone forever. But spend that $12,000 on buying a place, and when you resell it, you

should get most of that money back (and sometimes much more). This is why renting is sometimes called "throwing your money out the window."

STARTING SLOW

The dreary realities of health—financial or physical—just aren't sexy. But if you want to start saving the big bucks, you gotta start somewhere. Having savings means that if something happens, you won't have to freak out, scramble, beg your parents, or rely on those evil credit cards. And a debt load of nearly zero is sexy as hell to banks (who'd give you the money for a mortgage).

The first task to get things on track is to really assess your situation. Is your debt out of control? Are you living check-to-check, and if so, where does your money really go? Make a list of your monthly "nut"—the money you *have* to spend. Start with the basics, like rent, utilities, transportation, and phone. Include groceries, but keep in mind that it's a number that can change drastically.

Take your income and subtract that nut. The leftover money is your "discretionary income," the stuff you can spend. Now comes the hardest part: figuring out where that cash goes every month. If you spend a lot with your bank card or credit card, you can probably look at your bank statement (or online) to see where it all went. If not, you'll have to walk around writing every stinking penny down for a week or two. "I did this for two months and it became like a game—the Cheapskate Game," Yochim says. "I probably wasn't that fun to go out with, but it made that stomach-churning feeling go away—and I felt more in control. I called the result of my investigation my 'spendy-total.'"

After two weeks of obsessively tracking your pennies, take the spendy-total and subtract

it from your "discretionary income." We'll call the remaining number "the Naked, Horrible Truth." If your spendy-total is bigger than your discretionary income, things are going to get shitty. If you have some left over, you're in good shape to start saving. Either way, once you've confronted the realities of where your money goes, you can put it in other places. Smart places.

A BAY OF PIGGY BANKS

The secret to trackable, easily organized investing is to have a lot of different accounts set up for specific purposes—that way you can keep your different nest eggs separate. Here's the ideal setup:

1 Your checking account. Come up with a two-week budget, and only keep what you're allowed to spend—on bills and on discretionary fun—in there. "This is basically an allowance," says Gichon. "You're giving yourself money for the week, and you're free to spend it all on one big dinner, or eat nothing but yogurt and have extra money next week."

2 Your holy-crap money. Make a regular contribution until you have three to six months' worth of expenses saved up. Put it in something like a money-market account, which you can get to if you have to, but not so easily that you'll do so on the spur of the moment.

3 Your short-term-goal account. Whether you're saving up for a down payment, a car, a pair of Blahniks, or a trip to Amsterdam, you've got to put that money where it'll earn interest. And since you know pretty much exactly when you'll need it, a good place to put it is in a CD, or certificate of deposit, available from your bank. You buy these in blocks of time, typically anywhere from 3 to 12 months—promising not to withdraw during that time, or risk a huge penalty—so there's really no chance of cheating. Another way to go is a Roth IRA. You can withdraw up to all the money you put in (but not the earnings), so these accounts are ideal for saving up for a down payment.

4 Your retirement account (this is your 401(k) and/or your SEP IRA).

5 A regular savings account. Anything that doesn't go into items 1 through 4 can go here, and maybe you can up your allowance—or just save more.

So how do you break up your money so you know how much to put into each piggy bank? Experts have rules for this, too, and the most widely used comes from a guy named Richard Jenkins. He recommends a breakdown called "the 60 Percent Solution," and it goes a little something like this (all amounts are for gross income—before taxes are taken out):

- 60 percent to "committed expenses" (your monthly nut)
- 10 percent fun money (discretionary income)
- 10 percent irregular expenses (your holy-crap fund)
- 10 percent retirement fund
- 10 percent to debt reduction—if that's done, it can go to savings

You might have heard that, say, you're not supposed to spend more than 25 percent of your income on rent and thrown up your hands in utter frustration at that stingy amount. It's true; in urban centers, that's just not a realistic figure. "However," points out Yochim, "since you're not in the suburbs, you're probably not making car payments or [automotive] insurance payments—so you get screwed on rent, but you come out ahead in transportation." As long as your nut stays under the 60 percent mark, you can still come out ahead.

WHERE TO SAVE

You've probably heard about "the latte factor," even if you didn't know it was called that. That's when those annoying articles tell you that if you don't buy a two-dollar gourmet coffee each day, and instead drink the office swill or make it at home, you'll save $500 a year, which is a healthy nest-egg contribution.

The good news on that is that you are allowed to indulge where it really improves your quality of life. "Spending is like dieting," says Gichon. "Excessive diets don't work, and neither do excessive budgets. Just prioritize what's really 'necessary.'"

DEBT DIVAS

Debt is riding the general public like an oversized jockey weighing down an exhausted thoroughbred. You have to get that jockey off your back, Seabiscuit. Stay on that allowance, no matter what, and cut up your credit card until it's paid off. If you've got student loans and credit-card debt, it's worth looking into a student-loan consolidation. Essentially, it means refinancing all your student loans into one at a lower interest rate and extending your repayment period out to 15 or 20 years. That way, it's less of a strain on your monthly nut.

WORK IN AN OFFICE?

If you have a desk job and a regular income, do they offer a 401(k) or a 403(b) plan? A 401(k) is a savings plan that you can't touch till you retire. The plan is run by an outside investment firm, such as Fidelity, that gives you a choice of mutual funds and money markets to put your money in. The money comes out of your paycheck before taxes, which means your taxable income goes down. You won't have to pay taxes on the money you put away until you retire, at which point you could be in a much lower bracket. Basically, it's free money, albeit money that you can't yet touch. A 403(b) plan is the same thing, only for teachers, government workers, and people who work at nonprofits.

If you have the chance, put as much as you can stand into that 401(k). Many companies "match" those funds; they pay into your retirement at the same rate you do—that's more free money. You may think you're too young to invest, but every expert cites the example of the girl who started saving at 25 instead of 35. Basically, she has a shitload more money because she started earlier, and if she'd started later, she'd want to kill herself for being such an asshole at 25. Take heed.

If your office doesn't offer a 401(k), you can set one up for yourself; it's called an IRA, or an Individual Retirement Account. There are a few kinds. A deductible IRA works just like a 401(k)—you can put up to a certain amount in your account each year tax-free (in 2010 it was $5,000). You can tell your bank to put 10 percent of each paycheck automatically in your IRA before you even touch it—just like a 401(k) does. The more you can automate, the better. If you don't see the money, you get used to not spending it.

FREELANCE WOES

What if you freelance and never fricking know when the next check is coming? Then it's extra important for you to set up a holy-crap savings account—the one that you'll fall back on if something horrible happens, like you don't work for three months. "It's your safety net," says Yochim, "and you should have it whether you have a regular income or not—but if your income is irregular, it's even more important." The rule of thumb is three months safety net if you have a full-time job, and six months if you are a freelancer. To even start accumulating that safety net, you have to get a handle on your spending and your income. The only way to do that is to come up with an approximate, realistic yearly income and divide by 12; that's your monthly budget, and you just have to do your best to live within it. (Having the holy-crap money will help; you can borrow from that, as long as you pay yourself back the minute the checks roll in.) Make sure you think about yearly taxes, too, and set aside the amount you'll owe so you don't have to dig into your real savings when tax time hits.

Once you build up your safety net, you can set up your own retirement account— a SEP IRA. It stands for Simplified Employee Pension, but think of it as the Self-Employed Plan.

girls just wanna have funds

START A WOMEN'S INVESTMENT CLUB // Hope Swindle

Are you a member of that meek herd of people who go blank when you think about the stock market (if you think of it at all)? Grab a gaggle of girlfriends and start a women's-only investment group, and you too can play the game. Soon, your collective desire not to end up penniless, clueless, and dependent on fathers or cunning bandits for financial security can be made into reality. To get started, all you need is a small nest egg to invest, a few on-call "consultants" for their expertise, and the desire to flex your financial muscles.

GETTING IT TOGETHER

First, get a group of women together who are equally clueless but inspired to change that fact. Writers, pediatricians, yoga teachers, opera singers—whatever. Have each member contribute an equal share each month ($40 is a good place to start); take this money and invest-invest-invest. Use a broker, who will actually purchase the stocks for you, and have fun as you take a risk on the stocks you have a feeling about. Dow101.com has a complete list of stocks available in the Dow Jones Industrial Average Composite Index ("the Dow"). Hot tips from *Forbes* might find their way into the mix. Maybe you'll decide to buy shares of a young upstart juice company because someone's boyfriend worked there. Perhaps you'll invest in a software manufacturer that someone

had read could be red hot. Maybe you'll even read a blue-chip company's annual report. Combine monthly buying and selling sessions with a potluck feast and you'll be doing it all in style.

KEEPING THE BALL ROLLING

If, by the next meeting, the software company has dropped 10 points, don't panic. Think of investing, even in stocks, as a plan for the long haul. While it's tempting to pore over the returns, don't be too much of a market watcher. The Dow Jones Industrials, for example, don't represent each company, just an average, and if that's anything like average weight/height ratios, we know never to trust those things. And here's the biggest secret of all: Diversify! Remember never to have all your collective money in one area of the market in case it tanks.

ONCE YOU'VE GOT MOMENTUM

Need to increase membership so you can invest even more? Hold info-gathering sessions where you share your knowledge. Invite women veterans from the industry's front lines to share their sage wisdom about the market and how you, too, can benefit from investing in stocks and bonds. These ladies are tough: power suits, frosted highlights, pert diagrams—all of it straight from the trenches. Break the code. Learn the lingo. Make it rain and put away your own little pots of gold. Maybe you'll still occasionally fantasize about marrying money, but at least you know you'll be the one calling the broker.

mad money

GIVE BAD SITUATIONS THE FINGER WITH A FUCK-YOU FUND // Tara Bracco

You may already be building an emergency fund and putting money into a retirement account, or at least planning to, but chances are you're still missing an important financial security blanket: The Fuck-You Fund.

The FU Fund is a stash of cash that allows you to ditch a crappy job or a harmful relationship without money being an obstacle. It's that pile of money that lets you turn your life around, even if it's not technically an emergency. And it's cooler and more empowering than an emergency fund, because it enables you to make proactive, healthy choices about your life. "The FU Fund is the financial equivalent of a mental-health day," says Manisha Thakor, coauthor of *On My Own Two Feet: A Modern Girl's Guide to Personal Finance.* "It's about taking back the power and saying, 'I deserve to be happy.'"

Ideally, gals should have enough cash to give themselves the freedom to make proactive choices and to respond to life's unexpected crises. The right amount of savings varies for each woman, but in general, Thakor says, it makes good sense to shoot for having three months' worth of essential living expenses reserved in an emergency fund and three months' worth of expenses set aside in a Fuck You Fund. With this level of financial security, ladies are less likely to feel stuck in bad professional or personal situations.

The idea of an FU Fund is not new. Financially intelligent guys know they need access to cash if they want to up and leave their jobs, but this theory is not part of the female vernacular. Maybe the ladies are more accustomed to the concept of an emergency fund, but this sets up the idea that savings are just a cushion in case of a crisis. As a result, women are hesitant to use their stockpiled pennies in ways that might further their goals or happiness, because it feels irresponsible to spend emergency money in this way. This reluctance, Thakor says, mostly stems from women having limited nest eggs to begin with. Boo to that. But yay to FU! Think of it this way: having an FU Fund could mean the difference between dragging your ass to that awful job day in and day out and having the flexibility to move on to a life you'll love.

emergency room

GETTING HEALTH CARE WITHOUT HEALTH INSURANCE // Emily Farris

Everyone knows it's a good idea to have health insurance, but sadly, that's a luxury not all Americans can afford. If you're one of the unlucky ones, here are ways to get the care you need without going into crazy debt.

IN CASE OF EMERGENCY

If you've wrecked yourself on the roller rink, skate straight to a public hospital. They're required to treat everyone—with or without insurance—and many public hospitals can be found around the country. Unless you're insanely broke, you'll have to pay something, but public hospitals often offer sliding scales and payment arrangements. To find one near you, visit the Membership Directory page of the National Association of Public Hospitals and Health Systems' Web site (www.naph.org).

LADY PARTS

A lot of ladies' reproductive organs are covered because they qualify for low-cost ob-gyn care through Planned Parenthood. Many of their U.S. locations offer sliding-scale payments based on Title X, a federal program that helps provide low-income U.S. residents with family-planning services. You qualify for discounted fees for annual exams, pregnancy and STD testing, and contraception if your annual income is within 250 percent of your state's poverty level. Call your local Planned Parenthood to see if you're eligible (1-800-230-PLAN).

WHAT'S UP DOC?

Free health clinics offer basic health-care services at no cost to those who don't have insurance, regardless of income. They're the perfect option when you need non-emergency treatment. It might take a little persistence to get an appointment, but the care these clinics provide is "very similar, if not identical, to a private provider" says Peg McKee, director of development at the Kansas City Free Health Clinic in Kansas City, Missouri. Locate one in your city at www.freeclinics.us.

GRIN AND BEAR IT

Dental schools are a fantastic option for people without dental insurance. "Visits with dental students tend to take about three times longer than if you were visiting a private dental practice," says Sandra Shagat of the UCLA School of Dentistry, where the cost of care is about half of what nearby private practices charge. But "the person working on your mouth will be closely supervised by someone who's been practicing for several years." To find a local American Dental Association–accredited school, go to the Dental Education Program page at www.ada.org.

tax broad

AVOIDING AN IRS MESS // Eva Rosenberg

When it comes to taxes, most of us think about them as little as possible—and try to pay as little as legally possible. But navigating through allowances, deductions, forms, and filing is no picnic. That's why we tapped tax professional and founder of TaxMama.com, Eva Rosenberg, for advice on reducing the pain factor, whether you work for the Man, for yourself, or someone in between.

WORKING FOR THE MAN

Clocking in on somebody else's dime means you got a W-2 in January that has all the info you need to file your taxes. If you usually end up with a refund, update your W-4 form with your company's payroll department: for every $2,500 you get back from the IRS, increase the number of allowances you're taking by one. Sure, a refund can seem like an awesome windfall, but if you increase your allowances, that means you, rather than the IRS, earn interest on your money. So take that extra cash you'll see in your paycheck and send it straight to a savings account.

There's nothing worse than owing taxes. If you fall into that category, update your W-4 form reducing your allowances by one for every $2,500 you owe. This will increase the amount of taxes your company withholds, so you'll see a bit less in your paycheck, but it will be worth it come next tax time.

TAKING CARE OF (YOUR OWN) BUSINESS

Being self-employed means no W-2 for you, which can make tax time a little more complicated. Especially with Uncle Sam tightening his grip on small-business owners—who the IRS has determined are most likely to underreport their income or underpay their taxes.

If your gig involves performing services, each of your clients should have sent you a 1099-MISC form in January, which shows the full amount they paid you during the previous year. Many clients will ask you to sign a W-9 form before they pay you for services, so they can use that information to fill in the 1099-MISC. To reduce the potential for identity theft, give them an Employer Identification Number (you can get one at www.irs.gov) rather than your Social Security Number. If your business sells goods, you won't be getting 1099s from anyone, so you have to track your own income and report those sales on your tax return.

Being your own boss means paying your own taxes, which you should do by making quarterly estimated payments—you may face underpayment penalties by waiting until the end of the year. Since the payments are due on odd, hard-to-remember dates, automate them to come straight outta your bank account by signing up for the IRS's free Electronic Federal Tax Payment System at www.eftps.gov. Chapter 2 of *IRS Publication 505: Tax Withholding and Estimated Tax* provides info on how much to pay, but here's a calculation shortcut: you need to pay self-employment taxes of 15.3 percent of your profits in addition to income tax, so depositing 20 to 30 percent of your profits (money you make after deducting your expenses for materials, office space, utilities, etc.) will usually be enough, depending on your tax bracket (the higher your taxable income, the higher your tax rate).

BEST OF BOTH WORLDS
Some folks run a business in addition to holding down a job. Obviously, you have to report and pay taxes on all the green you glean. But rather than making quarterly payments on your self-employed income, make it easier on yourself by simply increasing your withholding at your job.

Now a little info about deductions. Everyone should keep records, whether you're self-employed or work for someone else. You never know what will be worth a deduction, and it's much easier to save a receipt than re-create it. For information on what's deductible, *IRS Publication 17: Your Federal Income Tax* is a good starting point. The key is organization. The Tax MiniMiser (www.taxminimiser.com) is a perfect tool for keeping mileage records, holding receipts, and summarizing expenditures.

CH-CH-CH-CH-CH-CHANGES
If you happen to move to a new state, you may need to file in two places. Multistate tax returns are sticky business, so it's best to have those prepared by a professional. You may think you're saving money by doing it yourself, but you'll probably end up paying twice as much in taxes as you should.

If you tied the knot, the IRS wants to know about it. Even if you said "I do" a minute before midnight on December 31, for tax-return purposes, you've been married for the whole year. Generally, your best option is to file a joint return. But if your spouse has any unpaid IRS or state taxes, child support, alimony, student debt, or certain other kinds of government debt—hightail it to a tax professional. They'll let you know if you're better off filing separately.

wage slave

A DAY-JOB SURVIVAL GUIDE FOR ARTY GIRLS // Michelle Goodman

Not every working girl dreams of clawing her way to the corner office. Instead, you might fantasize about getting paid piles of cash to write travel articles, design clothes, photograph celebrities, or illustrate children's books. Nevertheless, art junkies do have financial obligations—school loans to pay off, housing and car payments to make, trips to Europe to save for—so we need a day job to pay the bills. Which is precisely when creative atrophy can set in. But having a day job doesn't mean you have to sell your creative dreams down the river. You just need to make time to create and psych yourself up to do it. It's about developing a habit—until you couldn't turn back if you wanted to.

SO WHAT DO YOU DO?

Let's get one thing straight: there's no shame in having a steady gig that covers your rent, keeps you debt-free, and lands you some decent health insurance. "I think the glamour and romance that we once assigned to being a starving artist is so over," says Heather Swain, who wrote the first of her published novels while teaching third grade at a New York City school. "You have to balance and compromise for art, and there's dignity in that."

The idea is to find a stable, decent-paying job that doesn't make you stay late, commute too far, or collapse to the floor in a twitching heap. After all, a girl only has so much energy. For your nine-to-five or nine-to-one job, take something completely removed from what you do creatively.

Ask any art junkie who's paid her dues, and she'll show you a resume filled with temp, secretarial, bartending, and dog-walking jobs—all gigs you can stop thinking about the second your shift ends. But a noncreative job in your field can yield great perks, too. For example, a musician working as a lackey at a record label could learn her way around the business and make priceless contacts.

RIGHT TO CHOOSE

No matter how low-key your day job is, you're still bound to have crappy days that threaten to squelch your creative drive. "It's very easy to tell yourself you don't have time," says Swain. "But it's never an issue of time—it's an issue of priority."

In other words, waiting for the time, energy, or inspiration to strike is like waiting for a couple thousand dollars to miraculously appear in your bank account. Think about it this way: If you were saving for a three-month trip to New Zealand, you'd cut back on sushi dinners, concerts, and new shoes, right? So, you just need to trim the fat from your nonwork schedule to make room for your creativity fix. Sacrificing sleep, meals, and exercise doesn't count, but a few other cuts do. You don't really need as much TV as you've been watching. You also don't need to talk to your friends for 40 minutes a night and be their shrink.

To see where your biggest time hits are, Keri Smith, a former bookstore clerk who penned *Living Out Loud: Activities to Fuel a Creative Life* and now works full-time as a freelance illustrator in Toronto, suggests taking an inventory of your nonworking hours for a week—a sort of "where did all my bleeping time go?" list. You'll probably discover you spend untold hours instant messaging friends, rearranging your closet, and reading online personal ads—time you could devote to something a tad more

creative. That's not to say you should nix all your downtime or become a hermit. Just see where you can scale back, if only by an hour a week.

Even the less frivolous probably spend at least a couple of hours a week waiting for something or someone—like the subway or a friend who's late for dinner. If you drive to work, bring along a tape recorder to brainstorm ideas. Better still, ditch your car keys, grab a pen and paper, and hop on the bus. You know you've got however long your commute takes to kill, so why not spend it with your notebook?

BITE-SIZED PIECES

As Jill Badonsky, a creativity coach and author of *The Nine Modern Day Muses (and a Bodyguard): 10 Guides to Creative Inspiration for Artists, Poets, Lovers and Other Mortals Wanting to Live a Dazzling Existence* explains, feeling overwhelmed by creative goals is another reason you may have trouble leaping from burned-out wage slave to dedicated art girl. Perhaps your ambitions are so lofty (overnight literary sensation, NEA grant recipient), that you don't know where to begin. Or maybe you're too busy comparing yourself to more successful artists, an act that Badonsky says "is just deadly in the creative process."

All this angst is about as productive as expecting to sprout gigantic biceps your first week at the gym. The bottom line is that you've got to start somewhere, just like your art idols did (no doubt while mooching off their relatives or toiling away at a day job). Wading in s-l-o-w-l-y is your best bet. Badonsky suggests sitting down to at least three bite-sized chunks of creative time a week, even if they're only 15 minutes each. "Breaking things down seems to resonate with people," the California-based counselor of 25 years says. "The minutes start to add up and then you build this momentum that's so much easier to stick with."

Taking baby steps toward your goals can also help if you battle that nasty P word: procrastination. If you've ever glanced at your easel or sewing machine only to be overcome by an inexplicable urge to alphabetize your CD collection, you know what this means. Next time the P word strikes, just tell yourself you'll clean the bathroom after 10 minutes of creative time. Ten bucks says you forget all about the toilet bowl.

GIRL'S GOT A HABIT

As Smith, the *Living Out Loud* author, explains, the quickest route to addiction is to develop a creative routine. Your first order of business is to figure out when you do your best work. Are you a card-carrying vampire who's most prolific after midnight, or one of those annoying people who's insanely chipper at the crack of dawn? Swain, who swears she isn't a morning person, spent three years working on her first novel from five to seven a.m.—because they were her most productive hours. Just figure out what works best for you.

No matter what routine you adopt, "you have to be ruthlessly committed to your creative time," says Badonsky, the creativity coach. Here's where your "where did all my bleeping time go?" list comes in handy. Once you've freed up time slots for your creative fix, she explains, block them off in your calendar and "make it as important as a doctor's appointment."

Note to art fiends having the workweek from hell: it's okay to skip a creative appointment when the rest of your life is spiraling out of control. If you're not up to grabbing your pen or guitar pick, Badonsky suggests reading a magazine about your craft, doing some project research, or brainstorming. This still counts as being creative, so no need to flog yourself.

THE BUDDY SYSTEM

There's nothing like someone else's boot in your ass, be it a writing teacher or an art partner in crime, to help you get serious about your habit. Badonsky is an advocate of using night classes to keep your creative juices flowing. "If you take a class, even if it's after work, somehow you manage to psych yourself up," she says. The structure and the homework assignments help, as does the fact that you've coughed up cold hard cash to be there. More importantly, connecting with other members of your creative tribe can be invigorating.

But you don't have to break your piggy bank to get this camaraderie. Crafty clubs—from band practice to writing groups to stitch 'n' bitches—can be just as valuable, not to mention easier on the wallet. If you're not sure where to find like-minded creative types in your neck of the woods, start with the bulletin boards in cafés, bookstores, and artists' centers. Use the web, too.

GET A ROOM

Now you should be well on your way to resisting the charms of the TV after work. Still, a particularly mind-numbing day at a desk or on your feet might make you extra susceptible to the inertia that binds your derriere to the sofa like a tongue to a frozen flagpole.

That's when it's time to go straight to your room. Like Virginia Woolf's room of one's own, you need a comfortable, quiet, TV-free spot to work on your craft. Basements, garages, alcoves, walk-in closets, and spare bedrooms make great places to work without interruption. If you live in a shoebox, you might need to get creative.

Your "room" doesn't have to be in your home. In fact, the change of scenery after a hard day's toil can give you that much-needed creative shot in the arm. If you can rent a place outside your house to do your artwork, by all means go for it. Renting your own affordable desk space, studio, or practice area is easier than you might think. Many cities are home to warehouses converted into dozens, if not hundreds, of affordable artists' studios for rent. To find the good workspaces in your 'hood, check with your city or county arts commission, or the bulletin board at your hobby shop or art school. Ditto for your favorite arts publications, websites like Artisthelpnetwork.com, and that online hub of all things rentable—Craigslist.

If your wallet isn't up to renting a workspace but you want out of the house, go portable. Stuff your paints, laptop, or glue guns into your backpack and find a café table, park bench, or barstool of your own, or go into the office an hour early or stay an hour late to get your artwork done.

midday creativity snack

It's 11 a.m. and you're in your cubicle, bored silly, with no pressing projects to speak of. Your sketchpad, knitting needles, or sheet music are burning a hole in your backpack. Go on. Just take a hit. You know you want to. Rather than forwarding chain letters, try some of these midday art breaks.

the lunch date   Make a daily lunch date with your art and work on your novel or comic strip at your desk, go out for grub and bring along your favorite art magazine, do some research at the library or bookstore, pick up supplies from a nearby hobby shop, or take a mind-clearing walk and brainstorm.

the shameless plug   Have an upcoming art opening or performance? With the help of the company printer or photocopier, making flyers and other promotional paraphernalia is a cinch. Stay late and the copy room is yours. Just be discreet.

the fact check   Need to nail down some facts for a story you're writing? Trying to find a good deal on a luscious vintage fabric? The zippy Internet connection and free phone calls make your office the perfect place to get this research done. And remember your discretion: Go easy on the long-distance calls, stay away from websites that show nipple, and keep a work-related document open in case a coworker walks by.

the extra-credit project   Everything from negotiating a contract to mastering a new computer program can help further your creative career down the line. Bonus points if you can do this on company time—maybe as part of a training or mentoring program.

the bonus track   Trapped in a meeting or stuck on hold? Jot down a note or read an article related to your craft. Or make your weekly to-do or supply shopping list.

so legit you'll quit

GOING INTO BUSINESS FOR YOURSELF // Michelle Goodman

If you're sick of your day job, you don't have to sit idly by while your resentment builds. You can take the skills you're passionate about and go to work for yourself. Sure, your friends and family might think you're crazy—at first—but once they notice you don't have to beg for time off, struggle to stay awake during morning staff meetings, or grovel for a raise, they'll be convinced. Plus, you can make your own hours, choose who you work for and what projects you work on, take naps and Fridays off and 90-minute lunch breaks, and work in the pajamas you've slept in—for the past four days.

It takes a lot of persistence, an open mind, and a little gumption to jump into a freelance life, but once you start, you'll never want to go back to the office. Here are a few tips to set you on the path to employment freedom.

USE A SAFETY NET

Unless you have three to six months' living expenses saved (or you're about to inherit a windfall), don't rush to dump your day job. "Start slowly, without biting off more than you can chew," cautions organic farmer Annie Salafsky.

Before you kiss your paycheck good-bye, see if you even like playing boss—and if people want to buy what you're selling. Work for yourself nights and weekends, all the while stockpiling cash. If you're too busy to keep your nine-to-five gig, find a steady part-time job instead. The idea is to stay debt-free, so when the cash finally starts pouring in, you're not forced to use it all to pay off credit card bills.

GET THICK-SKINNED

People will call you crazy for turning away a steady paycheck. Don't listen. Most of them hate their jobs anyway (yet fear layoffs like the plague). Nina Frenkel, an illustrator who went indie after one layoff too many, makes a great case for self-employment: "There's more stability in being your own boss and having many clients. It's unlikely that they will all bail at once."

You also have to prepare yourself for repeated rejection. You may have to promote your business to 25 people just to land one paying customer. Don't take those 24 no's personally. Dust yourself off and move on. Remind yourself that you have amazing talent—and that you're giving up dress codes, insipid water-cooler banter, and regulated pee breaks.

BE SHAMELESS

Word of mouth spreads quicker than a California wildfire. So tell everyone about your new venture, from your grandma to your gynecologist. Find additional low-cost ways to get noticed, such as donating your services to charity events. (It's a smart way to gain extra experience, too.) And take advantage of the Internet, where you can lure clients from all over the world with your web site.

A good reputation goes a long way. The easiest way to promote yourself is to earn rave reviews—not to mention repeat business and referrals—from customers. As freelance editor Carly Sommerstein says, "Go that extra mile for a client and she's/he's yours."

DON'T BUY, BARTER

In the spirit of starting small, keep your initial expenses to a minimum. You can save a lot of beans by trading your services or goods with other independent professionals. For instance, you might be able to exchange your services for used furniture, business card designs, computer repairs, marketing advice, even massages. Before you pull out the plastic, ask yourself if it's really something you need for your first year in business. If it is, see if you can get it for free or next to nothing.

LEARN TO LOVE BREAD AND BUTTER

To make it working solo, you've got to bend a little. Don't turn up your nose at work that isn't your first choice. In leaner times, you may need to take some of the most hilarious jobs to stay afloat. For instance, a writerly freelancer may find herself editing Wiccan erotica or writing ad copy for the Dr. Ruth vibrator (yes, there really is such a thing). Sometimes a job is a job and you need to take it.

Trying to balance bread-and-butter work with your own craft can be tricky. Indie rocker October Crifasi, who doubles as a guitar instructor, keeps her mornings free for practicing and weekends open for performing. Assigning yourself deadlines for delivering your work is also helpful.

GET LEGIT

A few things are definitely worth paying for: Business cards so you don't have to write your phone number on a napkin, a P.O. box so your checks don't get ripped off, an accountant so you don't screw up your taxes, a city or state biz license so you don't get slapped with fines, and health insurance so if your appendix needs to come out, the sky-high medical bills don't send you running back to your full-time job.

The business side of things can be the hardest part, especially if you don't know squat about law and finance. If you need help, don't be afraid to ask. Most freelancers don't regret the day she hired her accountant or financial planner.

MEET THE LOCALS

Isolation is the quickest route to second-guessing your decision to go solo. For your sanity, regularly schedule face time with someone other than your postal carrier or cat. (E-mail junkies, this means you too.) Start with professional e-mail discussion lists, then work your way up to industry meetings and events. Talking shop with others in your field—self-employed or not—can help save you months of missteps and remind you that you're not in this alone.

FURTHER READING

If you're thinking about going indie and want more information on how to get started, check out the Resources on page 356.

baking for bucks

START A FREELANCE BAKING ENTERPRISE // **Lauren Mucciolo**

Sure, those birthday cakes go over well at friends' parties, but perhaps you've thought it would be too complicated to bake your way into business. Fortunately, breaking into the freelance baking industry is not as tricky as it may seem. With a little business know-how and bakerly invention, you can be mixing and folding your way to the stomachs of many in a town near you! Just follow these easy steps to get your enterprise on the move.

STEP 1: FIND A NICHE

The real obstacle to the freelance baking industry is not a lack of interest—most café owners like indie foodstuffs because they humanize their businesses in ways that their corporate competitors lack. But these small businesses can't afford to make arrangements with every rainy-day baker in the neighborhood. As with any other product one would develop to sell competitively, you need a niche. Maybe you're great at vegan cupcakes or swell with wheat-free pies. Whatever the specialty, you can bring joy to bellies if what you're selling is unique.

Of course, your niche should be something that fits your own personality; it's both easier and more exciting to invent a great recipe when your own taste buds are at stake. Do you want cookies with frosting? Half brownies, half cookies? Low-cal blondies? Take some time to explore your own identity and desires.

STEP 2: PERFECT A RECIPE

Maybe you're a fan of both oatmeal and chocolate chip cookies and will rarely turn down anything that marries the two. Use this ingredient love to make what you consider to be the world's most perfect cookie. Use friends as taste testers, fine-tune the recipe until it's right every time, and then consider yourself ready to take your works of art to market.

STEP 3: WIN OVER YOUR LOCAL CAFÉ MANAGER

Make some really exquisite samples of your product and assemble them in some sort of attractive presentation. Call your local eccentric café and find out when the manager is in. Pick a slow time of the day to go and trek those beauties to the front lines.

Now, here's the hard part—you have to know how to seduce the manager's taste buds quickly and efficiently. State your case and have her take a taste early on in your presentation. Explain how often you could replenish stock and what kinds of great ingredients you use. You may want to figure out your overhead charges before you suggest a price tag for your goods, so that when the subject of money comes up, you can explain how much you're putting into the product, and how much your labor and invention deserve.

STEP 4: MAINTAIN YOUR SENSE OF HUMOR

Sometimes your creations will fall flat, literally. Everything from the weather to

slight variations in your oven can cause massive batch failure. Because it's inevitable, be sure to keep extra ingredients on hand. And if you can't meet an order, tell a client honestly and quickly—that way there'll be time to find a backup baker or at least allow the client to plan for your goodies' later arrival. After all, you want to be known for your flaky crust, not a flaky disposition. That's what keeps them coming back for more.

So what are you waiting for? Get out your spatula, put on your oven mitts, and get baking!

make it work

LAUNCH YOUR OWN CLOTHING LABEL // Tara Marks

These days, countless boutiques and online shops are stocked with clothes made by indie designers—crafty, creative ladies who turned their love of style into stylish threads. If you've got an eye for design and a passion for fashion, you've probably wondered just how they did it. Turns out, whether you want to be the next Diane von Furstenberg or simply dream of hawking your handmade frocks at the local craft fair, it's something you can do too. Here's the inside scoop about what it takes to launch a fashion line DIY-style. (And if you're interested in learning even more, check out the Resources on page 356.)

TAKING CARE OF BUSINESS:
MONEY MATTERS AND MAKING A PLAN

Fashion may be fun, but launching a clothing line is first and foremost a business. Budgets and goals are just as important as hemlines and silhouettes. It's important to consider the realities of entrepreneurship so you can decide up front if you're game to do the legwork.

And let's cut to the chase—to start your label, you're gonna need money. Even the most DIY of divas has to pony up some funds to bring her brilliant ideas to fruition. You'll want enough dough to cover pattern and sample making, fabric and materials, and production and shipping, which could vary greatly depending on the type of clothes you make, how you produce them, and where you sell them. But the good news is, you can actually do it with very little cash. If you make reasonably priced clothes in simple materials with small manufacturing runs, your start-up costs won't be exorbitant. When it comes to choosing fabrics, think about how much money you're willing to spend, then design your pieces around your budget. If you're conjuring up a couture line at $25 a yard, you'll have to make a huge investment on materials alone.

Not everyone can launch a clothing line inexpensively, but it doesn't take as much as you might think. Nanette Lepore, for instance, started her business in 1992 with a $5,000 loan from her dad. Relying on personal loans from family members is a common way for budding designers to get their lines off the ground. "We started with a $10,000 loan from my dad in 2001 and repaid him after a year," says Deirdre Nagayama, who, along with partner Stacy Rodgers, launched the classic, comfy San Francisco–based line She-bible. "We've never taken out a bank loan, but we do lean on our AmEx from time to time." Applying for a business loan is also an option. Associations like the National Federation of Independent Business offer financial resources for small-business owners, and Accion.org is a good source for microloans. Whatever you do, don't quit your day job; if you're already employed, stay that way while you launch your venture so you can support yourself financially.

Before you thread a single needle, you'll need to create a plan. Write down your goals, whether that's opening an Etsy store with a couple of dresses, or creating a 10-piece collection that's sold in your favorite boutique. For help writing a business plan, consult the resources at the Small Business Administration web site (www.sba.gov) or see what courses your local community college offers. The She-bible gals took a "How to Start a Fashion Business" class at City College of San Francisco for cheap. There are also legal issues involved with running a small business, so if you're serious about turning your hobby into a possible moneymaker, read up on how to legally establish your company and find out any tax consequences that come with it.

SHE AND HEM: CREATE YOUR COLLECTION

The first step, of course, is nailing down your designs. Decide what type of clothing you want to produce and how many pieces you want to start with. Choose colors and fabrics (keeping in mind the cost of materials) and think about creating a cohesive look that lets your style shine. Create prototypes of your designs to see how wearable they are, or if garment construction isn't your forte, simply sketch your ideas and make notes about design details.

CUT IT OUT:
PATTERN AND SAMPLE MAKING

Once you know what you want your collection to look like, you'll need a pattern for each piece. It's imperative that the patterns are expertly made, since they'll be the blueprints for every item you produce; they're also the foundation for a good fit—a key element when it comes to selling your clothes.

If you have mad sewing skills, very little money to invest, and a desire to tackle patternmaking on your own, find a how-to book you can learn from (see Resources on page 356). Being able to interpret your designs and manage alterations will save you money and turnaround time. But because the technical craftsmanship of excellent patternmaking may elude even an experienced sewer, many designers leave this step to an expert. "Neither of us sews," says She-bible's Nagayama. "We usually start with a concept, or parts of garments that we like the fit of, and begin modifications from there. We also sketch our ideas and explain what we want to our patternmaker."

The most reliable way to find a patternmaker is through referrals. If you know someone in the fashion-design biz, hit her up. You can also contact fashion schools for students with strong patternmaking skills, but be wary. Working with student patternmakers may keep costs down, but you might pay for it during manufacturing. You can bring a really good patternmaker your crappy hand-sewn item and she'll know all the right questions to ask to create a professional-looking piece. Web sites for fashion professionals like InfoMat.com and Fashiondex.com also offer referral services—or try the classified sections of industry papers like *WWD*.

With patterns in hand, you can use the same search avenues to find an expert seamstress to create a one-off of each piece. Often, these samples are what you'll present to local boutiques to see if they have an interest in buying, so it's essential that no seam or hem is left unconsidered. Be sure to inquire about her expertise with the type of product you design, look at examples of her past work, and ask about turnaround time.

SELL IT LIKE IT IS: GETTING BUYERS

To make your line profitable, you're going to need buyers. And it helps to have them before you invest mucho dinero in producing items that may or may not sell. When it comes to boutiques, the shop owner is usually the one looking for the latest and greatest merchandise, so stop in or send a handwritten note to introduce yourself and your new line.

Getting your gear sold in boutiques outside your hometown, in department stores, or even internationally, however, is a bit more challenging and much more costly. Attending a fashion trade show (where designers set up individual booths to show off their wares to thousands of buyers) is the best way to do it. Because paying to flaunt your fashions doesn't ensure interest in your line, shelling out the dough can be quite a gamble; it's fitting that the most well-known fashion trade shows, such as MAGIC and POOL, are held in Las Vegas. If that seems overwhelming, start attracting buyers by opening an Etsy store to gauge interest. Or sell your gear at indie fairs like BUST's Craftacular, then take your profits and invest them in more expensive ventures like a trade show.

But before you start selling to anyone, you'll need to figure out how much to sell your threads for, making sure the price covers the cost of goods sold (COGS)—all production-related expenses like buttons, zippers, fabric, construction, labor, and shipping. A designer has two sets of customers: the retail store and the final shopper. Generally, retail shops mark up the wholesale price of clothing (what the designer charges the store) by double, plus 20 percent. Calculating your wholesale price can be complicated, but one of the best approaches is to apply the same markup principle. For example, if your COGS is $25, your wholesale price would be $55 ($25 x 2.2), and your retail price would be $121 ($55 x 2.2). If your retail price is too high compared to that of similar items on the market, you'll have to simplify the design, use less-expensive materials, or make production more efficient.

FACTORY GIRL: PRODUCING THE GOODS

Production is where your brilliant ideas become a real, live clothing line. Typically, many young, broke DIY designers with small orders to fill hire a freelance seamstress for production. It's a good way to keep costs down until your business grows to a point that it can't be handled by an individual.

Once product demand increases, most designers have their line produced by a factory, where industrial cutting and sewing machines crank out clothes much quicker and more precisely than someone using a home sewing machine. Generally, these plants don't advertise their services, which means it can take some digging to find one. And not every factory likes to work with new designers, since they tend to have more problems and pattern mistakes. Another thing to be aware of is manufacturing minimums. For instance, a factory may require an order for 200 pieces of each style, but that may include all sizes and several color options; make sure you understand their parameters. When starting out, it's best to choose a factory in the U.S., even locally if possible, so you can communicate clearly and oversee the process.

ACHTUNG, BABY: GETTING NOTICED

Without exposure, your collection will fizzle without ever seeing the inside of a fashionista's closet. Marketing and branding your business is as important as the design of your clothes, so you'll need a logo, business cards, and hang tags (featuring your label's name and secured by safety pin to each item of clothing) that are as cute as your collection. Call on your artsy friends to help you. Know a graphic designer? Enlist her assistance (in exchange for trade, if you can't pay her) or search Craigslist for affordable freelancers.

Consider creating a look book: a booklet that features photos of gals wearing your clothes, along with the name and style information of each piece. It's an important sales tool for buyers because they can see what your clothes actually look like when worn, and it's a perfect item to send to editors and bloggers who will hopefully want to write about your new line. Every penny counts, so sending out thousands of press kits (a nice folder including a look book or photos of your collection, a designer biography, a collection summary, and copies of any press clips) is out of the question. E-mail your info to anyone who might be interested, but be choosy about who gets a pretty, printed package.

In addition, create a simple web site for your line. If you're clueless when it comes to HTML, sites like Webs.com offer Web-design wizards and user-friendly interfaces that can walk you through it. That same graphic-designer friend can probably help make your site look good, and remember, keep the same color scheme and font selection throughout your branding.

Take any opportunity you can to talk up your business or show folks your collection. You never know what it may lead to. Relatively unknown California-based designer Bianca Benitez, of the sweetly feminine line Dear Creatures, sent one of her favorite actresses and singers, Zooey Deschanel, a few pieces from her first collection. Deschanel took a liking to the line and the next thing Benitez knew, Deschanel was starring in a cotton commercial that featured her Dear Creatures dresses, giving Benitez instant, free, international-level exposure.

Launching a clothing line is no small task. Don't be afraid to ask for help from friends, family, and more-experienced designers. Be prepared for a lot of hard work. You're guaranteed to make some mistakes along the way, but the day you see a stranger on the street rocking one of your original designs will make it all worthwhile.

shameless self-promotion

BE YOUR OWN PUBLICIST // Anne Leighton

Say you have an awesome band. Or a fabulous store. Maybe you crochet the best toilet paper cozies this side of the Mississippi. Think you need to hire a publicist to let the world know about your greatness? Think again. Here's how to do their job.

Publicity is simply the art of speaking up for something you believe in. Even if you're the kind of person who's shy at parties, you can publicize your creation if you believe in it enough.

The art of publicity boils down to understanding what's special about your project, then finding media outlets that can give it press—and convincing them that they should. Think about what your project is. Picture how it would look in a magazine or on a TV program or web site. Then contact the appropriate people and briefly tell them something specific about your project and how it could fit into their media outlet. Hopefully, one of them will give you some coverage. And you'll live on in glory forever . . . or, at least, sell a couple of books (or cupcakes, or knit hats, or whatever). The idea is to keep receiving media attention, so you can keep the public aware of your work.

Let's break it down.

STORY TIME

The first thing to do is to figure out what your story is. That will define what you say to media outlets and how you'll write press releases. Whether people praise you because you make amazing pastries or your record store features awesome bands playing live, you need to spend some time writing down what's special about your project. You know the saying that "Dog Bites Man" is not news, but "Man Bites Dog" is? Well, the same holds true here. "Girl Plays in Band" or "Girl Knits Hats" is not a story, but "Guitarist Offers Free Rock Clinics for Youngsters" or "Knitter Makes Hats out of Your Pet's Fur" could be. You need to offer something new, something timely, something trendy, or some kind of service. In other words, you need to figure out what makes your project newsworthy.

Once you understand what your project is about, figure out how to describe it. Media people don't have time to hear it all, so you should think of one or two points to focus on. What have people said about your work? For instance, if you've groomed the neighborhood dogs and everyone says how nice their mutts' butts smell, that's a selling point. If your macramé belts have sold well at a local boutique and a charity is asking you to produce a dozen for their fund-raiser, ask the charity to write a letter that elaborates how you helped and include a great quote in your press release. Or a film producer might talk about how his film won the "worst film" in the Artsy Fartsy Film Festival and remember quotes from the judges. After all, even bad press is press—they may not have liked the film, but they still talked about it. You just have to use the connections to your advantage.

Media outlets are inundated with press releases, e-mails, phone calls, and packages all competing for their attention. That's why you should be able to summarize why your work stands out. But don't let the idea that there's competition scare you off. The fact is that radio stations have 24 hours of programming to produce every day, and newspapers have thousands of words to pull together for each and every issue. This means that they are always on the lookout for stories to fill their pages and their airtime, and you've got as good a shot as anyone to be one of them.

PARTNER UP FOR MORE ATTENTION

If you can't quite figure out a story for your project, make one. One of the great ways to get a placement in the media is to collaborate with a venue or with other people because that can become a story. Why? Because you have someone or something else involved with your project and there is strength in numbers. Both consumers and journalists tend to feel story potential when two or more parties are working together to make something happen.

Playing at a local club can get you a calendar listing in the newspaper. But when you connect the event with a charity or announce that your club gig will be a CD release party, you might get a write-up with a picture. Displaying your artwork at a public library is a great collaboration because suddenly an intellectual organization believes you're talented. Incidentally, because people enjoy chowing down, having food at your event is a good idea. If you can arrange with the library to have a reception with drinks and food, more media people will come, especially if you can bring in a local drink company or store as a sponsor.

OFFER FREEBIES

Another way to create a story is to offer up a service. If you're a hairstylist known for cutting great shags, you might offer tips on how to avoid getting a mullet by mistake. If you own a restaurant, you could write up a seasonal recipe. If you own a bookstore, consider compiling a list of your recommendations of the best children's books of the year and send it around to the media before the holidays.

3-2-1 CONTACT

Now that you've got your story, start gathering media contacts. Put together a database on your computer or in a notebook. Start with the local media: daily papers, radio shows, morning TV shows, and free weeklies that cater to your area. Call and ask for the department that's closest to your field. Performers can talk with the theater, music, or features editor. TV shows have either assignment editors or producers; generally, you'd call the news department to get started. Radio shows have producers for individual shows.

Sometimes you'll get an assistant on the phone. Ask them these questions: Who gets information about my project? Can you please spell their name? What's their mailing address? What's their e-mail? Do they prefer phone or e-mail follow-ups?

Also find out if they want to receive your product, just a photo, or merely information about your event. If they want the product, send it, but understand that whenever you mail off a product, you're probably not going to get it back.

Once you've hit all the local media, you can consider approaching national media. This includes magazines, TV, radio, and newspapers that are distributed all over the country. These types of media outlets usually only cover universally popular topics and celebrities that most people have heard of, so as a relative unknown, getting coverage there is a long shot at best. Nevertheless, a national media outlet might be interested if someone famous is involved with your project. For instance, if Hilary Swank buys your crafts, send a press release to the "Page Six" column of the *New York Post* and to *Premiere*. Another reason to approach a big outlet is if you have a surefire contact who writes for them. A surefire contact means this person is a real friend who calls you just to chat.

WRITE A GREAT COVER LETTER

Okay, you've got your targeted media list. Now you need to put together your pitch. You should always type a three-paragraph cover letter when pitching to big media outlets. Use a standard business format: Put your address at the top of the page, then type the address of your media outlet. Type in the date you're mailing the letter. And until you get to know a stranger, always begin with the polite salutation "Dear Ms." or "Dear Mr." Then follow the three-paragraph format:

Paragraph 1

In the first paragraph, introduce yourself and your project in a simple way that makes it relevant to their media outlet. If you want a cooking magazine to print your recipe, let them know that you've written the recipe up in the same format used by the magazine. Tell them how many people come to your restaurant each week and order this special food.

A musician will write about her CD and explain that she's playing shows weekly in different towns when she writes to XM Radio's Billy Zero for the Unsigned Bands Channel, because he likes bands who are actively performing shows. "Enclosed is my band XXY's new album, *The Unpredictable Chromosome*, for consideration on XM's Unsigned Bands Channel. We've played out in Washington, DC, and other Mid-Atlantic states, and are actively booking ourselves in New England every weekend."

Paragraph 2

The second paragraph gives extra information on the project, establishes your credibility, and should seduce the journalist. If you're a performer, include significant credits. In one sentence, describe your philosophy. Write a sentence that shows how your goal to be in this outlet is relevant to their purpose. So the unsigned band would tell Billy Zero, "XXY has opened for Antigone Rising and has performed on Dave Space's show on Manhattan Cable. We've organized benefits in Northampton for Habitat for Humanity and will continue to do so every month until there is no homelessness in the state of Massachusetts. We'd appreciate it if you could help our causes (our music and ending homelessness) by playing our record, please."

The Finish

The last paragraph should optimistically encourage the journalist to connect with you. Use a positive phrase like "I look forward to talking with you" or "I hope to be in your magazine." Then include your e-mail and phone numbers, including your cell—make it easy for them to get in touch with you.

Close your letter in a friendly way, like "Very truly yours," "Sincerely," or "Thank you." Then type your name and sign.

Ask one or two of your literate friends to read your hype before you send it, because it's hard to edit yourself and you don't want to send a letter with typos or different names in the address and salutation.

THE PRESS RELEASE
Like cover letters, good press releases have formats. Try to divide your release into five sections:

Contact Info
In the upper left-hand corner, always include the publicity contact information: your name, e-mail, and phone number.

The Headline
The headline should list your product and then the most famous thing connected with your event and the date. For instance, if your record store features live bands, start your press release with the headline "Mary's Record Store Features Band Rock Sox Playing Live, April 10."

Paragraph 1
Paragraph one will show the "who," "what," "when," and "where" of the event, plus "how much it costs." So, you might write, "Rock Sox will be playing at Mary's Record Store, 223 Main Street in Shreveport, Louisiana, at 7 p.m. on April 10. Admission is free, as this event will help promote Rock Sox's new album, *Smell the Sox*, which is available at Mary's. The store number is 555-555-5555."

Paragraph 2
The second paragraph will give more information about your specific project. Since you're Mary's Record Store, you'd write about the types of music you sell and why you present live bands.

Paragraph 3
The third paragraph includes more information. Describe Rock Sox. Explain how other bands can play at Mary's. If a paragraph has more than four sentences, split it in half. It's fine if a press release has five or six paragraphs, but it shouldn't be longer than one page.

I CERTAINLY ADMIRE YOUR PERSISTENCE
The biggest rule after you send your pitch is to follow up. Be concise and nice. First, place a follow-up call to see if they received your package, then ask, "When may I follow up to see about a story?" In your database or notebook, jot down their directions so you can follow up in a way that's appealing to them. If a journalist says, "I'll pass," wait four or five months. Send updates when you have events or dramatic career progressions.

If you don't connect with anyone and the event is happening in the next two to four weeks, give a call the next day. Then wait about a week. If your event is about nine days away and it's a weekly paper, do one last follow-up. Two days before the event, invite them.

PERFECT TIMING
Put yourself in the shoes of a producer or editor and think of the calendar. From planning to publication, it takes four or five months for a magazine to put together an issue. It takes two or three weeks in TV and radio to plan a feature for a show. If you're a dog groomer and it's summer in six months, tell a national magazine you'd like to offer canine cooling tips. Submit your restaurant's red, white, and blueberry cheesecake recipe to a women's publication in February for the July issue.

résumé rehab

POLISH UP YOUR BIO AND KISS UNEMPLOYMENT GOOD-BYE // Angie Ross

Tough times got you pounding the pavement for a job? Then your résumé's got to be spot-on, since it will probably be one of hundreds the hiring managers receive. A well-written résumé is key to securing the coveted face-to-face interview, so follow these tips to make sure yours stands out from the pack. (In a good way.)

PROOFREAD
You don't want your résumé to end up in The Folder—the place where recruiters keep bad résumés to be mocked by colleagues, friends, and the family dentist. Typos are a surefire way to get there. Read your résumé. Read it again. Seriously, read it one more time. Then have a friend read it. Even the smallest typo can knock you out of the running.

KEEP IT SHORT AND SWEET
Your résumé is a marketing piece, not an extensive recap of your job descriptions.

Focus on what matters for the job opening. Aim for one page, definitely no longer than two.

TRASH THE OBJECTIVE
No one cares that you "want a job with growth opportunities where your professional and academic background will be of value." Switch it up with a summary of qualifications, a short paragraph detailing the skills you have that are most relevant to the job. This moves the focus from what you want to what you bring. It may be a subtle difference, but it's a powerful statement about your priorities. Be sure to tailor the summary for each job opening; recruiters hate junk mail as much as you do. You have only a few seconds to capture their attention, so make them count.

GET SOME ACTION
Focus on what you've achieved, and explain how you did it using action-oriented language. Scrap the more passive "responsible for" and start with an action like "streamlined operations" to add impact. But don't overdo it. You want to sell real accomplishments, not try to make Shinola out of, well, you know. You are good. You can do this job. Believe it and sell it. A résumé isn't a job application—it's like an advertisement for your awesomeness.

speak easy

SUREFIRE SPEECH-GIVING TIPS // Tara Bracco

If you were asked to give a speech to a roomful of people, could you do it? For lots of women, public speaking is scary stuff. But if you back away from the challenge, you may be missing out on things like impressing your boss with a killer presentation or giving a moving toast at your BFF's wedding. Anyone can be a good public speaker, even if the thought makes your palms sweat and your heart pound. The hardest part is saying yes when given the opportunity. Once you've done that, focus on one or two of the following tips at a time while practicing your speech and pretty soon, you'll feel like a pro.

ENTER WITH ENERGY

Leave your fear behind by walking into the space with enthusiasm and eagerness to share your message, even if you feel hesitant. Spend time visualizing yourself beginning the speech in this way and imagine the audience smiling back at you with friendly attentiveness.

SPEAK UP

Women tend to speak in soft, high-pitched voices that get even higher when we're nervous. Talk in a deep, clear voice to convey confidence and remember to project.

PACE YOURSELF

If you are a speedy speaker, your audience won't have time to process what you're saying. Take deep, even breaths to help control the pace of your speech and calm your nerves. Pay attention to punctuation by pausing at the ends of your sentences. Pauses can be very powerful.

GIVE UP THE VALLEY-GIRL TALK

Many of us fill our speech with "like" and end definitive sentences with an upward inflection, as if asking a question. In a speech, this keeps people from taking you seriously. Also, stay away from other fillers, such as "um" and "you know."

CONNECT WITH THE CROWD

Make eye contact with your listeners and use purposeful gestures to engage them. Avoid pacing the room and using excessive hand movements because it will distract from what you're saying.

DRESS FOR SUCCESS

Whether you wear a new suit or your favorite frock, have a dress rehearsal to make sure your outfit is comfortable. You want to be able to focus entirely on your speech, not on whether your skirt is riding up or how much your feet hurt.

there she goes

HOW TO TRAVEL SOLO // **Michelle Snider**

If you're like most folks, you've probably always hit the road in a pair or a group. But why not go away for few days by yourself? Instead of fearing what might or might not happen, take the risk. You never know where you'll end up.

BEGIN WITH A SENSE OF WHAT YOU WANT FROM YOUR TRIP
Create a context for your experiences to help tie everything together. Do you hope to have some kind of epiphany about your career? Do you feel a need to connect with your sense of intuition or push yourself to be more outgoing? Having a personal goal (in addition to having a great time) can give the trip greater meaning.

START SMALL
If you've decided you want to try out traveling on your own, don't feel like you need to plan a trip to cross India on foot. If it makes you more comfortable, go to a place where there is a lot to do. Then, if it feels right, branch out from there and encourage yourself to take on something more challenging. Using your first solo experience to boost your self-esteem will ready you for longer trips.

TAKE PUBLIC TRANSPORTATION
While renting a car in a foreign land will gain you access to remote and relatively inaccessible countrysides, you're a lot less likely to meet any of that country's inhabitants. Consider taking trains and other forms of public transportation instead of secluding yourself in a rental car. You'll be sure to meet heaps of locals and independent travelers, and there is no better way to come into contact with so many interesting and different people. Plus, it's cheaper!

NO MATTER WHAT YOUR AGE, STAY IN HOSTELS
Yes, they can be somewhat chaotic at times, but they are a great way to meet people from the entire planet. Contrary to popular perception, most hostels are clean, have decent showers and good locations, and provide shelter for friendly people of all ages. You will encounter tons of people and, especially as a solo traveler, you will have the opportunity (as well as the openness and

flexibility) to get to know some of them in a meaningful way. But it is virtually guaranteed that you will have someone in your room who snores, so bring your earplugs. You can find out the cool places to go and the places to avoid by talking to the people you meet and the people who run the place.

BRING A BOOK WITH YOU TO MEALS BUT BE WILLING TO SHARE A TABLE

Eating alone can sometimes be a real bummer, especially if there are groups of friends and couples having a grand (and loud) time around you. Bringing a book to dinner might help you focus on something other than the feeling of loneliness that can come with that empty seat across the table. Sometimes, if the restaurant is busy, the host may suggest you share a table with another single diner. Who knows? You may end up having a great conversation with someone you never would have met if you had been traveling with a companion.

DON'T RUSH

Traveling alone is a unique opportunity to find your own pace and blend into the groove of day-to-day life in the place where you are staying. Try to experience a city as if you lived there. Go to the same place for coffee every day and see how it starts to feel like home. If you find a city you like, don't get caught up in trying to see everything. Just stay where you are—it will only begin to reveal itself to you when you give yourself the time to see it. You can take pictures of landmarks as you pass them, but sometimes the best things about a city aren't on postcards.

SIT NEXT TO PEOPLE WHO SEEM INTERESTING, AND MAKE IT OBVIOUS THAT YOU ARE TOO

It is unbelievably easy to meet people abroad, especially when you are on your own. The challenge is to meet people you truly connect with. You might overhear someone talking about one of your favorite movies while waiting at a train station. Eavesdrop gracefully and start up a conversation if you find yourself on the same train. Be open to meeting people in your travels and you can form friendships that span continents and cultures.

LEAVE ADDRESSES WHERE PEOPLE CAN WRITE TO YOU

If you'd like to keep in touch with your peeps back home (and have them know where the hell you are) you can have real, physical mail sent to the main post office of almost any town in the world. Most places will hold your mail for about a month, and if you've moved on to the next stop, some will even forward your mail for a small fee. A package from your parents with three big boxes of Junior Mints might be just the thing to cure a case of homesickness.

REMEMBER, YOU CAN ALWAYS CHANGE YOUR PLANS OR COME HOME

Sure, you probably won't want to come home early, but consciously making the daily choice to continue or end your journey truly makes it yours. It sounds so simple and logical, yet knowing you have the possibility to stop at any time can empower you in your travels. Having this option can remind you of one of the greatest things about traveling alone: you get to do everything you want to do. If you want to stay in bed all day or blitz through five world-class museums, you can do it. It's your trip and you can make it anything you want it to be.

liking it rough

LEARN TO LOVE CAMPING // Heather Menicucci

If your idea of roughing it means heating up leftovers instead of having food
delivered, it's time you had an "in-tents" experience. Here you'll find everything
you need to hit the trail, from digging cat holes to chugging campfire cocktails.
Consider this not just a camping guide, but a city girl's call of the wild. Let's get
primitive!

A PATCH OF PARKING LOT TO CALL YOUR VERY OWN

From mountains to plains, beaches to forests, all kinds of nature await you and your tent.
When the weather warms up, start looking at the map for any green areas within a few hours'
drive of home. And no matter where you go, a watery spot to splash around in can be a
bonus. While no place offers as much water as shoreline campsites, seaside camping will test
your limits—skinny-dipping and sleeping on the beach are romantic, but the sun and wind
are harsh and the sand exhausting. A swimming hole under a canopy of evergreens can be
equally exciting.

Site Camping

Site camping is just that—a designated area divided into sites for tents, sometimes with
room enough to park a car. The presence of other campers, fire pits, running water, and even
outhouses make this the most manageable way for a newbie to start. Private campgrounds
are the height of site-camping convenience and can be found near major roads in every
state. They are, however, a far cry from the Tarzan-and-Jane experience you might be after,
as many resemble quartered-off parking lots, complete with painted yellow lines. Parks
and forests can charge anywhere between $4 and $20 per night for a site, and private
campgrounds can cost twice as much. Reservations are almost always required, and the most
secluded and waterfront sites are snatched up early in the summer, sometimes as soon as
spring, so book ahead.

Backcountry Camping

For the most pristine wilderness and roughest roughing it, try backcountry camping.
The procedure is pretty simple—most times you can pick a forest on your map, park at
one of the many entrances, hike for about five minutes, walk off the trail, plop your stuff
down, and camp. Rules can vary, but usually you're allowed to pitch your tent anywhere,
as long as you're at least 150 feet away from water sources and trails. It may be intense
and challenging—you will likely have to drop trou and crouch behind a tree to go to the
bathroom (a.k.a. dig a cat hole)—but how far would you go for your own private waterfall?
With backcountry camping, it's really up to you. Rough it a lot or only a little. Some parks and
just about every forest offer dispersed camping for anywhere between $0 and $20 a night.
Permits are occasionally required and can be obtained at ranger stations.

Get as fanatical with gear, gadgets, and supplies as your wallet allows, but remember you'll be packing and carrying it. Great deals can be scored at thrift stores, yard sales, and in classified ads; camping superstores can fill in the gaps where the Salvation Army fails.

First, You'll Need a Tent

Be prepared to spend anywhere from $50 to $500 for one that sleeps two or three comfortably. More expensive equals more streamlined, lightweight, and weather-resistant. Check for a durable waterproof floor and good ventilation. Most tents guarantee three-season comfort (spring, summer, fall), but new campers may want to stick to summer camping at first. Just make sure there's a rain fly—a raincoat for your tent. Otherwise, if it starts to pour, you may find yourself running for the car. A tarp or an old shower curtain is also essential for keeping the party going when it's raining. Tie four corners to trees for a canopy, drape two corners on waist-high stumps for a lean-to, or throw it on the ground and splash it with water to make an impromptu Slip 'N Slide.

Next, Something to Sleep In

While sleeping bags are the classic camping bed, you won't need one if you have a tent and aren't camping in cold weather. Roll up two blankets tightly with cord and tie them to the bottom of your pack. Balled-up clothes and towels can double as pillows. If you're into getting properly outfitted, though, you can score a three-season sleeping bag for anywhere between $30 and $250.

Then, the Backpack to Carry It All

You'll need one with a frame that's about twice the size of your basic school pack, which provides the support you need. There are two types: those with external and those with internal frames. External frames are meant for long hikes and are sturdier for lugging a lot of gear, but unless you're climbing Mount Everest, an internal frame will be fine. You can find one for $25 to $400.

burn, baby, burn: be your own firestarter

Building a fire is more than a necessity; it's an art and a source of pride. Here's a basic formula for a tried-and-true method.

Build your fire in the same spot as the campers before; look for charred ground and an old fire ring. Finish the ring with large, flat rocks or make a new one if it's been broken down. Smooth out a shallow pit in the center. Start with tiny twigs and bark. Pick twigs that snap when you bend them, and only take fallen branches. Pile pencil-sized twigs in a loose teepee formation. Add bigger branches as you work outward. Stuff paper and dried bark in the open spaces. Light the paper and bark first and fan it lightly. When things start heating up, add bigger branches and eventually logs. You'll need to fiddle with it pretty constantly to keep the fire roaring. Before you fall asleep or leave camp, pour on enough water to be sure every ember is snuffed.

Other Assorted Needs

Some beach sites prohibit fires, and wind and rain can also prevent a fire from getting strong enough for cooking, so you may want to bring along a camp stove. Call your friends and see if you can borrow instead of buy. If you do buy one, get one that runs on propane. Butane/propane mixture stoves are more compact, but also more expensive, and refill tanks are a little harder to find. Again, prices range widely, from $15 to $150.

Don't forget to tote along some potables. You can schlep five gallons of fresh water weighing forty pounds to last you just two days, or you can splurge on a water purification system which will turn most stream, river, and lake water into drinking water. Grab a few water bottles so you can carry some of the wet stuff along with you on hikes.

Here are some other odds and ends to buy:

• Pocketknife, can opener, and corkscrew
• Basic first-aid kit
• Lighters and matches
• Small handheld garden shovel for digging cat-holes
• Toilet paper and paper towels (take the cardboard rolls out so they take up less space)
• Bug spray (bring a few different brands just in case the bugs you encounter are immune to a certain kind) and citronella candles
• Dr. Bronner's biodegradable soap (it can be used as body soap, dish soap, and toothpaste—just don't swallow—and is as environmentally friendly as soap gets)
• Sunscreen
• Flashlights (check the batteries and bring extra)
• Trash bags (can be used as hats, tarps, jackets, even shower caps)
• Rope (can come in handy as a clothesline, tarp-hanger, or belt)
• Duct tape (of course)

SKIRTS, PANTIES, AND FEMININE WILES

If your pack isn't making your knees buckle yet, throw in some clothes. Revel in the knowledge that no one will be there to make sure you match. On a warm-weather weekend excursion, you can make do with one pair of pants, two T-shirts or tank tops, a hoodie, a skirt (okay, or shorts), a swimsuit, and about five pairs of socks (make sure one is knee-high for hiking in tall grass). Take extra panties so you can change liberally, which will help you feel fresh and clean, despite the lack of showering. Use a designated plastic grocery bag for all the dirty unmentionables. Tie it up tightly and stash it in your pack.

Hardcore campers might claim otherwise, but good sneakers are a fine substitute for hiking boots. Flip-flops are essential when bathroom emergencies strike in the middle of the night. A cowboy hat camouflages bad camping hair and really completes the nature-girl fantasy, but pigtails and braids also have a cute Pocahontas appeal. Sexy saltwater locks are another clear benefit to beach camping, but if you're in the woods, lightly dusting your hair with baby powder will cut down on grease. Baby wipes keep things fresh down below.

the city girl's camping motto: go prepared

Here's a quick list of tips to avoid offending the granola crowd and ensure that you'll impress the owls. Again, common sense and research prevail.

• If you're site camping, try to position yourself away from other people or at least use your quiet voice. Everyone's out there looking for their own Walden, and it probably doesn't include you.

• If you're backcountry camping, pick a pre-existing site. A fire ring or a clearing is an excellent clue.

• Check the weather religiously before you leave. Bad weather doesn't have to spoil the fun if you're ready for it.

• You don't want to be sent packing just when your marshmallows start toasting. Check online or call the ranger for any necessary permits and fees.

• Don't keep food in the tent unless you fancy wild beasts in your pajamas. To keep food from bears, you may have to hang it from a tree, about 10 feet up and 10 feet away from the tree trunk. Every place will have detailed animal warnings and precautions, so again, call first.

• Everything but paper, which can be burned, must be carried out. The saying goes, "Take only pictures, leave only footprints."

• Plan to arrive with at least two daylight hours to set up and get your bearings. You don't want to wake up to find your tent on top of some stinky deer pellets.

• If you don't find level ground for the tent, you'll have a major headache in the morning. Remove any stray rocks or twigs, and beef up the padding with leaves and dirt. Stakes can pull easily out of sand, so look for a grassy area or bring extra-long stakes.

• Dump wastewater, even biodegradable soap, at least 150 feet from water sources.

• To make a cat hole, dig a hole at least 6" deep and wide, and 200 feet from water, trails, and sites. Stick a shovel or branch in the ground standing up in front of you for support. After you fill the hole, cover it up again with dirt. Carry out the used toilet paper in a designated plastic bag for yucky waste, as it doesn't decompose that fast. Be thankful your cat isn't there to see you.

• For even more info on what to bring and where to go, check out the Resources on page 356.

FOOD, BOOZE, AND MEDICINAL PLANTS

Campfire cooking is a sport. Mincing garlic on a plastic plate balanced on your thighs while ants head for your Muenster will be a test of your culinary skills. Plan recipes for each meal so you don't overpack. If you aren't hiking far and have the luxury of bringing ice, you can be more decadent. If not, you can still indulge in delicious eats, have your morning dark roast, and go to sleep nice and soused.

Foodstuffs

Dry beans, pasta, and grains are lightweight and make versatile dishes, but canned beans are certainly easier to cook if you don't mind carrying them. Garlic, onions, broccoli, and peppers have lasting power and don't need to be kept cool, and dried foods like sun-dried tomatoes are flavorful and nearly weightless. Don't forget a small plastic bottle of oil, and don't be ashamed to stoop to ramen when you're feeling lazy. Fill film canisters with various spice combinations: red and hot; sweet and cinnamony; complex and exotic.

A few bricks of cheese and a loaf of bread will supply lunch for at least a few days, but prepare to develop a taste for melty, air-temperature cheese. Fruit is filling, healthy, and makes you feel all naturey; it can be heavy, though, so prioritize. A few naughty snacks like chips and chocolate are fun to look forward to—if your companions don't eat them all during the car ride.

Cooking Supplies

One old soup pot, two plastic dishes that can double as cutting boards, two spoons, and a sharp knife are all you need to create a spread for two, but don't even try to go at it without a few pieces of aluminum foil. A barbecue grate is light and provides an easy cooking surface, but heating up some flat rocks will do the trick, too. Don't forget a trusty cup for coffee and wine. Coolers are marvels of the modern world and are great for trips where you won't be hiking far, but if you are, you'll have to rethink anything that requires cooling.

Liquid Indulgences

When it comes to treats of the chemical variety, get your caffeine fix with tea bags of coffee. Skip the cream or bring a small container of the powdered stuff. If a cooler is feasible, you can bring a few cans of beer for the first day. After that, if another ice trip is out of the question, switch to red wine for days two and three. Wine is heavy, though, so the hard stuff goes farther. By day three and beyond, move on to tequila—it goes down just fine warm with plenty of limes. Remember, any substance that increases the likelihood of cosmic staring off into space is perfect for camping.

At the end of every camping trip, reward all your hard work with a decadent meal. Camping is work. But it's not work the way most of us know it. It's the kind of labor that forces you to sleep deep and hard, actually produces thirst and hunger for physical rather than habitual reasons, makes your armpits deliciously smelly, and gives you that sneaky little euphoric suspicion that you can do anything.

tag, you're it

SPRUCE UP YOUR SUITCASE WITH CRAFTY LUGGAGE LABELS // Valerie Rains

A good suitcase is hard to find—especially when it's rotating around a baggage carousel in a tidy row with all the other black, nylon, wheeled suitcases. The simple solution to the problem? A distinctive and dutiful luggage tag to help you spot your stuff. Here are two great ways to make your own.

pinning away

materials

Button-maker tool
(available from
www.badgeaminit.com)

Printout or photocopy
of a map of your area

Scissors

Fine-point pen

1 To make this tag, borrow or buy a button-maker tool. Then take your map and use the template from the button kit to trace a circle around the portion of the map containing your street.

2 Cut out the map and write your name and address on the circle, being careful to keep all the writing at least ¼" in from the edges of the circle.

3 Follow the button maker's instructions for converting your contact information into a slick pin and attach it to the front of your luggage.

roller coaster

materials

2 paper coasters
of the same shape

Pen

Cutting mat or buffer
cardboard

Utility knife

Translucent plastic (office
sheet protectors work well)

Craft glue

Hole punch

Index card

Ribbon, shoelace, or
ball-chain key ring

1 Choose one coaster to be the front of your tag. Trace around a driver's license or credit card in the center of it (or in a space that works with the design on the coaster). Place a sheet of cardboard or other buffer material underneath your coaster and cut out the shape with the utility knife to make a window.

2 Cut a section of plastic ¼" larger than the window on every side and glue it to the inside of the coaster.

3 Once the glue has dried, punch a hole at one end of the windowed coaster and place it on top of the second (whole) coaster. Mark where the hole was punched and create a corresponding hole in the second coaster.

4 Apply a thin line of glue around three-quarters of the perimeter of one coaster (or around three edges of the perimeter if your coasters are square), leaving the portion of the coaster with the hole in it unglued. Affix the second coaster to it, and allow the glue to dry.

5 Cut an index card down to a size that will fit between the coasters through the unglued opening, write your address on it, and slip it in. Attach the finished tag to your suitcase with the ribbon, shoelace, or ball-chain key ring.

baby got bike

PICK WHEELS YOU'LL REALLY USE // Jennifer Skorcz

Selecting the right bike can be daunting, so here's a primer to help you make your choice. For all styles, check out the women-specific bikes—their geometry and tailoring make them a smart pick.

TRAIL BLAZER

If rugged riding sounds up your alley, you'll want to buy the lightest mountain bike you can afford to make climbing and maneuvering easier as you build strength. Opting for front suspension will make your bike fairly easy to negotiate through moderately technical sections of trail, while full suspension is designed to flow through demanding technical terrain at higher speeds. Suspension is a performance feature, not a comfort feature—it's heavy and will feel sluggish on pavement, so it's best to keep this beauty on the trails.

ROAD WARRIOR

Road bikes are intended to be ridden long distances for fitness, touring, and competition. The curved handlebars provide several torso-position options—a necessary feature when you're on the saddle for hours—but most put the rider in a forward-leaning position meant to provide aerodynamic benefits for competitive cyclists. If you're cycling for fitness, try a compact-geometry road bike (a frame with a sloping top tube, which promotes a more upright and comfortable riding posture). Because road bikes are intended for pavement, they have skinny, smooth tires. If you desire a bit of tread, have the tires switched for cross tires.

COMMUTER

A commuter bike is your best bet for getting to and from the office. It combines the comfort of a mountain bike's flat handlebars with the efficient large-diameter wheels and skinny tires found on a road bike. When deciding what features you need, keep a few things in mind. A flat route does not require the same gearing as one with hills; if you'll be riding at night, make sure you add lights; if you plan to carry things with you, such as clothing or a laptop, get a rack and pannier.

THE CRUISER

Perfect for leisurely rides through the neighborhood, lifestyle bikes are not typically designed for long rides—they tend to be heavy and built with relaxed, cruiser geometry. For a short, slow pedal along the boardwalk or a quick jaunt to the farmers' market, a lifestyle bike is the way to go.

READY TO BUY?

Purchasing a bike at a shop means you can work with a knowledgeable person who can answer questions, measure you and the bike to make sure it's properly adjusted for fit, and fine-tune any components that affect comfort. Leave room in your budget for accessories: a helmet, lights, a bell to let others know you're coming up behind them, and, depending on the biking you'll do, riding gloves or padded cycling shorts.

road ready

KEEP YOUR BIKE RIDING FINE WITH THIS MAINTENANCE GUIDE // Jenny Rose Ryan

So you finally saved enough to buy yourself a new set of wheels. While your new bike will surely save you cash on transit, that doesn't mean you can neglect it when it's not in motion. Ignoring basic maintenance means repairs will come faster, be more complex, and be a whole lot pricier. Follow these tips and you'll be upright and ready to respond. If your regular maintenance still won't stop that clunky sound, you can always bring your bike to the bike shop for a tune-up. Or, tune in to the awesome how-to videos on BicycleTutor.com.

BRAKE LEVER

BRAKES

FORK

SPOKES

CRANKS

DERAILLEUR

SEAT POST

SEAT TUBE

RIM

TIRE

COG

ready your rubbers

For tire maintenance, get a big floor pump and a smaller one for travel, and be sure to check your tires weekly. If there's too little air, your tires are prone to punctures and you won't be able to go as fast.

1 Lean your bike against something sturdy like a wall (or have a friend hold it). Find the tube stem along the inside of the rim (that thingy with the black cap) and unscrew the cap. If yours doesn't have a cap, you're already ahead of the game. Attach your handy-dandy pump to the valve and lock it in place.

2 Check the tire's sidewall for the recommended PSI (pounds per square inch) and aim to fill the tire to about 80 percent of the maximum. Keep an eye on the gauge as you pump and stop when it reaches the desired PSI. Fill it too much and little bumps will feel like you're going over railroad ties. Fill it just right and not only will you be fast, but your ass will thank you too.

3 Unlock the lever, remove the pump, and replace the black cap. Now take your bike for a spin on the air you put in it.

fix a flat

In the event of a flat, you'll need to patch your tube. With your handy mini bike pump, a tire lever, and a patch kit, you can even fix it on the road.

1 Remove the tire from the rim by gently pushing the tire lever in between the rim and the rubber and pulling outward on the tire with your other hand. Continue all the way around the tire until everything comes apart; it'll make a satisfying zipping sound. Set the tire aside.

2 Remove the tube from the tire and deflate it with your hands, feeling for the puncture as you do so. If you have a pen, mark the spot. If not, don't forget where it is.

3 Your kit will come with a piece of sandpaper. Use this to gently sand the tube around the hole, roughing up an area slightly larger than the size of the patch.

4 Apply a thin layer of glue on and around the hole.

5 Place the patch gently on the center of the hole, applying pressure from the inside and smoothing as you go. Apply consistent pressure on the patch for about a minute.

6 Wrap the tube around the rim and push the valve through its designated hole in the rim. Wrap the tire around the tube.

7 Using your hands and the tire lever (for tight spots), push the walls of the tire back into the rim starting at the valve. Work all the way around the rim. Often the last six inches are the most difficult part to get in.

8 Once the tire is around the tube and is completely in the rim, inflate the tube to the desired PSI (see above).

brake like a fool

Braking creates a lot of friction that, over time, can wear down brake pads on rim and disc brakes. This makes stopping harder and your ass less safe. If your brakes don't seem to be responding like they used to, test them by lifting the front tire off the ground and spinning the wheel. Squeeze the front tire hand brake. It should stop the wheel almost immediately. Repeat the lifting and spinning procedure for the back brakes. If the brakes don't work quickly on the wheels, check the brake pads where they contact the rim. New pads have deep grooves. If the grooves are worn away, your brake pads need replacing.

If you don't know what to get, bring your bike to your local bike shop and ask for help. There are two types of brake pads: cartridge and bolt-on. Cartridge pads require no tools to install, while bolt-on pads, duh, bolt onto the brake. Always replace both pads on a brake at the same time.

Now let's get started. Grab your pads (and a wrench or screwdriver, if your brakes are the bolt-on variety).

1 Disconnect the brakes by removing the brake cable from the brake clamp. To do so, press the brake pads together and pull out the cable (figure 1).

2 If you have cartridge pads, slide the cartridge from the clamp. Remove bolt-on brake pads by using a wrench to unfasten the bolt that holds them in place (figure 2).

3 Place the new cartridge pad into the clamps with the grooved side facing the rims (figure 3). If it's a bolt-on, place the pad so it contacts the rim when the brakes are activated, and fasten the bolt.

4 Reassemble the brakes by replacing the brake cable, and take a short ride to test the alignment. If things don't hit the rim as they should, adjust the angle and placement of the pad. Make small adjustments and keep testing as you go. If you're still having trouble, time to wheel yourself in to the local bike shop.

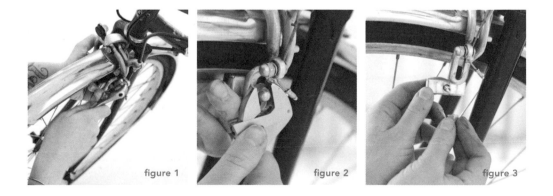

figure 1   figure 2   figure 3

lube your chain

Aside from your wheels, the chain is what makes your bike go. Keep it running smoothly by keeping it clean and lubed just like your Saturday night. Make sure you're in clothes you don't mind getting a little greasy, and turn your bike upside down so you can move the pedals freely. Don't spill degreaser on any paint jobs, though, or you can take that clear off, too.

materials

Latex gloves

Biodegradable degreaser (Simple Green is a good one to try)

Water

Plastic bottle or bucket

3 clean rags (cut up old T-shirts work great)

Old toothbrush

Chain lube from your local bike shop (under no circumstances should you use WD-40—it's actually a degreaser and solvent, not a lube)

1 Put on your gloves, then mix one part degreaser to two or three parts water in the plastic bottle or bucket. Don't make a bunch at first; you can always whip up more.

2 Dump some of this degreaser/water combo on a clean rag. Soak it, but don't drench it.

3 Grip the chain with the rag in one hand and pedal backward with your other hand (figure 1). Pass over the chain once or twice, then rotate the rag to a clean part (and soak it with more degreaser if you need to).

4 Keep backpedaling and holding the chain, pausing periodically to check for caked-on junk. Use the toothbrush and some more degreaser to scrub off these gross bits (figure 2). Try to make everything as shiny and new as possible.

5 Once the chain is as clean as you want, wash it off with water, dab it with a clean rag, and allow to air dry.

6 Immediately after the chain is dry, dab it with the chain lube, making sure to get all the links (figure 3). Use the last clean rag to wipe excess oil from the chains, and you're lubed and ready to go.

figure 1

figure 2

figure 3

meals on wheels

ENJOY LUNCH ON THE GO WITH A BIKE BAG YOU CAN SEW // Lenore M. Edman

materials

½ yard canvas or another sturdy fabric, like oilcloth or vinyl

Sewing machine with matching thread

3 Velcro cable ties (available at hardware and electronics stores)

Velcro tape

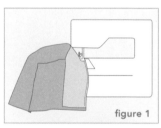

figure 1

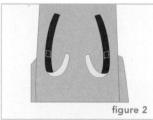

figure 2

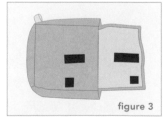

figure 3

Whether you're commuting to work with leftovers in tow or biking to the park for an outdoor sammie, skip the backpack and store your meal in this easy-to-sew lunch bag. Just the right shape for an entrée-size plastic container, it hangs from the top tube of your bike (or your handlebars if your top tube slopes) and fits perfectly in the frame, so it won't slow you down when you ride like the wind.

1 Cut your fabric into an 8" square (for the front of your bag), an 8"-by-13" rectangle (for the back and flap), and a 3"-by-22" strip (for the sides and bottom). For all the sewing that follows, the seam allowances are ½".

2 With right sides facing, sew the strip around three edges of the square piece of fabric, making sure the strip's short edges are flush with the raw edge of the square (figure 1). At each corner, put your sewing machine needle down, raise the presser foot, and pivot the material so you can sew the next side (after lowering the presser foot again).

3 Create a rolled hem across the top of the fabric by folding the edge over ¼" and ¼" again. Sew it down. Canvas holds a finger crease well, which makes a rolled hem fairly easy.

4 Now attach the back and flap of your bag. With right sides facing, match a short edge of the rectangular piece of fabric to the bottom of the bag, and sew along the sides and bottom, putting your sewing machine needle down, raising the presser foot, and pivoting the fabric at the corners like you did before. There should be about 5" of fabric left to form the flap.

5 Create a rolled hem on the raw edges of the flap by folding each side over ¼" and ¼" again (fold in the tips of the corners before rolling the sides to create a neat point) and hem.

6 It's Velcro time! Velcro cable ties are ultra-thin (so they won't interfere with the cabling on your bicycle), easy to sew, and hold extremely well. Sew two ties to the top of the bag (each about 4" from the end of the flap, about ½" from each side) (figure 2). These will attach to the top tube of your bike. Sew one more tie to one of the bag's sides (about 1" from the bottom) that will attach to the seat tube.

7 To make the flap closable, sew a 3" piece of Velcro tape to the middle of the inside flap (about a ¼" from the end of the flap and about 3" from each side) and to the corresponding spot on the outside of your bag, so the pieces match up and easily secure. Sew 1" of Velcro tape to the inside corner of the flap that points to the front of the bicycle (opposite the side of the bag with the cable tie) with a corresponding piece on the front of the bag so they match up and secure (figure 3). You'll want that extra bit of Velcro on the side to keep the fabric from flapping as you zoom along.

hit the road

TIPS FOR PLANNING A BIKE TOUR // Michelle Dobrovolny

Maybe you want to test yourself by pedaling from your city to a friend's neighboring town. Maybe you want adventure. Maybe you're sick of cars. Or maybe you want a trip that is less about the destination and more about getting there. Anywhere you can go by car, you can go by bicycle, and anyone who plans well, takes a few precautions, and is prepared for the unexpected can hit the road on a bike. Now, where do you want to go?

THE ESSENTIAL FACTORS
Here are a few important things to keep in mind while planning your trip.

- **Season:** You don't want to be pedaling in snow or grueling heat.
- **Wind Direction:** This varies by region and season. Pedaling against the wind wastes energy, so it's worth figuring out which way it will likely be blowing.
- **Elevations:** Take into account the reduced energy you'll experience on days requiring uphill travel.
- **Distance:** Mileage between water stops is important to consider. Plan on carrying extra water until you learn how much fluid your body needs. Generally, try to avoid routes that require cycling through uncivilized stretches spanning more than 30 miles.

HOW ARE YOU GOING TO GET THERE?
Low-traffic, paved routes are best. Gravel roads are rideable, but only with the right tires. Some interstate highways have wide shoulders ideal for cycling; on others, cycling is illegal. You will benefit from following roads that someone has cycled before, though the route may be indirect. The Adventure Cycling Association

(www.adventurecycling.org) has more than 37,000 miles of cycling routes mapped throughout the U.S.

HOW LONG WILL IT TAKE?
Whether it's a three-day tour or a two-month one, it's important to plan out your ride. First-timers won't want to pedal 100 miles a day, even if they can handle it physically, because grueling exertion isn't the point of the ride. Take a little time to see things along the way, commune with nature, and relax with the pace of the road.

WHERE ARE YOU GOING TO SLEEP?
Some cyclists will plop down a sleeping bag in whatever area is semisecluded. For those who are not so brave, check a guidebook to find out what's available along the way. You may want to call ahead to make sure the campground will be open or that there will be a vacancy. For more luxurious accommodations, plan a trip through towns where you have friends and/or family and catch some Z's on someone's couch.

HOW WILL YOU STAY SAFE?
A culture of fear has long infected women. Its dicta are well known: "Don't talk to

strangers." . . . "Don't walk alone at night." . . . "Don't ever go anywhere by yourself. You will be raped and killed." . . . "You are a victim." We carry this burden of fear throughout our lives. But not only is the fear unjustified, it is in fact also dangerously misdirected. There's no need for you to be scared to leave your home and have an adventure. Just take some basic precautions: Keep in contact with a close friend or family member while you're on your journey. Check in. Tell the person about anything weird you encounter. And, if at any time you feel in danger, pedal to a public place and call 9-1-1.

Staying safe extends to the ride itself, of course. Keep hydrated. Eat often. And anytime you feel like you need to stop, listen to your body. You're not trying to race through France, after all.

WHAT WILL YOU BRING?

- Bicycle multitool
- Patch kit, extra tire tube, and tire levers
- Padded cycling shorts
- Baby powder (to absorb ass sweat)
- Helmet
- Cycling gloves
- Water pack
- Side bags (for carrying your gear)
- Food, food, and more food
- Compass and maps
- Air horn (to scare off unfriendly dogs)
- Sense of humor (for dealing with headwinds, rainstorms, broken spokes, and stupid cars that won't share the road)

Now, start planning and pedaling. For more in-depth information about planning a bike trip, check out the Resources on page 356.

hod roddin'

BUYING A VINTAGE CAR // **Sunny Chanel**

Sure, a car just gets you from point A to point B, but sometimes a gal wants to get there in style without spending a year's salary. That's where the vintage automobile comes in. Most old cars were built to last, and with the right care and consideration, a vintage car can potentially swing for a few more decades.

CLASSIC CAR PITFALLS

It's true that there are risks in buying an old car. Like that boy at the bar, you have no idea where a used car has been until it's been tested. So when you check out the steel-hearted stallion of your dreams, make sure to take it for a vigorous drive. Trust your senses—eyes, ears, nose, touch, and common sense. Hear any grinding, banging, or other bizarre sounds? Consider them warning signs. Examine the car inside and out (even better: have a car-smart friend do it, too) to make sure everything looks satisfactory. Keep an eye out for rust, a bent frame, oil leaks, smoke in the exhaust, or an engine covered in oil. An auto that needs a new transmission, head gasket, or even an entire engine is one you'll definitely want to avoid. Other repairs can be easily and economically fixed. The cost of any and all repairs is dependent on the make, model, and malady; parts are often the biggest bite. That 1965 Ford Fairlane will be much easier to find parts for than an '81 DeLorean DMC-12 (since Ford designed Fairlanes for the middle class and sold zillions, while there were only something like 9,000 DMC-12s made). With more common American vintage cars, it is amazing what you can pull from your local neighborhood junkyard.

HOW TO FIND YOUR DREAM CAR?

Before you start looking, figure out what you want, be it a '70s muscle car, a '50s lead sled, or a '60s slant back. Also keep in mind that an American car will generally be cheaper to maintain. Then check your local papers, periodicals like *Auto Trader*, and the Internet and make sure to keep an eye out for those sale signs in car windows. Don't get any fancy ideas about buying your used car on an opposite coast and breaking it in on a cross-country road trip—that's trouble just waiting to happen.

AVOID A LEMON

When it comes down to it, use your instincts. If the deal sounds too good to be true, it probably is. Don't be afraid to have your own trusty mechanic check it out before you throw down the cold hard cash. If the seller has nothing to hide, then he or she won't have an issue with having others examine it. If you play your cards right, you'll not only have saved a whole lot of moolah, but you'll also have made a magnificent mobile match.

so sue me

WHAT TO DO IF YOU'RE IN A CAR ACCIDENT // Jenny Ramo

Automobile accidents are terrifying, and if you're lucky, they only leave you shaky and disoriented. Just about the last things on anyone's mind in such situations are lawyers, courts, and money. Yet what you don't want to do in this state is set yourself up for a lawsuit or jeopardize your rights to compensation. Even if it is your fault, here are a few things personal injury attorneys recommend you do if you are involved in a car accident.

1 Take photos. Grab your camera phone and photograph the accident scene. This provides an indisputable record of the facts and helps ensure that nobody involved in the accident later deviates from the story.

2 Never admit fault. This sounds like a horrible lawyerly suggestion, but the fact is that your idea of what is your fault may not actually be your fault under the law. Admitting fault simply stops the investigation into the accident prematurely and could cost you dearly.

3 Always wait for the cops. Cops are good, not evil (sometimes). Of all the times you might need a police officer, this is it. They will make sure anyone who needs medical attention gets it, sketch the scene, assign fault, and make the whole thing less traumatic.

4 Don't talk to the other driver. Another evil lawyer suggestion, but it's true. It's okay to make sure the other person is safe and not injured, but the more you speak to them, the more you will discuss what happened, and the more likely it is to lead to a misunderstanding. Be friendly, but be quiet.

5 Don't leave the scene. Never leave the scene of an accident, even to go across the street to get something. The police will still consider that leaving the scene. You must exchange information, and if you have called the police, you should wait for them.

6 Ask to see the other driver's information. Make sure to copy down all of their relevant details, even if you think you will never use it. Get a business card, their home and work numbers and addresses, the car's vehicle identification number, proof of insurance and the name and phone number of the insurance company, their driver's license number—anything to identify this person should they fail to return your phone calls when it comes time for their insurance to pay up, or if it turns out their insurance has expired. If they don't have insurance, it's even more important to get all their information—and to call the police. Your insurance company will go after them first with police-verified information, but if they can't collect, they'll still cover your losses.

With these tips, you should be able to get your car fixed quickly and turn away from that fender bender. Just make sure you remember to signal.

run baby run

TIPS TO HELP YOU STOP HATING RUNNING   //   **Jenny Rose Ryan**

If you hate running, it's probably because (A) you think it's boring, (B) it's just too much work, (C) it makes you feel like you're having a heart attack, or (D) all of the above. But it doesn't have to be like that. If you take it easy at first, build your endurance gradually, and incorporate elements of fun (your dog, a special running-music mix, a shiny new sports bra), running can be more than just a fast way to get your workout done. Check out these tips on how to stop hating running and you'll be ready to slip on some sneaks and hit the streets.

START WITH SHORT DISTANCES

If you've never run before, or you hated it too much to keep going, you need to start small. Run to the corner store first or take a jog to the coffee shop. Try alternating one block of running with one block of walking to ease you into the feeling. If you're running on a treadmill, alternate a couple minutes of running with a couple minutes of walking. As you get stronger, increase the time you spend running and soon you won't have to stop at all.

Running too much, too hard when you're first starting out is a big reason people decide to hate running. Try running one day and walking the next. Give your body time to adjust to running's unique sensations and challenges and you'll be a whole lot happier (and less sore).

DON'T TRY TO BE THE FASTEST

Sure, running is faster than walking, but you shouldn't be sprinting. You're not an Olympian (yet) and you don't have to make your lungs and legs burn to feel the benefits. Pace yourself so you can have a conversation without getting breathless. A jaunt around the park shouldn't feel like fight or flight.

THINK ABOUT YOUR BREATH

Being mindful of your breath will help keep you from panting. It also keeps your running efficient, which helps reduce stress on your joints. Just inhale for three steps and exhale for two, so you're exhaling on alternating steps. It will take some getting used to, but it will become second nature once you get the hang of it.

MAKE IT FUN

Sprint to a tree. Walk when you want. Skip or hop. Mix up your pacing to add variety and keep it interesting—this will also help you get faster. A special mix of running tunes can make all the difference when you work out. Craft a mix that follows the flow of your workout. If you need extra motivation in the beginning, start with some upbeat tunes. If you want to zone out and meditate, calm it down after that. And change the mix often so you can stay focused and interested. You can also take some time to map out routes you want to try. Make short ones for days you're just not feeling it, and try a long run that's on a transit route. That way, if your motivation exceeds your ability, you don't have to hobble home or call a cab.

Staring at your feet as the blocks click on is exhausting and makes every step feel like a hundred miles. Keep your head up and watch the world around you. You might even get a smile or two from runners passing by or from that cutie in the gym.

DON'T STRESS ABOUT SHOES
Sure, it'd be nice to spend a Benjamin on a killer pair of kicks, but you can run just as well with an old pair of Sauconys. Your pacing and breathing matter more. Once you get the basics down and realize you love it, head to a specialty store and get fit for the fancy ones.

CREATE A SCHEDULE
When it comes to running, the key is to create a pattern that becomes so second nature, you'll forget it's a schedule at all. If you're more of a morning person, slip on your shoes before breakfast. If you like to go at night, wear a reflective vest (and stay on populated trails or sidewalks). If you normally walk your dog at four p.m., try runing Fido instead. (You can get special leashes that strap onto your waist so you don't have to worry about carrying them—and remember, some dogs need to warm up to running, too, so go slow at first.) If you're really lucky and have a place to shower at work, the noontime run is a great way to break up the day. Plus, then you can be lazy when you get home. Once you establish a running routine and keep it up for a few weeks, you might even feel weird if you skip a run.

SET A GOAL
Have a neighborhood 5K you've always wanted to support? Sign up for the event, then start training. The Couch to 5K program is a good guide (www.c25k.com). Need some friends to motivate you? Get them to sign up too. Running might seem like a singular sport, but it's even more fun with a group.

MIX IT UP
Don't feel like running one day? Don't do it. No one is testing you. Go for a bike ride. Swim in a pool. Or spend the evening on the couch with a good book. Even hard-core marathoners take days off from their favorite sport, and you should too.

REWARD YOURSELF
Think of yourself as the donkey in pursuit of the carrot, or the mouse after the cheese, and reward yourself after a run with something that makes you happy. It can be gluttonous or relaxing, but what matters is that it's something you only do after you run.

sk8 or die

A BEGINNER'S GUIDE TO BOARDING // Amy Gunther

Some people may think of skateboarding as a guy sport, but with so much of the action based on hip movement, it's actually very womanly. It just takes a little psyching up and a lot of focus. Another awesome thing about skating is that you don't have to join a team to do it; you can go out skating day or night by yourself and learn a trick or two. Think you're ready to take a spin? Here are some basic things to keep in mind when first stepping on a board.

BUYING YOUR RIDE

When looking for a board, make sure you're getting one that's the correct width—anywhere between 7 ½" and 8 ¼" wide is good. Choose whatever feels most comfortable when you're standing on it. The trucks—which are what attach the wheels to the board—should not be too tight or loose; test this by standing on the board and rocking back and forth heel to toe, making sure there is some give. Tight trucks may feel better at first, but they make it hard to turn. Better to start out with trucks that are looser than you'd like; it will make you a better skater in the long run. Finally, make sure the wheels are the right size. Small wheels are good for technical tricks and staying slow and stable, while bigger wheels go faster and are better for skating on mini ramps. A 53- or 54-mm wheel is good for beginners.

BEST FOOT FORWARD

Figure out whether you're "goofy foot," which means you like your right foot in front, or regular stance, left foot in front. You can test this by standing on the ground with your feet together, and having someone push you from behind. Whatever foot goes forward naturally is usually your lead foot.

STAND BY ME

Stance on your board is really important; you want to be as relaxed as possible. Stand with your feet sideways, about shoulder-width apart (they should be over the bolts of the board). Bend your knees—almost uncomfortably at first—and hold your arms slightly out to the sides.

ROLL YOUR OWN WAY

The first actual "trick" to learn is just pushing. Keep your front foot on the board and push with your back foot as far as you can. Find a mellow street and just get comfortable riding down it. Lightly use your toes and heels to balance. Practice stopping by using your back foot as a brake. Just drag it to make a stop. Remember to breathe!

STEER IT UP

Push toward your toes to steer the board in the direction that they're pointing (to the left if you're goofy, to the right if you're regular stance) and lean back on your heels to steer the board in the opposite direction. Here's where you'll really notice if your trucks are loose enough or too tight. Don't be afraid to tweak the trucks with a skate key or wrench if they feel too tight.

TUMBLE FOR YA

If (and when) you fall, try to land on your side, not your hands! The body can take way more impact than your fragile wrists. Avoid using wrist guards, because then you'll think about using your hands to fall. Practice falling by tucking your hands in and using the momentum of the fall to land on your side. Other protective gear is totally optional. Wear knee pads if you're going to skate on ramps, though. The impact of falling from over five feet is a lot, and you can teach yourself to land on the pads.

Keep practicing and soon you'll impress all the skaters with your radical tricks. Take that, boys club.

pumping iron

WEIGHT TRAINING FOR BEGINNERS // Jenny Rose Ryan

Feel like Olive Oyl and wish you were more like Popeye? You don't need to get a gym membership to pump yourself up. Just follow these simple at-home weight-lifting tricks that'll increase your strength, give you more energy, and improve your other workouts—no gym required. The next time you have to move a sofa or lift heavy boxes, you won't be the weakest link. And by working out at home, you won't have to suffer through whatever someone else picked on TV.

figure 1   figure 2   figure 3

BEFORE YOU START

Before you start lifting weights, run your new exercise program by your doctor, who may suggest modifications to your planned exercises to ensure that you stay injury free.

PICK OUT YOUR WEIGHTS

Weight lifting relies on overloading your muscles so they have to work hard to overcome the resistance. If you give yourself too little resistance, your muscles won't have to work as hard. Too much resistance, you might find that you're swinging the weight in order to get momentum to lift it (which is a no-no). The weight should be heavy enough that you can ONLY achieve the number of repetitions (reps) you plan to complete. Get a set of free weights (a.k.a. dumbbells) in your desired weight—10 pounds each is usually a good starting point. If you suspect this might be too much or too little, get a couple different sizes.

WARM UP

Always warm up before you start lifting. Do a few jumping jacks or wait to pick up your weights until after you've done your cardio workout. You want your muscles to be primed to go.

WHILE YOU'RE LIFTING

Remember never to hold your breath while lifting; you don't want to strain yourself. Keep your abdominal muscles tight, maintain a straight back, and lift using the muscles only, not the weights' momentum.

Lift 1: Shoulder Muscles

To do a basic overhead press, stand (or sit) up straight with elbows bent and hands at eye level, holding the weights with your palms facing away from you. Push the weights overhead without arching your back, then lower the weights to where they started (figure 1). Do 12 to 16 reps.

Lift 2: Work the Back

This exercise, called a row, works the muscles on either side of the body. To do a basic row, stand with your knees bent and lean forward about 45 degrees at the waist. Hold the weights with your palms facing away from your body and let the weights hang down. Using your back and arms, bend your elbows and pull them back and upward, to torso level (figure 2). Do 12 to 16 reps.

Lift 3: Work Your Arms

Stand with your feet about hip distance apart. Hold the weights in front of your thighs, wrists facing away from you. Squeeze your biceps and bend your arms to curl the weights to your shoulders (figure 3). Keep your elbows stationary. Do 8 to 15 reps.

Perform this series of three lifts, then rest and repeat. Take a day off, take a warm bath, and let your muscles adjust to their power. After a day, you can go again. Warning: When you first start, you will be sore. But that's what happens when you break down and rebuild muscles.

toy story

MAKE YOUR OWN SEX TOYS // Erika Bardot

Hello, sex kittens. Today's lesson is about sexual imagination and looking at the world through kinky-colored glasses. It's time to spend a Saturday shopping for sex toys in unlikely places. Do it alone or bring your lover to share in the search. In discovering the sexual potential in nonsexual objects, you and your lover will open new lines of communication and develop new ways of relating. Just remember: never let shame or embarrassment prevent you from asking for what you want in bed or anywhere else. Be open to new things, but never be afraid to demand respect for your boundaries. Most importantly, let yourself have fun. Now, get out there and find these goodies that will surely tickle your fancy.

PLAYING WITH YOURSELF

Let's start at the toy store, where everything is nontoxic and nonstaining. Bathtub or finger paints turn bath time into fun time. Think about what one could do with a squirt gun and warm bathwater. Ping-Pong paddles are good for spanking. Toy handcuffs have the benefit of being easily breakable. Around Halloween, you can find sequined masks, tiaras, feather boas, wigs, and other fun role-playing stuff. Don't forget the candy aisle!

SEX IS ART

Next stop—the art-supply store. Find the softest paintbrushes you can afford, and choose a few different sizes. Use these, wet or dry, to lazily trace along your partner's skin. "Write" erotic things on your partner and have them try to read your message by the sensation. Think of all the yummy liquids you could use for paint. Chocolate sauce, perhaps? Crème de menthe? Get some low-melting-temperature (not dripless) wax candles. Test the heat of the melted wax before you play. Warm wax being dripped onto (hairless) skin is startlingly exciting. Also, buy some sheer chiffon and experiment with blindfolding.

HARD(ON) WEAR

On to the hardware store. Here, you will find rope by the yard. White nylon rope will satisfy all your bondage needs with little danger of rope burn. Get a very long piece. If you prefer chain, the store will cut it to any length you want. Those quick-release double key rings come in handy, too. Check out the cleaning supply section. That's not a feather duster, honey, that's a bum tickler! And the wiring section—that's not electrical tape, that's your new push-up bra!

COP A FEEL

But wait! There's more! Make a special trip to the cop store (Google local sources for "uniforms") for real handcuffs, nightsticks, and those supersexxy police hats.

CLAMP DOWN

The drugstore holds a few surprises too. Spring-hinged hair clips make gentle and effective nipple clamps and cloth bandages make great bondage wraps.

DOGGY STYLE

The pet store has cute dog collars and leashes. Cat collars are good for wrists and ankles.

FOODIE FUN

Hungry after all your shopping? Time to head to the grocery store. Food and sex are natural bedfellows, especially when hands aren't allowed. Some of these items may stain the skin temporarily, but they'll wash off in the shower. They may also stain your clothes and bed linens, so before you get naked, put down that plastic sheet. And if you are prone to yeast infections, avoid using the treats containing sugar directly on your lady parts, because they may upset your pH balance. Other than those rules, don't concern yourself with calories or fat grams. You'll be working it off anyway.

- **Lick It Up:** Mix any flavor of instant sugar-free pudding with enough water to dissolve the powder and make it a spreadable consistency.
- **Ready for This Jelly:** Mix any flavor of sugar-free Jell-O with enough boiling water to make it the consistency of hair gel. Pour it into squeeze bottles and use it before it congeals completely.

- **Shiny Happy:** Mix light corn syrup with food coloring. This paint is shiny and has a pleasant taste that's not too strong.
- **Chocolata Ya Ya:** Bring a half cup heavy cream and one tablespoon sugar to a simmer in a saucepan. Stir until the sugar dissolves. Pour the mixture over six ounces semisweet chocolate chips and stir until the chocolate melts. Let cool before using.
- **Slip 'n' Slide:** Combine a quarter cup glycerine (available in drugstores), a quarter teaspoon honey, and a quarter teaspoon clear vanilla extract in a bottle. Use it to massage back, arms, and legs—but keep it away from anyone's bits.

Give yourself the freedom to be curious and creative with your lovemaking.

pleasure chest

MAKE A BOX FOR YOUR TOYS // Yuki Hayashi

materials

Magazines or old books you can cut up (try some erotic pictorials, kinky prose, hot celebs, what-evah!)

1 round hatbox or rectangular photo box in rigid, heavyweight card stock

Removable tape (if needed)

Popsicle stick or paintbrush

White craft glue, thinned by 4 parts glue to 1 part water

Clear polyurethane spray coating

Soft chiffon or organza (optional)

Are all your sexy-time things cluttering up your closet? Are you tripping over your Rabbit while hopping out the door? While it's superfantastic that you're comfortable with your sexuality, you'll protect your toys and your clumsy ass by building them an elegant home. You won't find this project in anything by Martha Stewart, but it's easy, elegant, and a gosh-darned good thing.

1 Cut out pictures or bits of text from the magazines and arrange them across one side of the rectangular box. If you have a round hatbox, use little tabs of removable tape to hold the cuttings in place and cover approximately a quarter of its girth.

2 Once you're happy with the composition, use the popsicle stick or brush to apply a thin coat of glue to the back of one of the cutouts and position it on the box, gently smoothing out air pockets and excess glue with your fingers. Continue this procedure around your box, making sure the cutouts have some overlap. Don't allow the base to show—especially since these boxes are usually cheesy.

3 At the top of the box, fold your graphics over into the box, and glue them in place. Make sure there are no air pockets or excess glue. Cover the lid of the box in the same way. (Note: Be careful to keep your work very smooth and flat so the lid will fit properly.)

4 Let the glue dry for several hours. When it's bone dry, spray a layer of clear polyurethane over the box and lid (separately, of course, so they don't stick together). Follow the drying time suggested on the polyurethane container; repeat to add a second coat. The wipe-clean polyurethane will protect the artwork from any, er, spills.

5 Finally, if you want, use some soft chiffon or organza to line the box so you can nestle your toys inside.

body and soul

GO TANTRIC AND GET MORE BANG FOR YOUR FUCK // Elizabeth Randall

Tantra isn't just for crystal-carrying, patchouli-scented hippies or New Age-y celebrities. Anyone can benefit from this ancient set of sacred principles that encourages sexual awareness. Tantra, which originated in India, promotes enlightenment through the senses by interconnecting sexuality and spirituality. It's based on the idea that feminine and masculine energies—yin and yang—reside in all of us. "She" is the source of all power—the creative life force—but "he" brings consciousness to the power and guides it. One of the goals of Tantra is to foster a healthy marriage between the two. Tantra is also about being conscious in your body and leading a sexy life—in the bedroom and outside of it. As you awaken sensually, colors will be brighter, food will taste better, your sheets will feel softer! Tantra is a complex practice that can take a long time to master, but a few simple exercises will immediately shift your thinking. Try these tips to expand and deepen your sexual repertoire and inspire more balanced, connected, and satisfying partnerships.

BE CONSCIOUS

While having sex, be aware of the person you're having it with, how your body feels, and how your breath moves. Is it pleasurable? Fulfilling? In Tantra it is said that the deeper the pleasure, the deeper the emotional and spiritual healing. Afterward, reflect. How did the sex make you feel? Did you do something you didn't want to do? Did unexpected emotions arise?

DO SOMETHING DIFFERENT

Think about your sex life: What are your habits? Do you always use that cute pink vibrator on your clit or are you a strictly manual-stimulation kind of gal? Dare yourself to change it up. Try a new position. Rewrite your fantasy.

MOVE IT UP!

One Tantric principle is that energy ascends and descends along your chakras, the energy centers in the body (you can't touch them, but you can sense them). When having sex, you don't have to keep all that juicy energy in your genitals, where the first (anal area) and second (G-spot area) chakras are. Think of them as erotic generators that get your energy flowing, and then use your breath and intention to guide that energy up into your higher chakras, which are thought of as more spiritual. When you're feeling pleasure in your genitals, as you inhale, imagine that energy moving up your body and filling your heart. You'll heighten your awareness and possibly find a deeper connection to the feeling.

lassies for lasses

ADOPTING A DOG OR CAT // **Victoria Wells**

When you're looking for a furry friend, there's no need to drop a wad of cash on a fancy-ass breeder. There's an animal overpopulation issue in every city in America, and thousands of dogs and cats at animal-control facilities, shelters, and rescue groups urgently need homes.

Take time when choosing a pet—do research and visit the shelter a number of times to make sure there is a strong connection between you and your future companion. Shelter animals can be adopted for the cost of a donation or basic medical costs, usually $50 to $100 or less. Begin your search by logging onto www.petfinder.com, where you can check out a database of animals available for adoption in your neighborhood.

AGE

Puppies are cute and cuddly, but they have to be fed three times a day, they urinate what seems like every 10 minutes, and they get into everything if not supervised or contained in a safe area. A puppy is a great choice if you work at home or have a very flexible job. "Teenage" dogs (six months to one-and-a-half years) may seem to have limitless energy, but with proper training and a set of house rules, they are a good match for a person looking for an exercise companion. Adult dogs are a wonderful option for a busy lifestyle. While they do require daily aerobic exercise, their energy levels will most likely be lower than puppies'.

Kittens are not self-reliant and need supervision. If you are out of the house for most of the day, you may come home to find your kitten literally climbing the curtains. Grown cats require food, water, love, and a place to poop, but are more independent. For those who have love in their hearts but not as much time as a dog or kitten requires, grown cats are perfect pets.

BREED

Some people choose dogs according to their cuteness factor, but check that impulse. Pick up a book on breeds and their characteristics to help you find the right match for your situation. Shelters have primarily mixed-breed dogs up for adoption, but they are in every way as wonderful as purebred dogs. Consider that some landlords have weight restrictions you'll need to abide by.

PERSONALITY

Many shelter animals have a history of abuse or neglect and thus may have a certain amount of emotional baggage, such as resource guarding, separation anxiety, fear-based issues, and so on. While most animals will outgrow this, an animal with problems may be too much to handle for someone with little pet experience. Choosing a shelter that conducts temperament testing on its adoption animals is always a smart idea. Or hire a certified dog trainer to accompany you when choosing a pet to identify behavior problems. Contact the Association of Pet Dog Trainers (www.apdt.com) for a referral.

pooch purse

MAKE YOUR DOG A POCKET // Jennifer Knapp

materials

Scissors

6"-by-8" piece of vinyl

3"-by-8" piece of vinyl in a contrasting color

Sewing machine and matching thread

2 small plain rivets and rivet-setting tool

Several small decorative rivets

Epoxy craft glue

Contrasting color of thread

Self-adhesive Velcro dot

Poochies may not come with pockets, but that doesn't mean they don't have stuff to carry! Make your pup a stylish pocket to attach to his collar or leash. It's just the right size for a couple of treats, a poop bag, and a house key. Make it to match your outfit—or your dog's favorite jacket—and you and Fifi can prance to the park in style.

1 Using scissors and the larger rectangle of vinyl, cut a silhouette of a dog's head in the center of one end and cut two parallel slits on the opposite side (figure 1). Center the smaller piece of vinyl under the larger rectangle so you can see it through the silhouette cutout and stitch along the edges of the vinyl strip. Stitch around the silhouette.

2 Using the rivet-setting tool, add rivet eyes and a jewel collar. Cut a tiny nose out of the scraps from your main color of vinyl and use epoxy craft glue to attach it. Add a mouth with contrasting colored stitching.

3 Fold the two long sides to the center (figure 2) and stitch around the perimeter of the wallet (figure 3).

4 Fold the wallet over and attach the self-adhesive Velcro dot just inside each end to create a closure. Slip the dog's collar or leash through the slits on the back.

figure 1　　　　figure 2　　　　figure 3

here comes the indie bride

GET HITCHED ON THE CHEAP // **Michelle Goodman and Erin Dejesus**

You merge CD collections, purchase matching Tibetan rings at the local flea market, and declare your undying love for each other. You agree to keep the wedding simple, nontraditional, affordable. And then, blissfully, naively, you announce your engagement to the world.

Soon, married coworkers begin leaving back issues of *Modern Bride* on your desk. Your oldest college buddy sends you three wedding-planner books that "saved her life." Worst of all, the nagging questions from well-meaning relations pile up like unpaid credit-card bills: Have you set a date? Picked a venue? Started shopping for a dress? Drawn up the guest list? What about the band/photographer/caterer/flowers/seating chart/color scheme?

No matter how you respond, this unsolicited advice is enough to make any would-be bride fantasize about running off to Vegas. But with a little conviction and know-how, you can have the alterna-wedding of your dreams and avoid becoming another statistic in the $100-billion-a-year wedding industry.

GOING LEGIT

If you're planning a DIY wedding, all you really need is an officiant (the person who performs the wedding), the papers, and the love of your partner. Everything else—and we mean everything—is totally optional. Wedding laws, including who can do it, vary by county, municipality, and state, but the general legal process is actually quite simple. Here are the two things you'll need to do to make your marriage legit.

Apply for a Marriage License

Grab your partner and head to the county clerk's office—in the county you plan on getting married in—to apply for your marriage license. To be safe, do it at least one month before the ceremony (many states require couples to wait a few days after applying before receiving a license). The location of the clerk's office varies—it could be at a courthouse, the city hall, an independent office space—so Google the address of the one you need to go to. Each state has its own set of requirements, but you'll likely be asked to provide identification, proof of residence, and information about prior marriages; some places require blood tests. The web site USMarriageLaws.com is a good place to get started learning your local law, but your county clerk should provide the most up-to-date legal info.

Get Someone to Officiate

To make the marriage license valid, it must be signed by someone qualified in your state to perform marriages: a clergy member, justice of the peace, or other state-certified officiant. If you're skipping a traditional, denominational wedding and would like a friend or family member to perform the ceremony, he or she can legally register to do so through the Universal Life Church (www.ulc.net). Take note: Some municipalities have regulations stating that you must be married by someone who was ordained in-state. As far as the ceremony goes, the only thing that must legally be included is the Declaration of Intent—the "I do's." Following the ceremony, it's the officiant's job to file your marriage license.

SHOW ME THE MONEY

Sure, the average American wedding costs more than $25,000. But DIY brides across the nation have thrown one-of-a-kind weddings for less than $5,000 . . . $2,500 . . . even $500, and if you're resourceful, you can too. To keep from starting your shiny new married life drowning in matrimonial debt, set a realistic, firm budget from the get-go.

Prune the Guest List

For starters, taking a machete to that rapidly growing guest list can drastically cut costs. "I think a lot of times, people get sucked into 'Oh, I really need to invite my coworkers, I really need to invite my dad's coworkers, I really need to invite my third cousin,'" says Lori Leibovich, editor of IndieBride.com. But once you wise up to the fact that you'll be picking up the bar tab for people you'll never see again, making the tough cuts becomes, well, a piece of cake.

Be Crafty

To avoid throwing a cookie-cutter wedding (and spending all your dough), steer clear of paying for any services, attire, decorations, food, or venues with the word "wedding" in them; they'll all be marked up astronomically. Take a cue from today's DIY brides: a centerpiece you concoct from supplies bought at your local hobby shop is still a centerpiece. And setting up a boom box and asking friends to bring homemade mixed CDs is cheaper than hiring a band or a DJ, not to mention infinitely more personal.

Shop Smart

If you're supplying your own food and booze, bulk-sale stores like Costco are your new best friends. So are international districts. And if you know anyone who makes a mean homebrew, go for it. Just be sure to find out if you need a liquor license to serve it.

Since official wedding cakes, especially tiered ones, cost a small fortune (and often taste like sawdust), you're better off buying your favorite cake from a local bakery. You can always jazz it up with your favorite '70s action figures, vintage Pez dispensers, or anything else your fluttering heart desires. As for flowers, you'll save yourself at least a couple months' rent if you send a pal to the farmers' market the morning of the wedding for some fresh bouquets.

AN AFFAIR TO REMEMBER

There's no rule that says you have to get married in a chandeliered ballroom with champagne flutes and glistening ice sculptures. In fact, the quirkier your wedding, the better time everyone will have.

If you have your wedding at a place where an activity is available—bowling alley, arcade, amusement park—you don't have to create a reception. People can just take part in whatever happens at that place normally. Options for unique, affordable wedding spots abound. The funky little venue down the road—be it the Elks Lodge or the Lithuanian-American rec hall—can be equally economical and charming (or at least kitschy).

To infuse the big day with your personality, have the wedding somewhere you usually go—a supermarket, a street corner, a movie theater, your own house, a restaurant, hiking trail, a store, a parking lot. Maybe you want to get married in a Buddhist community center or have a potluck in the backyard of your grandma's cabin.

WHAT NOT TO WEAR

Your wedding dress doesn't have to be new. A sweet frock from your favorite vintage shop is likely to be cheaper than an off-the-rack wedding gown. There are also sample sales, bridal consignment shops, eBay, and web sites.

While we're on the subject of couture, let's talk about those pastel-colored bridesmaid monstrosities we all hope and pray we never have to pay good money to wear. Rather than relying on matching outfits, let your friends wear what they want, or have them stick to a color scheme. Many indie brides nix the attendants completely and just have their best buds speak or read at the ceremony, toast or roast them at the reception, or put together a wall of shame—embarrassing baby photos and all.

KEEPING IT REAL

If you already have three toasters and wouldn't know Waterford crystal if it broke over your head, gently steer guests toward gifts beyond the home-furnishings aisle. Going camping on your honeymoon? Register at REI. Need some tools or craft supplies? Register at your local hardware or hobby shop. And if you find the whole notion of asking people to throw money at you distasteful, encourage your guests to make donations to a political advocacy group or charity you support. Give guests a couple of choices, in case gun-toting Uncle Harry just can't bear to give his hard-earned dollars to the Democratic National Committee. Registering with websites like IDoFoundation.org and JustGive.org makes it easy for guests to contribute to nonprofit organizations you choose.

Despite having told yourself you wouldn't lose your head—or your credit rating—over one dang day, you may still find yourself cracking under pressure ("But the women in our family have always carried a bouquet!"). That's when it's time to practice the fine art of saying no.

when wedding rituals attack

Before you blindly follow a tradition, consider its roots....

dad giving away the bride   This stems from biblical times, when a daughter was the "property" of her father until marriage, at which point she became her husband's commodity (not to mention his housekeeper and breeder). Traces of this arrangement linger in Western weddings, like when a father walks his daughter down the aisle (sometimes answering the officiant's question, "Who gives this woman?") or when a bride assumes her husband's last name.

bouquet toss   Flowers have forever represented fertility. By throwing her wedding bouquet to a sea of supposedly eager unwed females, the now "deflowered" bride shares her good fortune so that one of her "virginal" friends can be next in line to get hitched and immediately begin procreating.

shoes tied to the newlyweds' car   Tying shoes to the fender of the newlywed's getaway car—which has transmogrified into tying soda cans to the fender—can be traced to an ancient custom of dear old Dad giving the groom one of the bride's shoes. The gift of the shoe symbolized the transfer of ownership of the bride from papa to hubby. Nice!

diamond engagement ring   Though the first known diamond engagement ring was bestowed in Austria in 1477, diamonds were rare until the late 1800s. It's thanks to the brilliant marketing efforts of De Beers, the mammoth diamond purveyor, that this became a universal phenomenon. De Beers began a colossal marketing campaign in 1938; by 1950, half of all American brides sported diamond engagement rings, and the figure climbed to 80 percent by 1960.

The minute you start trying to please anyone but you and your partner, you might as well just toss up your credit cards and hire a professional wedding planner.

"Our wedding was exactly what we wanted," says Tammy Weisberger, who celebrated her nuptials with a casual backyard barbecue at her in-laws' Washington farm. The hundred or so guests sat on hay bales during the ceremony, feasted on salmon donated by her fisherman uncle and grilled by her professional-chef brother, and danced late into the night to a local bluegrass band. "So many people still tell me it was the most fun wedding they've ever attended. And people still call me to steal ideas."

labor of love

HAVE A POWERFUL, NATURAL BIRTH // Lynn Flanagan and Erin Dejesus

Unless you're in the room during a labor or giving birth yourself, it's hard to imagine the sheer strength of a mother during the birth process. Writer and mother Laura Stavoe Harm put it best when she said, "We have a secret in our culture, and it's not that birth is painful. It's that women are strong." And so, dear ladies, we'd like to let you in on the secret—here's the inside scoop on what it takes to squeeze one out.

READY, STEADY, GO

While women's bodies already know how to give birth, taking a class in childbirth prep can give you the tools you need to birth in awareness rather than fear. There are many types of classes, but it's important to remember that there is no one way to do it right. The Birthing from Within program, for example, offers holistic prenatal preparation by coaching a woman through her personal fears, and Hypnobabies uses hypnosis to help her relax during birth.

Be sure you prepare yourself for a wide variety of situations. Babies have been known to show up before the anesthesiologist, so it's still worthwhile for a woman planning to have an epidural to practice pain-coping techniques. And since babies can refuse to make an appearance in a birthing pool, a woman hoping to stay home for the event will also benefit from learning to feel safe and comfortable in a hospital environment.

Plan on starting a class in your third trimester, finishing about three weeks before your expected due date; this will leave the techniques you learned fresh in your mind and give you time to practice without cutting it so close that you risk missing the last class if the baby comes early.

LOVE IS THE DRUG

A study at the University of Helsinki showed that women who eat chocolate during pregnancy subsequently have calmer babies. And women who take just a couple of minutes each day to unwind and connect with their bumps have lower rates of premature labor. It's all because of oxytocin, the love and bonding hormone, which gives you that warm and tingly feeling when you eat something pleasurable, when you fall in love, and right after orgasm. So think of one thing for each of your five senses that gets your juices flowing—such as looking at your favorite painting, sniffing fresh flowers, getting a massage—and incorporate them into your daily routine during pregnancy.

Oxytocin also stimulates uterine contractions during labor, so whatever makes a woman release oxytocin in her daily life can help her and her baby during birth. As Ina May Gaskin, pioneer midwife and author, says, the energy that gets the baby in is the energy that gets the baby out. Making out, having pleasurable sex, and replicating a romantic experience can bring on labor and make it go faster. If you didn't conceive to Enya, maybe you shouldn't be birthing to Enya. If your in-laws, older brother, and next-door neighbor weren't at the conception, they might not make the best birth companions, either. Create a birthing environment that inspires you, not one that seems like it should.

ROAM IF YOU WANT TO

Women birth best where they feel safest and most comfortable. Some women prefer being at home because a familiar environment can ease stress. In most hospitals, you're pretty much restricted to lying on your back while pushing, but at home you can choose whatever position you want to give birth in— such as on your hands and knees, squatting on a birth stool, or in a birth pool or big tub, all of which help gravity work with your body rather than against it.

Another option is a birth center, which offers a home-birth environment with a similar style of care away from your humble abode and which are more likely to be covered by insurance than home birth is. In both cases, the birth can be attended by midwives (and more on them later), not obstetricians, so these options are best for low-risk women who feel comfortable with the birth process and the idea of forgoing medication. If an emergency situation arises, a woman in distress or one who decides she wants an epidural can opt for a hospital; in other words, you're not locked into your choice of venue.

MOTHER'S LITTLE HELPER

Along with the where and how of birth is the question of who. A doula is a woman who is professionally trained to provide physical, emotional, and informational support during pregnancy, birth, and into the postpartum period. Doulas do not provide medical services, but they are trained to teach mothers-to-be pain-coping techniques (such as visualization and breath awareness), provide help to fire up a stalled labor, and offer ideas for an easier birth (like helping the mother move into better positions and using massage, acupressure, and aromatherapy).

The most important thing a doula does is set the mood; she is familiar with birth, and her trust and faith in the process can reassure the woman and her partner. Studies indicate that women who use doulas have shorter labors and fewer Cesarean births, need less pain relief, experience less depression, and are more likely to breast-feed and to develop more responsive and affectionate relationships with their newborns.

Start looking for a doula around the second trimester, to give yourself enough time to interview several and then get to know the one who fits you best. Choose someone you feel comfortable with and whose opinion you respect. Some hospitals even have doulas on staff.

preparing for a diy-style delivery

These days, many pregnant women are choosing alternative birthing experiences so that they can take better control of their comfort and family involvement. This often means hiring a midwife to deliver the baby outside of a hospital or even at home. Choosing a nontraditional birth requires legwork and research, and each decision should take into account your health, your baby's health, and the wishes of you and your family.

do your research   There are big differences between doulas, accredited midwives, and lay midwives. A doula attends to a birthing woman (using massage, position changes, and other supportive measures) and many also offer postpartum support. Certified-nurse midwives (CNMs) are licensed health-care practitioners and often deliver in a hospital setting (though some do attend home births). Certified midwives are not registered nurses but have degrees in midwifery. Lay midwives received their training through an apprenticeship or training program. The Citizens for Midwifery web site (www.cfmidwifery.org) provides an in-depth description of the differences.

decide where and how you want to give birth   Do you want to be at home, at a birth center, in the hospital with a midwife? Some women prefer to give birth in a hospital—where a midwife can deliver your baby and facilitate family involvement with additional medical assistance nearby—just in case problems occur during labor. Like hospitals, birth centers are licensed, accredited facilities with medical professionals but are outfitted to mimic the comforts of home. Birth centers often offer mothers-to-be private rooms and welcome the entire family to participate. Make sure your birth center is accredited by visiting the American Association of Birth Centers web site (www.birthcenters.org).

Not all states have laws that mandate insurance coverage of home births, and midwifery—even by certified midwives—is still illegal in some states. (Conversely, most insurance companies, including Medicaid, contract with birth centers to provide some kind of coverage.)

start screening your potential doula and/or midwife   Once you've decided what kind of birthing assistance you want, several online organizations can help narrow your search. Doulas of North America (www.dona.org) and the Childbirth and Postpartum Professional Association (www.cappa.net) have databases and referral lists on their web sites, sorted by location. For midwives, certification requirements vary by state, so check a potential midwife's legal status at the American College of Nurse-Midwives (www.acnm.org). If you choose to give birth at home, make sure your midwife has both insurance and admitting privileges at a nearby hospital. If your midwife has no malpractice insurance, she will not be able to accompany you into the hospital.

In addition to scheduling and pricing concerns, take into consideration experience, references, and most important, her approach to birth. Make sure you're comfortable not only with the midwife but also with her site, if you choose to give birth outside your home. In addition, every midwife has to have a backup physician. Be sure yours does, and do some research on the doctor as well.

WHAT A GIRL WANTS

Just as you choose your support team, you also have a say in who will be delivering your baby. Midwives can deliver babies at home, at birth centers, or at hospitals, depending on their training. They spend time with women focusing on wellness education and can be found through local midwife associations.

Unlike obstetricians, many of whom treat pregnancy like it's a disease to be cured, midwives are trained to see birth as a normal process that most women can handle without medical interventions, such as induction and episiotomy, as well as how to tell when the care of a doctor really is necessary.

PUSH IT REAL GOOD

Sometimes birth is dangerous and a Cesarean section can be a lifesaving surgical procedure for both mother and baby—when, for example, the cord comes down before the baby, the placenta covers the cervix, or the baby is wrongly positioned. But such medical emergencies are uncommon—accounting for between 11 to 15 percent of births. Most Cesareans are unnecessary, and yet they're becoming increasingly popular: 30.2 percent of women had a Cesarean birth in 2005 and the American College of Obstetricians and Gynecologists is predicting that 50 percent of babies will be born by C-section by 2012.

Yet the short- and long-term risks of Cesareans are rarely discussed. Infants born via Cesarean to mothers with no medical risks or labor complications have more than twice the risk of death during a birth compared to those delivered vaginally. Higher rates of complications for the mother, such as infection, more severe and longer-lasting postpartum pain, and future reproductive problems are also associated with Cesarean birth. Control over the birth process, as well as avoiding pain, urinary

incontinence, and pelvic-floor dysfunction are touted as reasons for choosing a Cesarean, but there are no studies that have been able to show a correlation between vaginal birth and higher rates of urinary incontinence and pelvic-floor dysfunction. Having major abdominal surgery is much more invasive and can subsequently be more painful than vaginal birth.

Another common concern is the loss of a vaginal tightness, but Kegel exercises and self-care can help dramatically during postpartum recovery. What is most alarming about the Cesarean trend is not the choices that women are making but that women are often misinformed, and sometimes coerced, into those decisions. Although maternal request is often assumed to be responsible for the dramatic increase in surgical births, the majority of women who had Cesareans for nonmedical reasons reported that it was suggested by a health-care provider. According to the World Health Organization, more than half of the current Cesareans in this country could have been safely prevented. It's time to push hard!

KNOW YOUR RIGHTS

Making informed decisions during pregnancy and birth can have a huge impact on how confident a woman feels about being a mother, and it's her reproductive right to have safe birth choices available. Preparing for birth is like preparing for a pirate adventure across the ocean: you can't predict or control labor, just as you can't control the sea. But you have nine months to inform yourself on a variety of options, prepare for the journey, and make sure that you have the best crew and tools available on board with you. Just remember that it's your ship, you call the shots, and if some matey dares to tell you to be quiet during labor, show them the plank.

rest in peace

CARING FOR A LOVED ONE IN DEATH // Erin DeJesus

The average funeral costs thousands (and thousands) of dollars—not including cemetery fees. But for proponents of the DIY funeral, caring for a loved one after death rather than turning him or her over to a funeral director offers more than financial benefits, particularly if the death was an expected one. Depending on your state's laws, you can handle many of the things funeral directors typically take care of during the time between a person's last breath and the burial or cremation: completing paperwork, transporting the body from a hospital or hospice home, washing and dressing the body, planning and hosting a wake, and transferring the body to a cemetery or crematory. "It ameliorates the grieving process," says Beth Knox, founder of the Maryland-based home-funeral resource Crossings. "It's a tremendous comfort, knowing that you could just be with them every step of the way until they were gone—truly, as in final-disposition gone."

TO COVER YOUR BASES LEGALLY, RESEARCH YOUR RIGHTS

Caring for your dead is legal in all 50 states, though some enforce legal conditions. Pick up *Caring for the Dead: Your Final Act of Love* by Lisa Carlson, the go-to guide that provides a lengthy list of laws concerning DIY funerals. You can also visit the nonprofit Funeral Consumers Alliance (www.funerals. org) for a state-by-state breakdown of laws, which includes downloads of state-specific paperwork when applicable, or call your local Office of Vital Records or public health department. One universal rule: there is no law in the U.S. requiring a body to be embalmed.

OBTAIN YOUR LOVED ONE'S DEATH CERTIFICATE

Knox warns that many families looking to care for their own may face resistance from hospital employees, who are used to funeral directors handling the process, but all you need is for the doctor or medical examiner to sign the death certificate to state the cause of death. Because some states require it by law, Knox recommends finding a funeral director to file the death certificate for you.

OBTAIN A BURIAL TRANSFER (OR TRANSPORT) PERMIT

Some municipalities require a permit, issued by the town or county clerk, to transport the body from place to place—from the hospital to the cemetery, crematory, or the town or state where the funeral ceremony will occur. Check with your local clerk to see if one is required. Usually, all you need for a transfer permit is the death certificate and basic information about the deceased. When it comes to physically transporting the body, rules and regulations vary by state. In some, you must hire a funeral director to provide the service. But in many states, it is perfectly legal to transport your own dead, either in or out of a casket, in your own vehicle. Carlson's book covers the laws of each state, but be sure to call your health department or attorney general's office to confirm.

BEYOND LEGAL CONCERNS

Obviously, making the decision to care for a loved one during the time between death and burial or cremation extends far beyond legal concerns—handling the remains personally can prove to be a powerful final act of love. Though the thought of forgoing a funeral director might sound grisly, Knox points out that the opportunity to closely serve your loved one should trump our society-fueled fear of death. "It's just some too-many-zombie-movies kind of fear," Knox says. "Usually, it's not nearly as scary."

To prep the deceased for burial:

1 Decide on the body's final disposition, taking into account the deceased's wishes. If your loved one did not purchase a cemetery plot, research local burial sites and gather their requirements for preparation of the body; if the body will be cremated, make sure your local crematory will accept a body delivered by the family. Should you wish to bury your loved one on private land, laws and regulations will vary widely depending on where you live (local officials will take everything into account, including environmental impact and zoning property laws). Consult your local municipal officials for more information.

2 There's no U.S. law requiring an outer burial container, but if you'd like a casket for a memorial service or are burying your loved one in a cemetery (many will require one), select a casket or an urn. In a traditional service, the casket often accounts for much of the funeral cost, so be a savvy consumer by avoiding the funeral-home middleman and purchasing a casket or an urn directly from the manufacturer or craftsman. The Funeral Consumers Alliance website offers a list of affordable casket and urn providers (including many online retailers that offer ecofriendly options), as well as instructions on how to make your own.

3 The Crossings web site (www. crossings.net), offers a downloadable PDF that takes you through the washing and dressing process step-by-step. Should prepping the body be outside your comfort zone, some funeral directors may be willing to handle the remains while leaving everything else up to you.

4 Planning an at-home memorial service for your loved one is deeply personal. If you're not sure where to start, the Funeral Consumers Alliance web site has several downloadable pamphlets that give advice on such varied topics as how to plan a memorial service and ecofriendly burials. The links page directs families to several organizations, like Knox's, that educate visitors about the home-funeral process.

Resources

THE GREEN PARTY: THROW A LOCAL-FOODS POTLUCK *(page 240)*
Want to find out more about eating local?

- *www.100milediet.org*
- *www.localharvest.org*
- *www.slowfoodusa.org*
- *www.eatwellguide.com*
- *Animal, Vegetable, Miracle: A Year of Food Life* by Barbara Kingsolver, Steven L. Hopp, and Camille Kingsolver (HarperCollins)

THIS ALE'S FOR YOU: BREW YOUR OWN BEER *(page 260)*
Need to find a homebrew supplier?

- *www.brewapp.com* A New Jersey–based, mother-daughter fermentation supplier.

MEAN BEANS: ROAST YOUR OWN COFFEE *(page 262)*
Looking for beans to roast?

- *www.sweetmarias.com*
- *www.baldmountaincoffee.com*
- *www.nativecoffeetraders.com*

SO LEGIT YOU'LL QUIT: GOING INTO BUSINESS FOR YOURSELF *(page 298)*
Thinking about going indie?

- *www.anothergirlatplay.com* A site featuring the invaluable advice of self-employed women artists who live the creative life on their own terms. Be sure to check out the hefty resource page, too.

- *www.digitaleve.org* International organization for women who work in the digital arena. Check out the individual chapter sites for local resources and meetings.

- *www.nolo.com* Law for dummies. This site has all the necessary dirt on contracts, copyright, taxes, Internet law, and much more. Be sure to check out the small-business section.

- *www.score.org* A nonprofit offering free, confidential business counseling and affordable workshops nationwide. The site's loaded with resources for starting a business, including tips for women, minorities, and young business owners.

- *www.vistaprint.com* Cheap business cards that do the trick.

MAKE IT WORK: LAUNCH YOUR OWN CLOTHING LABEL *(page 302)*
Want to find out more about becoming a designer?

Trade Shows
- *MAGIC*, Las Vegas (www.magiconline.com)
- *POOL*, Las Vegas (www.pooltradeshow.com)
- *Project*, New York and Las Vegas (www.projectshow.com)

Fairs

- *BUST Magazine Craftacular* (www.bust. com/craftacular/craftacular-home.html)

- *Renegade Craft Fair* (www.renegadecraft.com)

- *Maker Faire* (http://makerfaire.com)

- *No Coast Craft-o-Rama* (http://nocoastcraft.com)

- *Urban Craft Uprising* (www.urbancraftuprising.com)

Fabrics and Production

- *Apparel Search* (www.apparelsearch.com)

- *American Apparel Producers' Network* (www.aapnetwork.net)

- *Style Source* (www.style-source.com)

- *The Evans Group* (www.evansgroup international.com) With factories in LA and San Francisco, they specialize in small-volume production, making them perfect for new designers.

Recommended Reading

- *The Fashion Designer Survival Guide: Start and Run Your Own Fashion Business* by Mary Gehlhar (Kaplan Publishing)

- *Fashion for Profit: A Professional's Complete Guide* by Frances Harder (Harder Publications)

- *Patternmaking for Fashion Design* (and DVD Package) by Helen Joseph Armstrong (Prentice Hall)

LIKING IT ROUGH: LEARN TO LOVE CAMPING *(page 314)*
Need more info on camping?

Places

- *The US Forest Service* (www.fs.fed.us)

- *The National Park Service* (www.nps.gov)

Gear and Shopping

- *Backcountry.com* The very best gear sold by folks with a backcountry spirit.

- *Federal Army & Navy Surplus, Inc.* (www.gr8gear.com)

Experts and Info

- *GORP* (www.gorp.com) Reviews of places organized by state.

- *Backpacker* (www.backpacker.com) Check out the forums.

- *SwimmingHoles.info: Guide to Swimming Holes and Hot Springs* (www.swimmingholes.org) Unbelievable labor of love and wonderful catalog.

Miscellaneous

- *Leave No Trace Center for Outdoor Ethics* (www.lnt.org) Nonprofit promoting strong stewardship principles.

- *Scoutorama.com* (www.scoutorama.com) Boy Scout–tested recipes and campfire songs.

Recommended Reading

- *Backpacking: A Woman's Guide* by Adrienne Hall (Ragged Mountain Press)

- *Lipsmackin' Backpackin': Lightweight Trail-Tested Recipes for Backcountry Trips* by Tim and Christine Conners (Globe Pequot Press)

HIT THE ROAD: TIPS FOR PLANNING A BIKE TOUR *(page 330)*
Need more info on planning a bike trip?

- *Adventure Cycling Association* (www.adventurecycling.org)

- *Mountain Equipment Co-op* (www.mec.ca)

Index

Credits

PHOTO CREDITS

© Glynis Selina Arban: Page 141; © Lynette Astaire: Pages 187, 195; © Burcu Avsar: Pages 21, 28, 29, 83, 148, 149, 154; © Marcin Balcerzak: Page 331; © L. Barnwell: Page 332; © Joe Biafore: Page 269; © Ruth Black: Page 301; © Jessica Boone: Page 246; © Sara Brownell and Nici Williams: Page 151 (right); © Amanda Bruns: Pages 30, 33, 134, 178; © Amy Cave: Page 237; © H. D. Connelly: Page 100; © Ryann Cooley: Pages 44, 196, 197 (top right); © Vincent Dilio: Page 184; © Edward ONeil Photography Inc: Page 254; © Allison Gootee: Page 95; © Kava Gorna: Page 129; © Eva Gruendemann: Page 258; © Karineh Gurjian-Angelo: Page 201 (top); © Heidi Hartwig: Pages 175, 182; © Jiri Hera: Page 271; © Meredith Jenks: Page 165; © Julie Kramer: Pages 223, 232, 235, 245, 251, 252; © Katarzyna Krawiec: Page 197; © Kate Lacey: Back cover (bottom center), page 131; © Jon Larson: Page 260; © Michael Lavine: Pages 176, 368; © Luis Louro: Page 112; © Jeaneen Lund: Back cover (top left), pages 248, 249, 250, 257 (bottom); © Michael Marmora: Page 61; © Jillian McAlley: Back cover (center), pages 107, 161; © Andrew McCaul: Back cover (bottom right), pages 13, 17, 48, 98, 163, 198, 263; © Sarah McColgan: Pages 133, 152, 153, 191; © Holly McDade: Pages 71, 221; © Marianne Rafter (styling by Karen Schaupeter; assistants Anna Su and Rachael Gray; clothing and props by Urban Outfitters and Buffalo Exchange): Pages 52, 55, 57, 58, 121, 122, 123, 124, 125, 127, 128, 136, 137, 143, 145, 146, 156, 158, 159, 203 (left), 277, 320, 321, 323, 325, 326, 327, 337, 342; © Gabrielle Revere: Page 171; © Dan Saelinger: Page 239; © Torsten Schon: Page 264; © M. Sharkey: Page 181; © Sharky: Page 225; © Shutterstock: Pages 273, 310; © Jen Siska: Page 151 (left); © Alpha Smoot: Page 228; © Tamara Staples: Pages 27, 64, 345; © Monica Stevenson: Page 18; © Danielle St. Laurent: Page 38; © Sarah Anne Ward: Back cover (top right), pages 15, 25, 35, 37, 41, 43, 47, 51, 65, 66, 139, 199, 219, 231, 233, 236, 238, 257 (top), 259, 265, 267, 268, 329; © Gordon Warlow: Page 355; © James Westman: Pages 45, 53, 69; © Terri White / Seven Acre Woods: Page 99; © Williams / Hirakawa: Back cover (bottom left), pages 167, 173, 193; © Anna Wolf: Page 240

ILLUSTRATION CREDITS

© Fontaine Anderson: Page 303; © S. Britt: Page 295; © Heather Culp: Pages 315, 318; © Genevieve Dionne: Page 351; © Julia Durgee: Pages 175, 181, 183, 193; © Helena Garcia: Page 341; © Susie Ghahremani / boygirlparty.com: Pages 72, 73, 74, 75, 76, 77, 93, 94, 96, 204, 205, 206, 209, 211, 212, 214, 216; © Marcellus Hall: Page 266; © Matthew Hertel: Page 105; © Jessica Hische: Cover, pages 3, 12, 106, 166, 218, 276; © Amy Karol: Pages 130, 132; © Julee Kim: Page 347; © Yoswadi Krutkolm: Pages 109, 117, 118, 119; © Omar Lee: Page 292; © Danny Luo: Page 274; © Sergio Membrillas: Page 79; © Andy Mora: Page 188; © Marcus Oakley: Page 6; © Saelee Oh: Page 81; © Kavel Rafferty: Pages 88, 89, 90, 91; © Shutterstock: Pages 298, 311, 316; © Elizabeth Carey Smith: Page 190; © Jon Spencer: Page 279; © Julia Staite: Page 16; © Holly Stevenson: Pages 108, 109, 110, 111, 169, 172, 173; © Rachell Sumpter: Page 243; © Anke Weckmann: Pages 84, 86, 283, 285, 287, 288, 307; © Erin Wengrovius: Pages 103, 114, 115, 164, 250, 338; © Adrienne Yan: Page 312; © Arkadiusz Zielinski: Page 291; © Marlena Zuber: Page 290

Acknowledgments

First and foremost, we'd like to thank our amazingly talented staff, both past and present, who have gone above and beyond to edit and design the stories in *BUST* and which appear in this book, including current staffers Emily Rems, Lisa Butterworth, Erin Wengrovious, and especially crafty lady Callie Watts, as well as past staffers Tara Marks, Elizabeth Carey Smith, Tracie Egan Morrisey, and Colleen Kane. But even with our amazing editors and designers, we'd have no book at all if it weren't for the brilliant and creative writers, photographers, and illustrators whose contributions are presented here. We thank them for their work, and for being a part of *BUST*.

We are so glad that one of our idols in the craft publishing world, Melanie Falick, was interested in doing a book with us; and we could not have asked for a better editor than Liana Allday. It was her clear vision and sharp mind that really made this book go from an idea to a reality. Like a literary sherpa, she carried much of the weight of this project and guided us through the process from beginning to end. We are grateful for the brilliant work that was done by Jenny Rose Ryan, one of our favorite crafty contributors, who massaged and molded all of the text, helping to push things along as necessary until it could all be delivered in perfect shape, like a literary midwife. And we are so thankful for the careful work done by our book coordinator, Jodi Doff, who compiled all of the text and managed the photographers and illustrators, like a literary choir director. We're especially lucky to have had the über-talented designer Jessica Hische on board as our cover designer. And, of course, big, big ups to the creative team at Stewart, Tabori & Chang who actually crafted this book with their own hands: graphic designer Anna Christian, copyeditor Ana Deboo, food copyeditor Liana Krissoff, proofreader Andrea Serra, and technical proofreader Chris Timmons, along with photographer Marianne Rafter and stylist Karen Schaupeter.

Laurie would like to thank her family, and a special shout-out goes to the two interns, Katie Oldeker and Larissa Dzegar, who helped sort through dusty boxes to find the old files. Debbie would also like to thank her family, especially her crafty mom, and the last-minute helping hands of Ryan Green, Jenni Radosevich, and Ingrid Coughlin, who helped get the final few crafts made.

Finally, we are forever grateful to the *BUST* magazine readers who have supported us all these years and allowed us to do what we've always wanted to do: publish a magazine that we love. We can't spell *BUST* without U.

About the Authors

Laurie Henzel and **Debbie Stoller** are two of the founders of *BUST* magazine, which was launched in 1993. Today they are its co-owners, co-publishers and co-creators—Laurie is the creative director and Debbie is the editor in chief. Debbie is also the author of the Stitch 'n Bitch knitting and crocheting book series and coauthor of the *BUST Guide to the New Girl Order*. In their LBB (lives before *BUST*), Laurie received a BFA from Parsons and ran her own graphic design studio, and Debbie earned a PhD in the Psychology of Women from Yale University and worked as a web programmer. Laurie lives in Manhattan with her husband, Michael, and her daughters, Olive and Penny; Debbie lives in Brooklyn with her dog, cat, and way too much yarn. To learn more about *BUST*, visit bust.com.